Blade Servers and Virtualization

Blade Servers and Virtualization: Transforming Enterprise Computing While Cutting Costs

Published by
Wiley Publishing, Inc.
10475 Crosspoint Boulevard
Indianapolis, IN 46256
www.wiley.com

Published simultaneously in Canada

ISBN: 978-0-471-78395-4

Manufactured in the United States of America

10 9 8 7 6 5 4 3 2

For general information on our other products and services or to obtain technical support, please contact our Customer Care Department within the U.S. at (800) 762-2974, outside the U.S. at (317) 572-3993 or fax (317) 572-4002.

Library of Congress Cataloging-in-Publication Data

Goldworm, Barb, 1958–
 Blade servers and virtualization : transforming enterprise computing while cutting costs / Barb Goldworm, Anne Skamarock.
    p. cm.
 Includes bibliographical references.
 ISBN-13: 978-0-471-78395-4 (cloth)
 ISBN-10: 0-471-78395-1 (cloth)
 1. Virtual computer systems. 2. Web servers. I. Skamarock, Anne. II. Title.
 QA76.9.V5G65 2007
 005.4@@sp3—dc22

                          2006037912

Wiley also publishes its books in a variety of electronic formats. Some content that appears in print may not be available in electronic books.

Blade Servers and Virtualization

Transforming Enterprise Computing While Cutting Costs

Barb Goldworm
Anne Skamarock

BICENTENNIAL
1807
WILEY
2007
BICENTENNIAL

Wiley Publishing, Inc.

I dedicate this book to my family, Karen and Zee, and my sister-in-law, Cindy, and her family, for their love and support and incredible patience as I disappeared for so many late nights, early mornings, and long weekends; to my father, who gave me a love of math, science, and logic; and to my mother, who gave me a love of language.

Barb Goldworm

I dedicate this book to my family, Bill, Evan, and Ethan, for their love, support, and patience; to my parents and brother for continuing to remind me I can do anything I put my mind to; and to my high-school English teacher, Mr. Harris, whose lessons I still hear every time I write.

Anne C. Skamarock

About the Authors

Barb Goldworm has spent 30 years in the computer industry, in various technical, marketing, sales, senior management, and industry analyst positions with IBM, Novell, StorageTek, Enterprise Management Associates (EMA), and multiple successful start-ups. She is the founder and president of Focus Consulting (www.focusonsystems.com), a research, analysis, and consulting firm focused on systems and storage. A frequent speaker at industry events worldwide, Barb created and chaired the Networked Storage Segment of NetWorld+Interop, has been one of the top-three-ranked analyst/knowledge expert speakers at Storage Networking World, and is a regular featured speaker for webcast providers including TechTarget and Ziff-Davis. Barb has published extensively, including regular columns for *NetworkWorld, ComputerWorld,* and *TechTarget,* as well as numerous business and technical white papers and articles on systems, storage and storage networking, and enterprise management. Barb can be reached at bgoldworm@focusonsystems.com.

Anne Skamarock has spent nearly 30 years in high-tech fields in various positions, including end user, systems administrator, scientific programmer, NFS software engineer, backup and recovery software engineer, technical sales, marketing, and product management, and industry analyst with SRI International, Sun Microsystems, Solbourne Computer, StorageTek, and Enterprise Management Associates (EMA). In addition to working with Focus Consulting, Anne is also founder and president of Skamarock Consulting, a technology, marketing, and research firm focused on systems and storage. While at EMA, she co-wrote *Storage Solutions: A Buyer's Guide* and wrote the weekly "Storage in the Enterprise" NetworkWorld online newsletter. Anne can be reached at askamarock@focusonsystems.com.

Credits

Acquisitions Editor
Carol Long

Development Editor
Kelly Dobbs Henthorne

Technical Editors
Craig A. Newell
Schley Stauffer Andrew Kutz

Production Editor
Sarah Groff-Palermo

Copy Editor
Candace English

Editorial Manager
Mary Beth Wakefield

Production Manager
Tim Tate

**Vice President and Executive
Group Publisher**
Richard Swadley

**Vice President and Executive
Publisher**
Joseph B. Wikert

Book Designer
Maureen Forys,
Happenstance Type-O-Rama

Proofreader
Rachel Gunn

Indexer
Ted Laux

Anniversary Logo Design
Richard Pacifico

Contents

Acknowledgements

So many people helped to make this book what it is; it is difficult to name them all. First, I want to thank Anne Skamarock for her collaboration, partnership, and long hours in researching, analyzing, debating, and co-writing this book and for helping me to keep my sanity throughout the project. Without Anne, this book would have been possible, but not nearly as good and certainly not as much fun. Second, I want to thank Winston Bumpus at Dell, because when I was deciding whether or not to say yes to Wiley and write this book, his sage answer was "Oh, go do it," and he convinced me I would be glad when it was done (and he offered his help and support). Thanks also for his great work on the management and standards issues and chapters and for connecting me with Prakash and other helpful people at Dell. Finally, thanks to Elliot Markowitz at Ziff-Davis and Russ Vines for connecting the folks at Wiley with me and suggesting I do this book. *—Barb*

Foremost, I thank my co-author, Barb Goldworm, for convincing me to help her write this book—I've never had so much fun writing before. Her good humor, her passion to get it right, and her ability to laugh under stress got us over some of the tough hurdles. I also thank Joan Wrabetz for giving me the final push I needed to go through with this project and for being a constant source of information and inspiration to me. *—Anne*

Thanks also from both of us to Andrew Kutz for his help in technical editing from a server-virtualization-implementation point of view and to Craig Newell for his help in technical editing from a blade-systems-implementation point of view. Both of them added strong insights and helpful additions, not to mention incredibly quick turnaround times, despite their day jobs.

Thanks to the following people, without whom this book would be missing key information: Prakash Ramkrishna at Dell for his help early in the project, giving both a historical perspective and a deeper look into the reasons behind blade architecture and management design points; Howie Goldstein for his expertise and written contribution on the networking chapter. Scott Rose at PANTA Systems (formerly at Veritas), who supplied us with valuable information about clustering technologies; Lance Levanthal for his work in organizing the Server Blade Summit and in helping us find key people to share their perspectives (and also for being around longer than we have, if only slightly); Michael Krieger at Ziff-Davis for his insight into the pre-history of blades, as well as his humorous perspective on this industry; Chris Hipp for his war stories and perspective on the official birth of blades; and Kelly Quinn at IDC for sharing IDC's statistics and perspectives, as well as her own thoughts on the blade market.

Thanks also to the folks at Wiley: Carol Long, our acquisitions editor, for helping to explain the process of doing the book and making it seem like the right thing to do; and Kelly Henthorne, our development editor, for her attention to detail and her patience in ensuring the quality of this book.

Finally, to the many product managers, architects, PR and AR staff (internal and external), executives, and IT managers from all the companies covered in this book, for their time, effort, and patience in providing us with the information we needed, and for all their work in delivering and implementing interesting and innovative solutions, including the following: Dell, Egenera, HP, Hitachi, IBM, Microsoft, PANTA, PlateSpin, PolyServe, Rackable, Sun, SWsoft, Symantec, Verari, Virtual Iron, VMware, Xen, and numerous IT user organizations. It was a pleasure working with them, and we gratefully thank them all.

Introduction

Technology changes over the last 30 years have come in many shapes and sizes. Some have dramatically altered the face of computing, while others were a flash in the pan. This book focuses on two technologies (one mostly hardware and one mostly software) that are rapidly becoming key building blocks for the next generation of data centers. Blade servers and virtualization, working together, provide the flexibility, high availability, and manageability to enable utility computing, where computing resources are provisioned as needed to deliver services on demand to users anywhere, anytime.

Blade server systems offer a highly modular, prewired, ultrahigh-density form factor for servers in the data center. With a design that allows shared redundant components such as power and cooling, network switches, and management modules, blade servers help reduce the number of components in the data center, as well as significantly increase the computing power per footprint.

Virtualization also offers both space savings and a reduction in the number of physical components by allowing multiple servers to be consolidated as virtual servers onto a single physical server. Virtualization eliminates the problem of large numbers of highly underutilized servers, and the space, management, power, and cooling that they require.

Both of these technologies are available in many forms from a variety of vendors, including major systems and software vendors as well as a number of innovative start-ups. Both have been successfully implemented in user environments ranging from small-medium businesses (SMB) to some of the largest enterprise data centers in the world.

This book provides an overview of the benefits of these technologies, an architectural view of each, an analysis of the major offerings, user case studies, and considerations and tips for selecting and implementing products. We hope you enjoy the book and that it makes your journey into implementing these technologies a smoother ride.

Who This Book Is For

This book is intended for those responsible for a variety of phases of evaluating and implementing blade server systems and server virtualization technologies. These phases include assessing your needs and evaluating the benefits of these technologies; analyzing the approaches and architectures of various alternatives; comparing and contrasting different vendor solutions; planning and preparing the data center for implementation; understanding trade-offs, pitfalls, and other considerations; and finally going into production.

About This Book

To help you find the information appropriate for the phase you are in, this book is divided into four major parts, plus the appendices.

Part I: Technology Evolution — Covers a brief history of related computing technologies, discussing a number of recurring themes. It then provides a more detailed history and timeline for blades and virtualization and their evolution since 2001 and discuses blades and virtualization as significant evolutionary steps, outlining the benefits they offer.

Part II: A Closer Look — Examines the architectures and specific features of blade server systems and their components, as well as the various types of virtualization and architectures/features. It also discusses related issues such as clustering, management, and pertinent standards.

Part III: Hardware, Facilities, and Software Considerations — Offers questions to think about when implementing blade solutions and virtualization, including blade hardware considerations, system software considerations (focusing on virtualization), and data center facilities planning (power and cooling).

Part IV: Solutions — Presents a matrix-based approach for applying decision criteria in differentiating products. This section includes a blade server system matrix and a server virtualization matrix, with available products assessed as of 2006. It also offers an analysis of available blade and virtualization solutions and discusses user case studies, with production implementations of blades and virtualization together. Finally, it offers a glimpse into the future of blade system and virtualization technologies.

Appendix A: Vendor and Product Information — Information in this appendix was provided directly by the blade and virtualization vendors to give an overview of their relevant product offerings and market focus.

Appendix B: Specifications and Standards — Relevant management and other standards and specifications are outlined along with online resources for more-detailed information.

Glossary — Quick-reference definitions of blade-server-system and virtualization terminology.

We hope you find these sections helpful as you decide whether and/or how to use these technologies to your best advantage. We also hope you find the book accurate, but we know that we are not perfect, and that mistakes do happen. If you find errors in the book or you have questions that remain unanswered, please let us know. We will attempt to make corrections available online at www.focusonsystems.com, and hopefully prevent others from sharing your frustration, while improving the quality of our information.

Technology Evolution

Blades and Virtualization – Building Blocks for Next-Generation Data Centers

Over the past 40 years, tremendous advances in the size, speed, costs, usability, and management of computer technology have been made. From the mainframe era of the 1970s, through the PC and workstation era, the client/server era, and the Internet era of the 1980s and 1990s, and now to the current consolidation era, computing has changed. As a result, the world had been transformed.

Many of these changes have occurred through a slow evolution; however, some technology advancements caused major paradigm shifts both within IT and in business operations. The commoditization of the PC, for example, created a paradigm shift in computing that is still evident today. The popularization of the Internet provides another example. The most recent evolutionary step in computing has been the introduction of blades and virtualization.

Today blades and virtualization, as complementary technologies, promise to be the catalysts for the next revolution in computing. Blades and virtualization are key enablers of true utility computing, an environment in which components are added (provisioned) *when* they are needed, *where* they are needed, and only *for as long as* they are needed — to give control back to businesses.

What Are Blades?

Blades are a new form factor for computer technology, which packages ultra-high density components including servers, storage, and communications interfaces in a prewired chassis with shared components such as power, cooling, and networking. In contrast to the traditional *horizontal* positioning within a rack (rack-mounted servers), blades are typically (though not always) installed *vertically* in a blade chassis, like books in a bookshelf.

In addition to the high density, prewiring, and shared components, an important differentiator between blades and conventional servers is the incorporation of remote out-of-band manageability as an integral part of each blade "device." This is fundamentally different from conventional servers (rack-mount or stand-alone) where systems management has been designed as an add-on capability.

The blade approach shown in Figure 1.1 offers considerable space savings over rack-mounted (1U) servers. For example, 60 blade servers can fit in the same physical space as 42 rack-mounted servers.

Figure 1.1: Example of blades in a chassis
Source: IBM

Server Blades and PC Blades

Most of the buzz about blades has focused on blade servers as an upgraded alternative to rack-mounted server farms. When one is implementing blade technology, blade servers are generally the starting point. However, there are other types of blades.

In addition to building servers on blades, a number of vendors have delivered PC blade products. In a PC blade implementation, end users operate with only a monitor, a keyboard, and a mouse (and/or in some cases a specialized client device), and the PC runs on a central blade. PC blades offer the ability to recentralize certain aspects of distributed computing. They offer improvements in physical security and manageability by locating the actual compute and storage components in a central location, allowing easy access for IT as well as centralized maintenance and management while providing a desktop environment for the end user, similar to having a local PC.

Storage and Network Blades

Blade technology also extends to other components of computing, including storage and networking. Since blade servers require access to information, the choice is whether to incorporate storage on the blade server itself, utilize storage or networking protocols to communicate with standard storage devices outside of the blade environment, or utilize storage blades. All of these options have pros and cons, of course, to be discussed in depth later in the book.

The same issues and options are true for general networking requirements. As blades have become more popular, networking vendors have seen the opportunity, and network modules (sometimes called *switch blades*) for both IP and Fibre Channel networks are available for blade server systems from multiple vendors.

Why Blades?

Since their introduction in 2001, blade systems have gained significant traction in the enterprise space. Reasons for implementing blade systems versus rack-mounted servers will be discussed in detail later, but here is a summary:

- Space savings and efficiency — packing more computing power into a smaller area
- Consolidation of servers to improve and centralize management as well as to improve utilization of computer assets
- Simplification and reduction of complexity (modularity, ease of integration, prewired configurations, shared components), ease of deployment, and improved manageability and serviceability
- Return on investment (ROI) and improved total cost of ownership (TCO) through increased hardware utilization and reduced operating expenses (OpEx)

What Is Virtualization?

Virtualization is the ability to create a logical abstraction of physical assets. In the case of server virtualization, it allows for multiple "virtual" servers to run on one physical server, thereby consolidating many physical servers onto one. There are several approaches to server virtualization, which will be discussed in detail later in the book.

Why Virtualization?

Since server virtualization allows multiple virtual servers to run on one physical server, by its nature it consolidates servers and applications. This increases server utilization and helps address the problem of server sprawl. A Gartner Survey in 2005 showed that 60% of users surveyed had consolidation projects underway, and an additional 28% were looking into it. Cost-reduction pressure, very low server-utilization rates (often under 5%), and the need for improved management have been key drivers.

Reduction in the number of servers from virtualization yields direct savings in hardware, power and cooling, and floor space, reducing both capital expenses (CapEx) and ongoing OpEx. In addition, the ease of deployment of virtual machines and advanced management capabilities in the virtualized environment contribute to reduced OpEx.

Why Virtualization and Blades?

Blade and virtualization technologies together provide critical building blocks for the next generation of enterprise data centers, addressing a two-fold challenge: The first is to deliver on the ever-increasing need for more computing power per square foot under significant IT operations budget constraints. The second challenge is the management of the geographic proliferation of operational centers, forcing the enterprise data center to operate and be managed as a single entity.

Blades bring savings in per-server costs due to consolidation of system resources into a smaller footprint (shared modules and simplified cabling, power and floor space). Virtualization brings additional savings through consolidation of multiple servers onto single blades. The modularity of blades within a chassis make them well-suited to implementation as groups of resources within a virtualized pool. These resources can then be provisioned for various tasks as needed. As requirements grow, it is simply a matter of adding or accessing more blades. This provides a much-needed solution to a very common problem — large numbers of poorly utilized servers and PCs coupled with an on-demand need for more computing power. Virtualization software efficiently manages the processing load on fewer computers running at higher utilization levels to handle the same burden, improving the ability to deliver on-demand while greatly reducing costs.

One user of virtualization and blades, when asked where virtualization had presented the biggest benefits, responded, "If possible, deploy (server virtualization) on blade servers....The configuration becomes so much more manageable and redundant, and that boosts efficiency even more. Why? Because blades not only take up half the space of traditional 1U servers, but they also share vital resources such as switches and interface cards, allowing for more-simplified, centralized management."

Conclusion

The high density and modularity that blades offer, together with consolidation of physical systems through virtualization, will allow data centers to pack substantially more computing power into their data centers, achieve higher utilization of that computing power, and reduce their CapEx costs. Racks of blades working together can deliver the equivalent power of supercomputers, and are built on modular components that can be added/subtracted/swapped as needed, at a greatly reduced cost. In addition, the modularity and manageability of blades together with virtualization allows for significant streamlining of operational and serviceability procedures, reducing IT OpEx costs. Furthermore, integrated remote management of blade systems and advanced management capabilities of a virtualized infrastructure allow for ease of deployment, redeployment, and serviceability in a centralized or distributed data-center environment.

This chapter introduced the concepts and some of the benefits of blades and virtualization as complementary technologies. In Chapter 2, "Evolution of Computing Technology — Setting the Stage," we will take a step back to frame the blade and virtualization technologies within the history of computers.

Evolution of Computing Technology — Setting the Stage

It is important to understand the context in which new computing technologies, such as blade servers and server virtualization, emerge. To that end, this chapter will look at common trends that have arisen throughout the history of computing, as well as the major evolutionary advancements in computing over the past four decades.

Recurring Themes

The progress in computing technology over the past 40 years has involved a number of key themes that occur over and over again. Many of these themes clearly apply to the introduction and adoption of blades and virtualization technologies.

Bigger, Better, Faster, Cheaper

With advances in computer-related technology, new computers, storage, and networking products are always introduced as bigger, better, faster, and cheaper. *Bigger* describes overall ability — generally increasing the computing power and memory or disk capacity. *Better* usually addresses increased usability, manageability, and reliability (lower mean time between failure [MTBF]). *Faster* relates to component speed — whether it's a processor, bus, channel, or network — and I/O speed. *Cheaper* is just that — less expensive but hopefully not cheaper quality. Blade and virtualization technologies offer these benefits in a variety of ways that are discussed in detail throughout this book. Clearly, the advances in processor chips are allowing more processor power and memory to fit onto circuit boards with greater reliability, yielding bigger, better, faster, and cheaper processor equivalents. Add in the virtualization and software management that enables blades to work together as a unified system, with components provisioned as needed, and the concepts of bigger, better, faster, and cheaper take on a whole new dimension.

Miniaturization

In 1965 Intel's cofounder, Gordon Moore, predicted that the number of transistors on a chip (i.e., *density*) would double every 18–24 months. This prediction became known as Moore's Law, and has continued to bring processing-performance increases, and decreases in size as well as costs. This law has also been reflected in disk capacity and memory, which now take up less space on a motherboard or in a disk array. Back in the 1970s a single computer filled a room, whereas today we are able to carry a computer in our pocket. Computer memory in the 1970s was counted in bytes, whereas today our computers support terabytes of memory. The size reductions and increased density possible with blade technology come directly from the miniaturization of the components that make up the blade servers.

Miniaturization has also had a significant effect on the software. The ability to put more memory and high-performance processors together has meant that software operating systems and programs can be more sophisticated. Most recently, server virtualization software has taken computing to a new level, to create multiple "virtual" servers where only one physical server used to be.

Decentralization and Recentralization

Back when computers were room-sized and required large amounts of power and cooling, they lived in glass rooms with raised floors, in one central location. People were required to go to the computers (either physically or via terminals) rather than taking them along with them like we can do today. As computers got smaller and cheaper, they moved out into people's offices and to locations remote from company headquarters, placing the computing power closer to the user and giving the control (and, generally, the responsibility) to the user departments. As more computers left the management and control of the Management Information Systems (MIS) organization (as it was called at that time), the decentralization of IT management began. It quickly became apparent that while decentralization often gave users' departments the ability to respond more quickly to business needs, it also created technical systems-management challenges that were often beyond the department's ability, resources, and skill level. Thus began the cyclical process of decentralizing and recentralizing IT resources. This included the computers themselves, the systems and application development work, and the management of the hardware, software, and data.

As the management of IT systems, networks, and storage has become increasingly complex, there has been a shift toward recentralizing much of the operational management of IT resources, regardless of where they are physically located. As organizations reap the benefits of both blades and virtualization software, the effects of this recentralization will increase.

Eras of Evolution

As poet and philosopher George Santayana put it, "Those who cannot remember the past are condemned to repeat it." It is helpful, therefore, to start with a brief history of the eras of computing — mainframes, PCs and workstations, client/server, the Internet, and now the consolidation era. We will then look at the promise of next-generation data centers, and whether they will deliver true utility computing enabled by blades and virtualization technologies.

The Mainframe Era

Commercial enterprise data centers of the 1970s were dominated by IBM mainframes. Other vendors involved in mainframes and minicomputers included Digital Equipment Corporation (DEC, now part of HP), Burroughs and Sperry (merged to form Unisys), Control Data Corporation (CDC), and Data General. CDC was a leader in scientific computing, along with Cray in supercomputers. In the commercial data centers, IBM virtually owned the market.

Large data centers consisted of room-sized mainframe computers, generally either IBM or IBM plug-compatible manufacturers (PCMs). Accompanying these large computers were strings of disk drives (also called direct access storage devices or DASD), strings of tape drives, printers, card readers, a system console, and a communications front-end processor. Virtually all of the hardware was either from IBM or one of a handful of PCMs. These included Amdahl (acquired by Fujitsu), Hitachi Data Systems (which had acquired National Advanced Systems from National Semiconductor), and Storage Technology Corporation (STC, now the StorageTek division of Sun Microsystems). Likewise, the systems software, including operating systems, utilities, database management systems, and application packages, all came from IBM or a small group of software vendors. These included Computer Associates International, Inc. (CA), and a small number of others, most of which were eventually acquired by CA. In many ways, IBM's dominance made for a simpler world, since it was all IBM — interoperability was not yet much of an issue.

The computer equipment lived in an environmentally controlled room, with a raised floor to create a place for the massive cabling required, as well as massive cooling (air or water) to address the significant heat output. Each string of disk was connected to a mainframe channel through a disk control unit, and each string of tape through a tape control unit. On the high end, certain mainframe CPUs were available in multiprocessor (MP) models, where two single processors were linked together.

All of the I/O device control units were connected to the mainframe via a byte or block multiplex channel, through bus and tag cables with four-inch-wide connectors and extremely stiff and bulky cables connected under the raised floor. The channel architecture offered a high-speed connection with little overhead, but the cabling imposed specific distance limitations for all devices.

Users accessed mainframe applications through a variety of terminals, ranging from line-at-a-time TTY terminals to full-screen terminals like the IBM 3270 product lines. See Figure 2.1 for an example of a mainframe data center from the 1970s. All software ran in the mainframe, with terminals acting simply as display and data-entry devices. IBM 3270 terminals were attached either locally to a mainframe or through a communications front-end processor via a 3X7X control unit. Although all the software executed in the mainframe, the control unit and terminals had the ability to perform limited local editing-type functions. Some terminals, called distributed function terminals (DFT), were designed to be somewhat more efficient, allowing some functions to be done locally at the terminal. This was the extent of distributed processing in the mainframe-terminal environment.

Figure 2.1: Mainframe data center — 1970s
Source: IBM Corporate Archives

Multiprocessing

As computing requirements increased, even the largest CPUs were not providing enough horsepower. In addition to needing increased capacity, data-center managers came under pressure for increased reliability and availability. To address both of these needs, IBM introduced multiprocessing (MP) versions of their largest mainframes. The MP models allowed multiple CPUs to work together as a virtual unit.

Two types of multiprocessing options were offered, with variations on how closely the two systems worked together. A tightly coupled multiprocessing (TCMP) system was composed of two processors sharing main memory and operating under the control of a single operating system, with a single system image. Loosely coupled multiprocessing (LCMP) operated as two separate systems, communicating through a channel-to-channel adapter and sharing disk storage and a single job queue. A component of the operating system, Job Entry Subsystem 3 (JES3), handled the job-sharing between the two systems.

Hardware features provided functions such as a heartbeat and a communications path between systems. Operating system software provided management functions such as managing the job queue to provide load balancing between CPUs for efficient utilization, and failover, so that if one half of the MP went down the other half could still operate as a standalone system. These principles are key requirements for multiprocessing today, which blade and virtualization technologies are leveraging.

Mainframe Operating Systems

The mainframe operating systems of the 1970s included many of the virtualization technologies and systems-management capabilities that posed challenges in the PC, client/server, and open systems environments that followed. Multiple IBM operating systems ran on the IBM S/370 mainframes, including DOS/VS (for small environments), MVS (Multiple Virtual Storage, for large enterprises), and VM/370 (initially, mostly for operating system conversions). Current versions of these are still in use today with IBM's VSE/ESA, z/OS, and z/VM. Since their initial releases, they have been updated to support and take advantage of the technology improvements of the 1980s and 1990s, such as extended architecture (XA), which expanded from 24- to 31-bit addressing, allowing virtual memory to go above 16MB. (This was later expanded to 64-bit addressing to increase memory capability even more.)

In the 1970s, these operating systems introduced the concept of virtual memory (then also called virtual storage) as part of the mainframe OS. This allowed the abstraction and mapping of real memory to virtual memory, and the specification of partitions or address spaces within the overall environment to each have access to a full set of virtual memory, separating and protecting the programs running in each address space.

The VM (virtual machine) operating system went to the next level of virtualization, and was the pioneer of virtual-machine environments. VM came from a combination of two components: Control Program 67 (CP67) and Cambridge Monitor System (CMS). CP67 allowed the mainframe to be divided into multiple virtual computers, with each virtual machine able to simulate a full mainframe and run a standard operating system in it. CMS was a single-user system that was ideally suited to run under CP67 as a conversational time-sharing system. CP and CMS evolved to become IBM's VM/370 product, used by huge numbers of IBM customers for migration from one mainframe to another or one operating system to another, since it allowed both the old and the new environments to run simultaneously under the VM hypervisor. This concept of a virtual machine is the same concept being used today by VMware, Microsoft, and Xen.

The communications functions of the mainframe environment of the 1970s were accomplished through a communications switch called a front-end processor, which ran its own software. Initially these switches supported only asynchronous and bisynchronous protocols to remote terminals, job-entry stations, or other front-end processors. This type of networking was replaced by IBM's Systems Network Architecture (SNA), which effectively added network virtualization. SNA defined logical units (LUs), which allowed different types of devices to live on the same communications line. This gave devices the ability to be accessed across multiple applications rather than being owned by a single application. The front-end processor and the software that ran in it paved the way for the intelligent switching and network virtualization software soon to come.

The Personal Computer and Workstation Era

During the mainframe heyday of the 1970s, another movement in computer technology began. A variety of microcomputers sprung up, based on Intel's 8080 chip and using a new programming language called BASIC and an operating system called CP/M.

When the first microcomputers were released, they had to be programmed directly in machine language (1s and 0s), like the very early mainframes. A new programming language called BASIC (Beginner's All-Purpose Symbolic Instruction Code) was created to help program these micros using a more English-like syntax. Various versions of BASIC with varying levels of functionality emerged. When a hardware vendor put out a request for a version of BASIC with advanced functions for their system, two Harvard students, Bill Gates and Paul Allen, met the requirements and sold the new BASIC to the company on a per-copy royalty basis. With this experience behind them, the two young men started a new software company and called it Microsoft.

Before the 8080 chip came out, Intel was interested in developing a version of PL/M (the language that mainframe system software was written in) to run on it. Rather than developing the 8080 emulator under DEC's operating system, the developer created a primitive operating system to run on the 8080 itself and called it CP/M (Control Program for Microcomputers). It was heavily influenced by the DEC operating environment, with features such as eight-character filenames with three-character extensions. Some of the features are still used by Windows today. Although Intel declined to market CP/M, it provided the basic foundation for the wide variety of micros coming to market at that time.

The combination of CP/M and BASIC needed just one more thing for micros to take off. The killer application for micros was end-user-oriented software for word processing, databases, and spreadsheets, and it came in the form of Word-Star, dBASE II, and VisiCalc. By the late 1970s there were at least 40 microcomputers in popular use and they were gaining traction in the market.

The next significant event in microcomputer evolution changed the industry and brought microcomputing to the enterprise arena. IBM was preparing to enter the microcomputer market in 1981 and went to Microsoft looking for help. From a small company in Seattle, Bill Gates bought an alternative operating system that was developed for the Intel 8086. Microsoft modified it for the IBM PC (Figure 2.2), calling it MS-DOS, and granted IBM a nonexclusive license. The IBM PC and DOS quickly became the industry standard for microcomputers and both began to find their way into corporate environments. As far as the explosion of the PC industry goes, the rest is history.

Figure 2.2: IBM PC 1981
Source: IBM Corporate Archives

During the rise of PCs in the 1980s, for the first time computer components could be purchased off the shelf and people could build their own microcomputers. In 1982, a group of four Stanford students — Andy Bechtolsheim, Scott McNealy, Vinod Khosla, and Bill Joy — saw this as an opportunity to build a computer that was as fast as the current minicomputers (bigger, better, faster) but was significantly less expensive (cheaper) and had a smaller footprint (miniaturization). Thus began the rise of Sun (Stanford University Network) Microsystems. The group delivered the first Sun workstation based on the Motorola chipset and the Berkeley UNIX (now called Berkeley Software Distribution or BSD) reference port and included a new networking protocol called TCP/IP, which sat on top of Ethernet. With the launch of their first workstation, they opened a whole new market that sat squarely between the historic mainframes and the emerging PCs. Sun's workstations caught on in the scientific computing world because they brought the power of the minicomputer to the desks of engineers and scientists. It didn't take long for the financial world to recognize the value of putting the power of computers at the users' fingertips. Soon there were many similar products available from companies like Apollo (acquired by HP), Silicon Graphics (SGI), MIPS, and IBM.

The Client/Server Communications Era

Soon the need emerged for these business PCs and workstations to communicate, both with other PCs/workstations and with corporate mainframes. This was the beginning of the client/server era, and two new types of communications: mainframe-based client/server communications and local area network (LAN) client/server communications.

Mainframe Client/Server Evolution

In many corporate organizations, users with 3270 terminals on their desks also now had a PC for local applications. Given the fact that PCs could accept added internal hardware cards and run software, it wasn't long before products emerged that allowed a PC to emulate a 3270 terminal. This gave users the ability to run their PC applications and access mainframe applications from the same device (but initially there was no way to share files between the two environments). This need created a related set of products that provided various types of file transfer between mainframes and PCs, known as micro-mainframe links. These products allowed a user to download a file from the mainframe, use that file locally on their PC from a PC application, and then upload it back to the mainframe. Although these products offered a new level of functionality and the beginnings of a new kind of distributed processing, they also created a whole new set of issues. First and foremost was data integrity — how do you prevent multiple users from downloading the same file, modifying it, and then uploading it back to the same host file? This file-locking problem is still a key issue in distributed processing and file management today.

Another method of micro-mainframe communications evolved around the SNA definition of an intelligent client, called advanced program-to-program communications (APPC). Instead of treating the PC as a dumb terminal, APPC allowed software running on the mainframe to communicate with software running on the PC through a more intelligent protocol. This allowed the development of coprocessing applications, which took advantage of the local intelligence of the PC and then communicated with the mainframe as needed. These coprocessing applications were the next step in distributed processing, and became known as mainframe client/server applications.

Local Area Network Client/Server Evolution

While PCs began the move into the mainframe world, another industry-changing trend was taking shape. In addition to connecting PCs to the mainframe, products were introduced to connect PCs and workstations to each other through what became known as local area networks (LANs). Initial PC connections were peer-to-peer, where the PCs were simply wired together and could see and utilize each other's resources. PC and workstation LANs were built using various topologies, including token ring and Ethernet. As workstations and PCs propagated out to the desktops of every employee, management of those resources became increasingly less centralized — and the decentralization movement of the 1980s was in full swing.

The next big leap came with the introduction of file servers. The concept of file serving allowed one computer system to make files available to other client systems and provided for file-system management and locking to preserve data integrity. This had two purposes: the first was to enable collaborative work through file sharing, and the second was to centralize data onto one server system for ease of file-management tasks (backup, recovery, etc.). The leader in this file-server movement was Novell, which at its peak owned 70% of the PC network market. At the same time, Sun Microsystems had developed a new protocol called Network File System (NFS) that allowed file sharing across multiple systems. Sun released the protocol and a reference port into the public domain in the mid 1980s. These file server technologies became the basis for future networked storage, and today nearly all network-attached storage (NAS) implementations are based on NFS or the Microsoft version — SMB/CIFS (Server Message Block/Common Internet File System).

As a result of these advances, the server market was born, creating the roots for many later variations, including application servers, clustered servers, NAS, and eventually blade servers.

The Internet Era

As the prices of PCs dropped, demand continued to climb. With the power of the computer available to the general public, the need to share information became paramount. Another major event that would change computing forever was in the works. The popular use of the Internet grew exponentially in the 1990s and across the turn of the century (Y2K), surpassing all expectations. The Internet was created in 1969 as part of a project of the U.S. Department of Defense. Originally known as ARPANET (Advanced Research Projects Agency Network), it linked four computer sites at various universities and research centers and was used by scientists. Its usage grew to universities around the world throughout the 1970s, making it an international network, based on the TCP/IP protocol.

As consumer products evolved to simplify access to the Internet, users in the general population discovered the power of using the Net. With the addition of the World Wide Web interface in 1990 — which delivered web pages containing text, pictures, audio, and video — more information began to appear and the Internet became a mainstay of both consumer and corporate communications. Companies like AOL, Google, Yahoo, and MSN sprung up to be the feeder services for all this information. These companies built and are continuing to build huge server farms, placed in rows and rows of racks to service billions of requests a day.

In addition to internal private corporate networks, a new type of communications emerged, allowing companies to communicate across the public Internet, with technologies to provide various levels of security.

The Consolidation Era

The ubiquity of end users having their own computers on their desks changed the way businesses operate. However, it quickly became clear that managing all of the often geographically dispersed systems was a nightmare. Backing up all the information on these systems alone was an insurmountable task. So began efforts at recentralizing operations. It started with the business-critical servers and applications, then moved to critical business information and associated storage and, with advancements in management software, moved to recentralizing the systems themselves or at least the management of those systems to avoid loss of productivity or data at the remote locations. Throughout the 1980s and 1990s, waves of recentralization and decentralization occurred.

When the Internet bubble burst in the late 1990s, the resulting economic downturn forced corporate IT management to begin slashing operational budgets. IT was responsible for managing large infrastructures based on a model where every server ran only one application (e.g., Exchange, SQL, etc.). Often these servers were running somewhere around 5% CPU utilization. Under severe cost pressure, it no longer made sense to continue to manage this large underutilized collection of servers, taking up unnecessary space and using extra power and cooling. Thus began the era of server consolidation. The use of blade servers, with their ease of management and smaller footprint, coupled with server virtualization, is helping to facilitate this recentralization of servers, applications, and management into a set of consolidated blade-server systems. The inherent manageability built into blade servers and virtualization software also enables further recentralization of management for remote systems.

Consolidation continues today in many businesses, not only with management of servers and applications but also with storage, centralizing information creation, and management in an effort to lower both CapEx and OpEx.

The Evolution of Technologies

As we've moved through these eras, interesting changes in particular technology areas have taught us lessons that apply to blades and virtualization.

Storage

The evolution of storage has followed many of the same trends seen with computers. As mentioned previously, core memory for the first computers was exceptionally small by today's standards. The ENIAC, hailed as the first electronic digital computer and recognized as the grandfather of today's computers, could only store 20 10-digit decimal numbers in its localized buffers — there was no *central memory*. Even as more capabilities were added to computers, including core memory, it was obvious that the ability to feed large amounts of data in and out of the processor was necessary; hence the development of input and output mechanisms and external data storage.

Before the advent of magnetic disk storage, programs and data were stored on punch cards, paper tape, and magnetic tape. Paper tape was a fairly inexpensive media that would normally hold about 400 bytes of data per tape and could be read at about 300 rows per second (8 channels per row).

Magnetic tape was first developed in Germany in the 1920s but was only a research project until the 1940s, when the U.S. Navy became more interested in it. The Navy then funded U.S. researchers at 3M (Minnesota Mining and Manufacturing Company) to create both a high-quality magnetic tape and a tape recorder, which they did in 1945. All of this was happening at about the same time the first commercial ENIAC-type computer was being built (later renamed UNIVAC) with magnetic tape input/output. Unfortunately, the money ran out and the project wasn't completed and tested until 1951. This test demonstrated the first commercial computer to use a magnetic tape storage system. It had eight tape drives, each of which was six feet high and three feet wide. It used half-inch tape that was 1,200 feet long and recorded data on eight channels at 100 inches per second with a transfer rate of roughly 7.2KB per second.

Then in the mid 1950s, IBM developed a radical new magnetic disk storage device they coupled with the RAMAC (random access method of accounting and control) computers called the 350 C disk drive. This new disk storage system had an extremely large capacity for the time, rapid access, and low cost. It stored 5MB on 50 24-inch disks with a maximum access time of 0.8 seconds.

Storage technologies have evolved (or have become extinct) over the past 50 years. As computers got bigger, better, faster, cheaper, and smaller, so did the storage technologies. For example, magnetic disk storage in the 1960s cost about $2,000 per megabyte. Devices had a capacity of 5 megabytes, with a form factor of 24 inches per disk platter, housed in disk drive devices that resembled washing machines.

As of mid 2006, magnetic disk storage costs less than $.005 per megabyte, they have device capacities in the terabytes (TB), and they are as small as a quarter. Access times for today's magnetic disks are on the order of three milliseconds, with maximum transfer rates of 96MB/sec. The MTBF for an individual drive is more than one million hours — roughly 150 years.

Not surprisingly, the theme of centralization/decentralization found its way into the history of storage. When computers decentralized in the 1980s and 1990s, so did their storage. With the advent of local area networks, file servers, and decentralization, came both innovation and challenges that arose with the first system crash or disk failure. Whose job was it to back up all the newly dispersed storage? Initially, individuals were tasked with securing their own data. When that failed miserably, there was a movement toward both centralized backup and centralized storage, thereby securing the valuable corporate resource — the data.

Following on the heels of LANs and LAN file servers, specialized storage servers were introduced as NAS appliances. These appliances started essentially as special-purpose, stripped-down file servers, which allowed a large amount of data to be stored on the appliance and shared by multiple servers and workstations. NAS appliances proliferated in an effort to decouple storage from individual workstations and centralize storage and storage management, yet maintain a decentralization of computing power.

Within a few years, in many enterprise data centers large amounts of storage began to be decoupled from computers and attached to networks called storage area networks (SANs). Steady advances in storage and storage network technology continue to contribute to the steady growth of SANs.

Virtualization has also been part of the history of storage, almost from the beginning. IBM used virtualization in the VM operating system to present both virtual disk and tape devices to the guest operating systems running as virtual machines, regardless of how many physical devices were attached to the computer. Today virtualization is used extensively with disk arrays. One aspect of storage virtualization is to present one disk interface for information lifecycle management (ILM) with hierarchical storage-management systems that move older, unaccessed data to cheaper, slower storage media automatically. Storage virtualization also helps in creating *hot copies* for business continuance scenarios.

Storage virtualization comes in three major flavors, categorized by where the virtualization takes place. Device-based virtualization is done within the storage arrays, providing a virtual device to the host, which is mapped to physical locations within the array. Network-based virtualization is done within the network itself, through intelligent switches or virtualization appliances. Network virtualization allows virtualization of storage across devices from different storage vendors. Host-based virtualization is done by software that resides in the host computer(s); it virtualizes storage across both networks and storage devices, providing vendor independence across network and storage vendors.

Storage continues to evolve along with computers. Just as blade servers are the latest and greatest form of computers, storage blades and blades booting from SANs are delivering better, faster, and cheaper storage, centralized and decentralized, leveraging improvements in virtualization to ease the storage administrator's management efforts.

Clustering

The principles of clustering came from the multiprocessing work that already had been done by companies like IBM and CDC. Computer clusters are loosely coupled multiprocessing implementations. Each computer in the cluster is a *node* with its own processor(s) (clusters can be created with multiprocessing nodes and often are), operating system, memory, and system storage. There may or may not be a shared storage pool; however, very few clusters today are implemented with shared data. Initially clusters were simply separate workstations on a network. However, with shrinking footprints and increased costs for space, often cluster nodes were rack-mounted, one on top of the other. Today blade servers enable clustering in even smaller footprints, as well as shared power and cooling.

The first commodity clustering product in the open-systems market was ARCnet, developed and released by Datapoint in 1977. ARCnet wasn't successful in the market and clustering lay dormant until DEC released their

VAXcluster product in the 1980s. With the introduction of cheap(er) computers, first with microcomputers of the late 1970s and early 1980s then with the workstations and Ethernet networks of the mid '80s, departments were able to make computer purchasing decisions on their own. In the mid 1980s this was especially true in universities, where some of the largest problems in computational physics were being researched on a shoestring budget. Without the funds to purchase the latest multiprocessor supercomputer, or even the more reasonable minicomputers such as the DEC VAX, an approach was developed that broke down the problems into parts that could be computed asynchronously in parallel across multiple workstations, using the network as the communications "bus."

In 1989, a group at Oak Ridge National Laboratory began work on a parallel virtual machine (PVM), which created a framework that allowed researchers to develop computational models that could take advantage of many heterogeneous computers working in parallel. The University of Tennessee released the first public version of PVM in 1991. The PVM software is free from netlib and has been compiled on everything from a laptop to a Cray. This eventually led to what is known today as high-performance computing clusters (HPCC).

In the mid 1990s businesses were discovering that the cost of computer downtime, for both scheduled preventive maintenance operations and unscheduled outages, was escalating dramatically. The question of how to keep business applications up and running, 24×7×365 became a high priority for IT management. High-availability (HA) clustering was born as a way to address this need. HA clustering allows two or more homogeneous computers, configured in a redundant fashion, to continue working when one system is down. The most common HA cluster contains two nodes, eliminating all single points of failure.

To understand clustering, it is important to note the communications required between clustered nodes to provide both failover and job sharing. A *cluster*, in its broadest definition, is two or more computers on a network, working together on one or more computational applications. Therefore, it is possible for the network, rather than being a local area network (LAN), to span across a wide geographical area — for example, the Internet. The communications issues are very similar to that of the LAN cluster; however, the Internet portion introduces obvious security issues. For instance, how are these geographically separate computers supposed to trust each other, especially in today's climate of hacking and viruses? This special case of clustering is the basis for *grid computing*.

Grid/Utility Computing

Like many of the technologies discussed in this book, grid (or utility) computing is a technology that is still evolving. However, it is fast on its way to realizing the vision of large-scale resource-sharing across geographically dispersed organizations. In today's global economy, especially with the amount of out-sourcing occurring, being able to share computational as well as data resources worldwide is imperative. By now businesses are all too familiar with the challenges of 24×7×365 requirements. Increasingly, IT organizations are being pushed to leverage all their computing resources together to deliver dynamic computational access across the globe to advance their business objectives.

The nomenclature *grid computing* brings to mind an electrical power grid, where a number of resources contribute to the pool of shared power to be accessed as needed. This is where the name *utility computing* originated. Although the promise of grid computing has not yet been realized, steady progress is being made. Grid computing is expected to see strong successes in financial services, oil exploration, medical research, security, entertainment, and mechanical engineering. Much like clusters, grid computing doesn't rely on high-powered computational engines; rather, it uses underutilized computational engines (workstations, PCs, mainframes, and so on), located on the network, anywhere in the world. As blade servers meet the criteria of being computational engines located on a network, along with their related blade component technologies, they will certainly see a bright future in grid computing.

Rack Servers

As decentralized enterprises shifted into the consolidation era and started ramping up centrally located groups of servers, the market was ripe for a more efficient and more cost effective way to store servers. The rack-mounted server market took off in the early 1990s as enterprises created high-end rack-mounted server farms, which resided in the data center, under the control of the IT organization.

The introduction of rack servers allowed users to configure racks of servers, networking equipment (for example, routers, switches, and firewalls) usually the size of one or two pizza boxes (1U and 2U), and storage devices (usually 9U) — potentially from different vendors — into a much smaller footprint than with traditional hardware. (See Figure 2.3.) With rack servers, devices are bolted in horizontally, and the user wires everything together behind the rack. Most of the major systems vendors offer rack-mounted versions of their products.

Although rack-mounted servers were an improvement over previous hardware options, wiring the components together often created a mess. Furthermore, as the rack-server market grew, the software side lacked maturity — in provisioning, virtualization, and systems-management tools. These areas have left opportunities for blade-server technology and server-virtualization software to deliver next-generation data center capabilities for the enterprise space.

Figure 2.3: Rack-mounted server cabinets
Source: Martin International Enclosures

Server Operating Systems

The evolution of operating systems involves a great deal of history repeating itself. Mainframe operating systems evolved in their user interfaces, their use of virtualization, their fault tolerance and systems availability, loosely coupled multiprocessing, failover, and load balancing. In addition, processes that were originally in the operating system, such as device handling and communications functions, were moved outbound into microcode and separate processors.

Windows

The evolution of PC and server operating systems experienced many parallel improvements. The growth from MS/DOS (PC/DOS) to Microsoft Windows in late 1985 added a graphical user interface, device-independent graphics, and the beginnings of a multitasking virtual environment (allowing multiple applications to run simultaneously), following in the footsteps of DOS/VS and MVS mainframe environments.

Throughout the evolution of Windows — Windows 3.1 (1992), Windows NT (1994), Windows 95, Windows 98, Windows and Windows Server 2000, Windows XP (2001), and Windows Server 2003 — the operating-system software grew more stable, and the "blue screen of death" for which Windows was famous (the error message that appeared when the OS crashed with a fatal error) became less and less frequent. Error handling improved and system availability increased. Device handling moved into device drivers and became *plug and play.* Windows Server added clustering with both failover and load balancing capability for increasing numbers of cluster nodes. This evolution continues, with virtualization capabilities being added into the OS, first to Windows Server with Virtual Server and eventually to the Longhorn release with Windows Server Virtualization. (This will be discussed later in more detail in Chapter 8, "Virtualization.")

UNIX

In the open-systems market, UNIX also grew up. From the geeky, technical gurus' operating system developed at Bell Labs in 1969 to run on multiple types of computers, UNIX has grown to become the basis for most high-end workstation environments, with its sophisticated OS features and a full-featured GUI.

Initially found only on mainframes, minis, and high-end microcomputers, several versions of UNIX were available for PCs by the end of the 1980s, but they ran so slowly that most people ran DOS and Windows. By the 1990s, PCs were powerful enough to run UNIX.

In 1991 a young man named Linus Torvalds took on the task of developing a free academic version of UNIX that was compliant with the original UNIX. Based on the POSIX standard for UNIX, Linux entered the scene and has today become a fully mature UNIX clone that can operate on workstations through high-end servers. Linux is now widely used as a stable and reliable platform for such applications as database servers, web servers, and proxy servers. Linux clusters are used for large-scale computing operations such as Internet search engines.

In general, server operating systems have evolved to support clustering with load balancing and failover in much the same way that mainframes developed this support. UNIX has evolved into virtualization as well, with the Xen open source hypervisor making its way into most UNIX versions going forward.

Conclusion

Many repetitive themes are involved in the emergence, early challenges, and adoption of new computing technology. Several of these themes have been discussed in this chapter:

■ Technology getting bigger, better, faster, and cheaper

- Miniaturization

- Decentralization/recentralization

This chapter provided a brief look at these themes, as well as a history of previous eras of computing and various technologies related to blades and virtualization. This history will provide a useful foundation for the next chapter, as we begin to look at the emergence of blade and virtualization technology, uses, market adoption, and reasons why blades and virtualization will be key to next-generation data centers.

CHAPTER 3

Evolution of Blade and Virtualization Technologies

Since the introduction of blade servers in 2001, the blade server market has grown to $2 billion (as of 2005). IDC expects the market to reach $8 billion by 2008. Blade servers were initially introduced as low-end servers, packaged into a small footprint for applications such as web serving. Over time, blade servers have grown up into a broader usage market, crossing vertical and horizontal segments, ranging from low-end to high-performance computing clusters (HPCC).

About the same time that blade systems were introduced, x86 server virtualization emerged and began to gain significant traction in the marketplace. Spending for virtualization-related activities will reach almost $15 billion by 2009, according to IDC. The virtualization market has evolved from infancy to adolescence, with big players on the field competing with open source technology. This chapter describes the history and evolution of blade and virtualization technologies, market adoption, usage, and reasons for implementation.

Timelines

The timeline in Figure 3.1 gives a high-level view of the history of blades and virtualization in the marketplace, along with related vendor areas and key vendors involved, issues driving blade adoption, and the value propositions that evolved over time.

Blade servers were officially introduced in 2001 by a small company called RLX Technologies (using the Crusoe processor chip from Transmeta) as a compact, modularized form factor, with low-end servers, well suited for scale-out applications such as web serving. *Scale out* is used to describe increasing processing power by running an application across many servers, versus *scale up*, which describes adding more processors in the same server (symmetric multiprocessing or SMP). The major server vendors (IBM, HP, Dell, and Sun) entered the space soon after blade servers were introduced, with varying degrees of effort. As Intel and AMD delivered new-generation (smaller form factor) chips, these server vendors began offering products using chips from both companies.

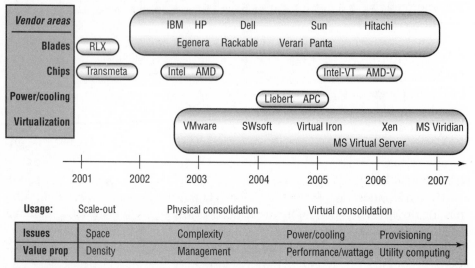

Figure 3.1: Blade and virtualization technology timeline
Source: Focus Consulting

With new processor chips, blade servers were delivered with more computing power, and blade usage shifted from scale-out web serving to broader-use servers and to consolidation of distributed servers into blade server farms. The ability to consolidate in a small space using high-density computing was crucial to the early value proposition. Fairly quickly, however, IT also saw that the architecture of blade server systems offered significant reductions in complexity and improvements in manageability.

IT continued to make progress with consolidation and started implementing larger blade farms. It became evident that there were issues with power and cooling. Vendors such as Liebert and American Power Conversion (APC) became important players in the blade space, offering products and partnerships to help with power and cooling in the data center. It wasn't long before the focus began to shift toward computing performance as it related to power, often quantified as performance per watt.

As these power and cooling issues are addressed, blade technology and its modular design will continue to be a key enabler in the move toward utility computing, where computing, network, and storage resources are provisioned on demand. The ease of provisioning and reprovisioning offered by blade systems, coupled with advances in virtualization, will lead to the next phase of virtual consolidation (where all resources are managed as a virtualized resource pool) and toward the goal of true on-demand utility computing.

In parallel to blade development, x86 server virtualization technology has evolved as well. VMware delivered the first x86 *desktop* virtualization product in 1999 and then released the first x86 *server* virtualization product in 2001. SWsoft entered the space next with its OS virtualization solution, Virtuozzo, followed by Virtual Iron. Microsoft came out with its initial version of Virtual Server (Release 1) in 2004, with general availability in 2005. In 2006, Virtual Server R2, which supports multiple guest operating systems, was made available as a free download, beginning some major pricing changes across the board. Microsoft also announced plans for their hypervisor virtualization offering, Viridian, also called Windows Server Virtualization, in its Longhorn release. The other significant change in this space came in the form of open source, with the Xen community releasing its free hypervisor and forming XenSource, a software vendor delivering value-add management solutions for Xen technology. These virtualization offerings, particularly in conjunction with blades, are laying the foundation for the future — simplifying provisioning and enabling utility computing for next-generation data centers.

History of Blade Server Systems

At this point, we will look into the evolution of blade systems at a deeper level, including a detailed history and the phases of evolution.

Before They Were Called Blades (pre-1999)

Although the official introduction of blade servers did not come until 2001, early versions of a PC on a card actually existed several years prior to that. Before the Internet explosion and broadband access, the early bulletin board operators were beginning to morph into the first Internet service providers (ISPs). These companies needed lots of servers to support sessions for their dial-up customers, and standard tower or rack-mount servers just took up too much space. Many enterprises were also supporting remote workforces using remote access/control software, such as Carbon Copy or PC Anywhere, for employees or partners to access in-house network resources from a remote PC or terminal.

Several companies (Cubix, ChatCom, and CommVision) saw some initial success in this market niche in the mid 1990s, delivering PC-on-a-card servers that resided in a common chassis. By 1997, however, Citrix Systems had achieved dominance in the remote access/control marketplace, displacing the Carbon Copy dedicated-PC approach. Citrix's software, somewhat similar to virtualization software, served up multiple PC sessions from a single server to multiple remote PCs acting as terminals. Since Citrix charged a per-server license fee, not a per-PC user license fee, it was much cheaper for users to implement, and by 2000 the success of Citrix had changed the market and closed the window for these early PC bladelike entrants.

Innovators and Early Adopters (1999–2001)

The initial version of what is now a blade server began in 1999 with an idea for a new, compact server form factor, designed for Internet hosting and web serving, from a reseller and consultant named Chris Hipp. Borrowing on the notion of vertical blades in a chassis (used already in networking), his initial blade server concept was to share components such as power and switches and eliminate unnecessary heat, metal, cables, and any components that were not absolutely necessary for serving up web pages.

As a result, Hipp, whom some call the father of blade servers, formed a company called RocketLogix with the idea of building these devices. According to Hipp, by 2000, RocketLogix had filed six U.S. patents, with a total of 187 claims related to dense blade computing. With the addition of an executive team of ex–Compaq server executives including Gary Stimac, who helped legitimize the blade concept and raise substantial venture capital (including money from IBM), the company became RLX Technologies, Inc.

The first product, the RLX System 324, shipped in May 2001, with RLX Control Tower management software released shortly thereafter. The blade concept was well-received and recognized by the industry as a revolutionary step. RLX was named one of *Red Herring*'s Top 10 Companies to Watch in 2001. In May 2002, the Los Alamos National Laboratory demonstrated the "Green Destiny" project, a compute cluster made up of 240 RLX blades.

Impact of the Internet Bubble (2001–2002)

Along with RLX, another new company, Egenera, appeared in 2001, with its own approach to blades servers. By late 2001, the major systems vendors had announced their entry into the market, and HP, Compaq, Dell, and IBM were all shipping blade products by the end of 2002, with Sun joining in 2003. Numerous other companies jumped on the blade bandwagon, including Amphus, Centauri NetSystems, OmniCluster, Racemi, and RealScale Technologies. Intel joined the blade frenzy through its acquisition of Ziatech.

The initial growth of the blade market was fueled by the rapid growth of Internet data centers during that time. In addition to garnering the interest and attention of the major platform vendors, this growth also led a number of companies like Inifinicon (now SilverStorm), Mellanox, and others to join the fray. These vendors began to promote I/O aggregation via high-bandwidth switch interfaces like InfiniBand for blade systems. The initial furor of the endless need for both computing and I/O scalability, compounded by cost pressure (both for physical resources as well as IT skilled resources) led to a variety of additional blade-related companies and solutions entering the market.

Niche Adopters (2003–2004)

Right as the blade market began to take off and numerous vendors entered the game, the Internet bubble burst. As a result, the blade start-up companies struggled, and many disappeared. Others started focusing on niche areas in order to stay in business. RLX focused on HPCC. Egenera focused on financial processing and found substantial success. Amphus focused on management software. Transmeta focused on the low-power niche, sacrificing performance for power management and low power requirements. The InfiniBand players focused on efforts to move all fabrics to InfiniBand. Success during this time came through a variety of niche markets such as imaging, financial trading-floor projects, military projects requiring portable self-contained rack systems, and even shipboard gambling.

In 2004, RLX exited the hardware business, and in 2005 they sold the Control Tower software to HP. Dell, who had entered the market in 2002, did not refresh their product at all during this time. With the market being so soft, blades did not represent a new opportunity for Dell, and served only to cannibalize their existing server market. (As the market began to come back, Dell re-entered in 2004.)

Mainstream Re-emergence (2004–2006)

As IT budgets began to loosen and IT organizations had money for projects again, blades found significant traction. In 2005, blade server revenue exceeded $2 billion. This growth puts the adoption rate for blades on much the same growth curve as the adoption rate for rack servers. Figure 3.2 shows the adoption rate for blades versus the adoption rates for rack servers, based on the number of years from the introduction of each technology.

By this time, the market also had shaken out, with IBM and HP taking the lion's share of the market, with a combined total share of more than 70%. Dell and Sun remained as systems players, along with several smaller players who had reasonable success, including Egenera (who pioneered the concept of anonymous blades, which will be discussed further in Chapter 4, "Blade Architecture" and Chapter 7, "Blades and Storage") and Verari (originally RackSavers).

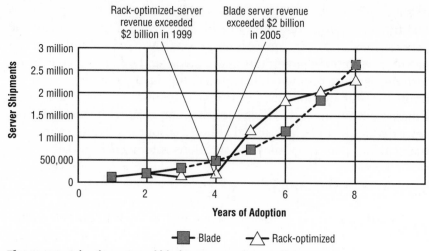

Figure 3.2: Adoption rates of blade servers versus rack servers

Source: IDC, End User Perspectives on Server Blade Adoption, Doc #TB20060525, May 2006

As part of the move to gain mainstream momentum, IBM and Intel opened up the specification for the IBM BladeCenter solution. As of mid 2006, more than 320 companies had received the BladeCenter specifications, with more than 600 technology and solution providers participating in the BladeCenter Alliance Program and Open Specification Program. According to IDC, in mid 2006 Blade-Center had been the leading blade server vendor in the industry for nine successive quarters, and IBM had shipped in excess of 350,000 blades since market introduction — more than any other computer maker had.

Origins of Virtualization

Now we will look more closely at the origins and history of virtualization. Although many think of virtualization as new technology of the 21st century, the concept of virtual computing goes back to 1962, when virtual memory was first used in a mainframe computer. In the early days of computing, physical memory, or *core*, was extremely small (64K–256K). This meant that programmers had to be highly aware of program size and resources, even to be able to run a program, and had to write programs that could overlay themselves in memory. To overcome this limitation, IBM introduced virtual memory on their S/370 models 158 and 168 in 1972 and changed computing dramatically. Virtual memory allowed the creation of a virtual partition or address space, completely managed by the operating system, stored on disk, and paged in and out of physical memory as needed. This concept is now used in many operating environments, including PCs, workstations, and servers, freeing programmers from the burden of memory management.

In that same era, virtual machines with virtual disk and virtual tape were used, as in IBM's VM/370 operating system, allowing system administrators to divide a single physical computer into any number of virtual computers, complete with their own virtual disks and tapes. The operating system simulated those devices to each virtual machine and spread the resource requirements across the corresponding physical devices.

All of these early capabilities are reappearing now in various forms throughout enterprise computing: virtual storage subsystems; virtual tape libraries; storage virtualization at the host, network and disk level; server clustering; and virtual server hypervisors are all part of today's landscape and are delivering the same type of significant improvements to technology as their predecessors did.

History of Server Virtualization

The early history of virtualizing CPU processing dates back to the 1970s with IBM's VM/370 mainframe operating system (see Chapter 2, "Evolution of Computing Technology — Setting the Stage"). VM/370 and its derivatives have run on all IBM mainframes since that time, providing the ability to initiate multiple instances of all IBM mainframe operating systems on a single mainframe (with the number of virtual machines limited only by processing capacity). VM was used extensively within the IBM enterprise customer base for testing of and conversion to new hardware systems, operating systems, and applications. To some degree, it also allowed users to migrate from older, smaller systems onto a newer mainframe and consolidate with other systems and applications.

As users moved to PCs and client-server computing, however, there was no equivalent solution for virtualization in the x/86 product line. In 1999, VMware delivered the first virtualization product for x86 workstations and then extended it to servers, creating a new market for server virtualization. Although a number of other vendors delivered PC and server virtualization solutions, VMware dominated the space, expanding their offerings to include hypervisor solutions (see the discussion later in this chapter), host-based solutions, and workstation products. In 2003, VMware was acquired by storage systems giant EMC, and now operates as a wholly owned independent subsidiary. Since VMware's initial product launch, other virtualization (and related) offerings have come from companies such as SWsoft who first delivered Virtuozzo for Linux in 2001; Virtual Iron, founded in 2003; and PlateSpin Ltd. (migration from physical to virtual), also founded in 2003.

More recently, two things occurred that have begun to change the server virtualization space significantly, perhaps leveling the playing field. An open source server virtualization project at the University of Cambridge resulted in the release of an open source virtualization solution called Xen. As of 2006, Xen has evolved into the fairly robust hypervisor Xen 3.0, built to take advantage of Intel and AMD hardware assists for virtualization. With the goal of becoming ubiquitous, Xen, which is available for free, continues to gain traction among big players such as IBM, Sun, HP, and Novell.

Also in 2003, Microsoft acquired a company called Connectix, which had several virtualization products, including Virtual PC for Mac, Virtual PC for Windows, and a virtual server product. Microsoft delivered Virtual Server in 2004/2005 and began offering it for free in 2006, causing others (including VMware) to follow suit with some portion of their product line. Microsoft has moved forward with a strong focus on virtualization, announcing plans for a hypervisor offering (Viridian) bundled into its Longhorn Server (as an add-on release; Longhorn Server is due out in 2007, but the hypervisor may not be released until 2009).

Server virtualization has achieved a significant amount of traction in the enterprise space and will be an interesting battleground for both big players and emerging companies.

Market Adoption

Market adoption of both blade and virtualization technologies has grown significantly since the early days of 2001/2002. Acceptance of these technologies has continued to grow substantially.

Blade Server Systems

According to IDC, more than 500,000 blade units were shipped in 2005, representing 63% growth over 2004. Blade revenue generated in 2005 was $2.1 billion, representing 84% growth over 2004.

Figure 3.3 shows the growth in the server blade installed base in the United States and worldwide. The growth rate of blades worldwide has been (and will probably continue to be) greater than the growth rate within the United States. One likely reason is that IT infrastructure outside the United States still lags, causing space and power availability to be even bigger issues outside the U.S. (particularly in places like India and China). Since blades offer significant advantages over rack servers in regard to these issues, their traction outside the United States is significant.

In the fourth quarter of 2005, blade servers (including x86, EPIC, and RISC blades) accounted for 4.6% of total server market revenue. Figure 3.4 shows the growth in blade server shipments relative to total server shipments from 2002–2005.

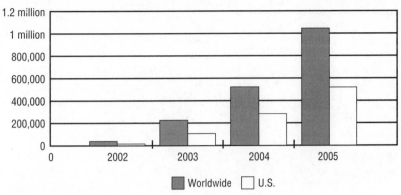

Figure 3.3: Server blade installed base from 2002 to 2005

Source: Worldwide and U.S. Blade Server 2005–2009 Forecast and 2004 Vendor Shares, Doc # 33631, July 2005

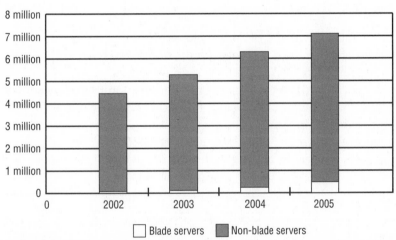

Figure 3.4: Blade server shipments versus total server shipments from 2002 to 2005

Source: Worldwide and U.S. Blade Server 2005-2009 Forecast and 2004 Vendor Shares, Doc # 33631, July 2005

Figure 3.5 shows the distribution of blade server revenue worldwide by vendor as of the first quarter of 2005. By the end of 2005, IBM had increased its lead in server blade revenues, with 42.7% of market share, while HP held with 35.1% share and Dell followed with 11.2% share.

"Market momentum in the blade market has continued, with blade volumes up 50% year over year," said Kelly Quinn, IDC senior research analyst, Worldwide Server research in early 2006. "Blade shipments increased more than 60% year over year in 2005 as IT managers began to adopt blades as a standard building block in their virtual IT infrastructures."

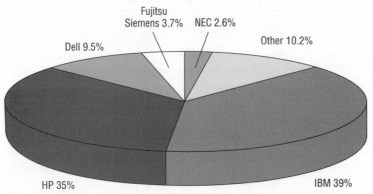

Figure 3.5: Market share of worldwide blade server revenue 2005

Source: IDC, Worldwide Quarterly Server Tracker, May 2005

Virtualization

According to IDC, more than 75% of companies with more than 500 employees are deploying virtual servers, and more than 50% of those servers are running production applications. A Yankee Group study indicated that 75% of all companies surveyed, regardless of size, already had or plan to deploy server virtualization over the next 12 months. Only 4% said they had no plans for virtualization. Worldwide shipments of server platforms with virtualization capabilities are forecast to reach 1.2 million units in 2009, with the number of virtual-server images forecast to reach 5 million.

Blade System Usage

From their initial target usage for web serving to a broader range of uses up through HPCCs, the use of blade systems has evolved.

Web Services

The initial vision that Chris Hipp of RLX held was based on high-density, low-powered blades grouped together for the scale-out function of serving up web pages in a bursting-at-the-seams Internet market. This became an early sweet spot for blades — users needed lots of servers, geographically distributed, with lots of I/O (input/output) and low CPU requirements.

As blades caught on in web services, many users liked the compact form factor, modularity, and cableless simplicity but had a difficult time paying more money for less computing power. They wanted higher-end processors

for uses beyond web servers. Although the OpEx costs are lower with
due to reduced management costs, the initial CapEx costs were h¹
server, even though they used slower processors.

HPCC and Application Servers

A number of innovations in blade CPU configurations contributed to
changes in blade usage. Blades were implemented with faster chips and went
from single to multiple CPUs per blade. In addition, advances in chip technology (such as dual-core chips) deliver almost double the CPU power in the
same footprint, with lower power and cooling requirements. This increase in
computing power allowed blades to move into more-CPU-intensive areas
such as scientific research, mathematics, rendering, and HPCC.

The addition of the second CPU, or coprocessor, allowed blades to evolve
from being used only as low-end web servers to being used also as high-end
application servers. Due to the additional I/O involved with application
servers, the second CPU is needed for assisting in I/O processing. In addition
to standard application server usage, one area of strong potential growth for
blade technology worldwide may be loosely coupled application servers supporting mobile and portable users.

Database Servers

When vendors started adding a second processor and high-speed interconnects, blade systems also became good candidates for parallel and clustered
database applications such as Oracle Real Application Cluster (RAC) 10g. Oracle 10g was designed as a scale-out database and its parallel design allows it to
run well on multiple processors at once, regardless of whether the processors
are on the same blade (server). For example, Oracle 10g can run on four two-
way blades or one eight-way server. Oracle RAC 10g also allows an administrator the ability to easily add blades to a database cluster, providing the ability
to increase (or decrease) the processing power allocated to the database cluster. The combination of multiple powerful processors and high-speed communications channels between blades creates an extremely high-performance
environment for these applications.

Standard databases, such as SQL or standard Oracle, although not designed
for parallel operations, will also run well on these high-end blades. Federated
databases, which are a collection of cooperating database servers running
autonomously (possibly even in heterogeneous environments), can run well
on blades also. One example is Exchange, running with multiple email servers
split across multiple databases and multiple servers.

Storage

Changes have also occurred in blade storage usage. Initially, when blade systems shipped, each blade contained some amount of disk storage. These first blade drives were all IDE (laptop-type) drives. The disks were very compact but had fairly high failure rates for hard-running servers. The next step for most vendors was to move to SCSI drives, as they got smaller (2.5-inch drives). This increased costs, but also reliability. As the market matured and blade usage expanded, a buzz started around a movement toward storage blades, which IBM delivered. Although storage blades were an interesting idea, they proved not to be flexible enough in a variety of ways — for example, you could not simply pop out drives, which hindered serviceability, and difficulties in connecting server blades to storage blades required a different kind of routing. The general trend now has been to connect servers to storage through networked storage (NAS or SANs) for a number of reasons. First, networked storage offers high performance, high availability, and redundancy. Second, connecting to (and booting from) networked storage can eliminate the need for storage on the blade, allowing the blades to be more interchangeable. (This will be discussed in more detail in Chapter 7, "Blades and Storage.")

Usage Evolution

As the market evolved, blade adoption began to grow in areas such as financial services, scientific research, retail, and health care. Egenera, which offered clustered single-system-image blade solutions, achieved tremendous success through porting of previously proprietary applications like those found on financial trading-room floors (from Sun or IBM systems) to their blade solution.

Early on, the guideline for considering the move to blades was more than five servers doing homogeneous work in scale-out applications. The number five was based on the up-front costs of the blade chassis and the fact that unless the chassis is roughly half-full, it is not cost-effective. Although there are differences of opinion on limiting applications to homogeneous work and scale-out, there is general agreement on the half-full guideline.

As blades have evolved, in many ways they have begun to more closely resemble their predecessor, rack servers, and have started being used for general applications. However, there are two key differences. First, very heavy CPU-intensive activity may still be better suited to rack-mounted servers since very high-end processors require more cooling and, therefore, more space for airflow. Second, the modularity, built-in management, and simplicity in wiring/cabling of blade systems provide significant benefits over racks in manageability, provisioning/reprovisioning, and serviceability in addition to space savings.

Data Center in a Box

A newer trend in blade usage comes from the modularity and simplicity of blade server systems. Because blade systems have the ability to house a group of servers and switches with minimal cabling and strong remote-management capabilities, they are an excellent solution for remote offices/mini data centers. As a result, numerous solutions have come to market, following the "data center in a box" and "retail store in a box" models. These solutions package together a variety of servers, each performing different functions. For example, a chassis may contain one blade that serves as a web server, one or two blades performing as application servers running software such as BEA or SAP, one or more database server blades, and blades for middleware, along with the appropriate switch modules. A number of components may be included for various types of uses. (Examples might include firewalls, VPNs, and load balancers.) This "data center in a box" can be dropped into a remote location and managed remotely.

Firewall/VPN Blades

When a blade system is used in the Data Center in a Box scenario, security is often a key requirement. As with any remote server environment, there is a need to provide a firewall and possibly a VPN. These solutions are provided through security software operating on a standard blade server, from security vendors such as Check Point.

Load-Balancing Blades

As part of delivering scale-out applications and in remote data centers where multiple servers are running the same application, a load-balancing function is needed to manage the distribution of work across multiple servers. The load balancer acts as a virtual server, representing and responding to a single IP address and port, and distributing the requests to a selected physical server within the blade farm. A variety of layer 4–7 switch modules from vendors such as F5 and Radware are available for blade systems to provide these types of services, as well as host-based load-balancing solutions.

Ruggedized Portable Computing

Another successful extension of the Data Center in a Box solution is for situations requiring ruggedization for remote locations. Examples of these include blades systems for use on a ship, for military applications, for seismic simulations, and so on.

Benefits of Blades and Virtualization

With all this as a backdrop, it is now useful to look more deeply at the reasons introduced earlier for considering blades and virtualization as complementary technologies. Although some of these have not changed since the initial vision of blades and server virtualization in the early 2000s, additional benefits have emerged and/or become more significant as the technology has evolved. Additionally, significant cost-reduction benefits can be achieved from implementing blades and virtualization, but it is not all about cost. Benefits of implementing blade technology include the following:

- Space savings and efficiency, packing more computing power into a smaller area

- Consolidation of servers to improve and centralize management as well as to improve utilization of computer assets

- Simplification and reduction in complexity (modularity, ease of integration, prewired configurations, shared components), ease of deployment, and improved manageability and serviceability

- ROI and improved TCO (increased hardware utilization, reduced OpEx)

Space

Packing more computing power into a smaller space was one of the main initial reasons for deploying blades. This reason is still significant for many data centers that are out of room. In an IDC survey of enterprise data centers in Europe in 2005, users ranked floor space as their number-two issue, surrounded by power-related issues as the number-one and number-three choices (see Figure 3.6).

As IT organizations have responded to ever-increasing demands for additional processing power and storage capacity, many data centers have grown their IT hardware to the point of maxing out their floor space as well as their power and cooling capacity. In many cases, blade systems offer help in this area by providing a way to replace larger rack servers with the same or greater capacity in a smaller footprint. In fact, as blade vendors have implemented faster processors, two-way processors, and dual-core processors (with quad-core processors in 2007), the computing power per square foot has increased significantly over early blade systems. For instance, 60 blade servers might now fit in the same physical space as 42 rack-mounted servers (these numbers vary from vendor to vendor). In some cases, users have been able to buy back space in the data center by converting rack servers to blade servers. This may allow IT to postpone or even eliminate the cost of building a new data center that would otherwise have been required. In addition, significant space savings may be accomplished through consolidation via virtualization.

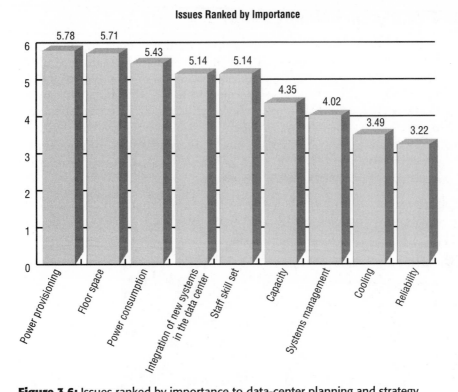

Figure 3.6: Issues ranked by importance to data-center planning and strategy
Source: IDC, End User Perspectives on Server Blade Adoption, Doc #TB20060525, May 2006

Consolidation and Centralization

Server consolidation has been a major driver for IT since the Internet bubble burst and budgets were tightened. Consolidation has been viewed as a way to reduce costs by increasing server utilization, reducing the number of servers needed, and reducing the time required to manage those servers. Consolidating legacy servers and centralizing server functions onto blades using server virtualization solutions accomplish all of these objectives. Blades, in conjunction with virtualization software, provide an excellent platform for physical consolidation (centrally locating all the blade servers) and virtual consolidation (consolidating multiple server applications onto the same blade under VMware or other virtualization technology). In addition, remote locations are relieved of any responsibility to manage their own servers (not to mention the fact that IT regains control over critical tasks such as backup and archiving for regulatory compliance).

Simplification and Manageability

Although rack servers provided a good option for improving space utilization over towers, for most data centers they also introduced a nightmare in terms of cabling. Figure 3.7 shows an example of a cabling nightmare using rack servers.

Figure 3.7: A server-room rack-server cabling nightmare
Credit: David Tabler

The prewired design of blade-server systems eliminates the cabling problems (as shown in Figure 3.8), not to mention costs, since the chassis provides the power distribution, connectivity between the server blades and switch modules (data and storage switches), as well as the management modules, and KVM switches.

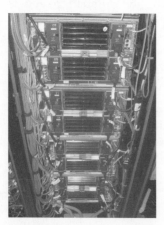

Figure 3.8: The cabling simplicity of blades as shown on a fully redundant IBM blade center with 84 blades, dual SAN fabrics, dual Ethernet switching, fully redundant power, and local and remote management for every blade

Source: IBM

The modular approach also makes adding/removing servers as easy as popping in a blade. If a blade fails, the LEDs indicate which blade it is, and it no longer requires a skilled tech to swap out the failing blade and replace it. The integration of the blade chassis management module allows for full remote-management operations, including power up/power down. In addition, various configuration options, including anonymous (diskless) blades that boot from a SAN, bring software deployment and server reprovisioning to a new level of efficiency.

This modular approach extends to virtualization solutions as well. The ability to provision and reprovision virtual machines based on business policies and application requirements eases the overhead associated with managing the virtual servers. If the application or business priorities change, simply move the virtual machine over to a higher performing blade to get the job done.

One way to look at the combination of blades and virtualization is, for each benefit a blade system brings, that benefit is multiplied by the number of virtual machines running on those blades, rather than on physical servers. For example, in a blade environment cabling simplicity is not only shared by the blades but also by all the virtual machines. If 10 blades are in a chassis, sharing cables, and each of the blades is running 5 virtual machines, 50 servers (albeit virtual ones) are sharing the cables as well as the modularity and simplicity afforded by the blade system.

ROI and TCO

Many of the reasons to implement blades and virtualization translate directly to money. These can be divided into ROI issues and reducing the TCO.

Reduced Infrastructure Cost

When considering an implementation that includes more than five or six servers, the overall infrastructure costs of blades versus other equivalent alternatives will be less. This is due to in part to the sharing of devices (switches, power supplies, and so on) and in part to the reduction of cabling and connector costs. Multiply all of that by the number of physical servers that can be retired (or purchases avoided) due to server virtualization, and infrastructure costs are drastically reduced. Because the CapEx is lower, there is a quicker ROI.

Time to Return

A significant portion of the benefit that blades and virtualization bring is in the area of ease of implementation, deployment, and provisioning. This benefit can be measured by what is called *time to return* (on investment) or *time to revenue*. The modularity and prewiring of blade systems described previously work together to dramatically reduce the time needed initially to deploy blade systems. Transitioning from rack servers to blades might mean that time needed to deploy shrinks from two weeks down to days or even hours. Additionally, blades and virtualization software make it easy to reprovision servers for use by another application or group of users, allowing resources to be reallocated based on business needs such as faster response to unexpected spikes in traffic.

Reduced Operational Cost

All of the management benefits described here can be translated (directly or indirectly) into reduced OpEx. These include everything from initial deployment to adding blades to reconfiguring and reprovisioning. Additionally, having complete remote-management ability eliminates travel in cases other than hardware replacement, while allowing management to be done centrally even when blade systems are geographically distributed. As one user put it, "Our staff was reduced due to a slump in business, and we are able to support hundreds of virtual servers with just a few people."

Reduced Serviceability Cost

Finally, the simplicity and manageability of blade systems and virtualization solutions changes the level of expertise of the repair staff. Since everything except for a hardware swap can be done remotely, when there is a hardware failure on a blade, virtualization software can automatically restart the VM on another blade (high availability), keeping the applications running. The blade hardware swap requires little to no technical expertise. It is said that even the Federal Express person could swap out a failing blade (and then ship it to the appropriate location for repair).

Conclusion

Blades and virtualization have both come a long way from their introductions in 2001. The adoption pattern for blades appears to be following a similar pattern to rack servers and continues to grow and expand into additional applications and vertical markets. Recent surveys show only 4% of users have no plans for virtualization. Both markets have evolved to include a full set of competitors, as well as vendors delivering complementary technologies. There are compelling reasons to consider blade and virtualization implementation, including strong financial reasons related to both ROI and TCO.

This chapter completes the "Technology Evolution" part of this book. Part II, "A Closer Look," examines the technologies involved in blade server systems and server virtualization, and provides architectural discussions and more-detailed looks at the various hardware and software components and issues surrounding blade and virtualization implementation.

PART

II

A Closer Look

Blade Architecture

The overall architecture of the blade server system was designed to minimize space requirements, simplify connections between computing components, and improve the manageability of the system components. The blade chassis leverages several principles from the chassis architectures, built for the telecommunications and networking industries, and applies them to servers. The most obvious of these principles is the placement of the blades into slots within the chassis (typically vertical, but not with all vendors). Another of these borrowed concepts is the sharing of common power supplies and fan assemblies at the rear of the chassis, which cool all of the blades. The chassis provides the interconnect between the blades and the switches, effectively eliminating much of the cabling mess created with rack servers.

The fundamental design objectives for blade server systems include the following:

- Aggregation of various components to be shared by the blades within the chassis, including power supplies, fans, I/O, and so on.

- Designed for manageability from the outset — introducing the idea of a chassis manager function, which delivers out-of-band management to all of the elements within the chassis. This enables one-to-many management of these components, either from the chassis manager itself or through integration with higher-level systems-management products.

- Redundancy of switches and chassis-management modules, going beyond redundancy of power supplies and fans.

- Shared modules (such as KVM and floppy/CD-ROM) primarily for use in diagnostics.

Blade System Components

The blade system comprises the following components:

- Chassis (including shared power supplies, fans, and so on)
- One or more blade servers
- Redundant switch modules
- Chassis manager module (also called the management module)
- Shared modules (primarily for diagnostics)
- Keyboard-video-mouse (KVM) interface
- Floppy and CD-ROM drive tray

It is important to note that although all blade systems from various vendors utilize these same building blocks, blades designed for one vendor's chassis may not interoperate with another vendor's chassis. Although interoperable blade systems would greatly benefit users, the evolution of blade systems involved independent development from various vendors, resulting in proprietary chassis and blade designs from both emerging technology vendors (such as RLX and Egenera) as well as major system vendors (such as IBM, HP, Dell, and Sun). Although a standard definition for blade server systems exists in the telco (telephone company) space (Advanced Telecommunications Computing Architecture or AdvancedTCA), no standard exist for blades outside of that specification. User pressure on the major vendors may eventually cause the vendors to address this issue and create standards and interoperability for blades. (This topic will be discussed further in Chapter 11, "Industry Organizations and Related Standards.")

Chassis

The chassis is the base component of blade systems and provides the following:

- Housing for all the components of the blade system
- Connectivity and plumbing for the various components via the midplane

The chassis includes the power supplies and the fans that provide power and cooling to the various components of the blade system. See Figures 4.1 through 4.4 for examples.

Figure 4.1: Fully populated HP BladeSystem enclosure
Source: Hewlett-Packard

Figure 4.2: Blade-server system and chassis from Dell
Source: Courtesy of Dell Inc.

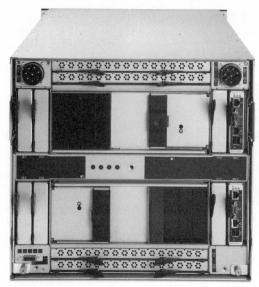

Figure 4.3: Blade chassis — back view
Source: IBM

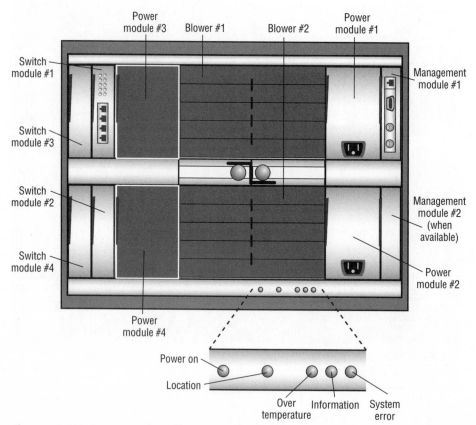

Figure 4.4: Blade chassis diagram — back view

As can be seen in the figures, the front of the chassis has blades that can be inserted and removed, and the rear of the chassis houses the fans, the power supplies, the shared switch modules, and the management module. The blade chassis is generally designed to allow the blades to be inserted from the front, and the switch modules to be inserted from the back, connected by a midplane. Because previous chassis architectures inserted everything from the front and all of the power distribution and connection functions were implemented on the back, these functions have traditionally been known as the *backplane*. In blade server systems, however, the backplane function often is implemented through the midplane.

Figure 4.5 shows an example of an open chassis. In the middle of the chassis is the passive midplane, providing the power-distribution line to each component, as well as the connectivity between all of the blade system components. The midplane typically has connectors on both sides that provide the connectivity to each of the components in the blade system.

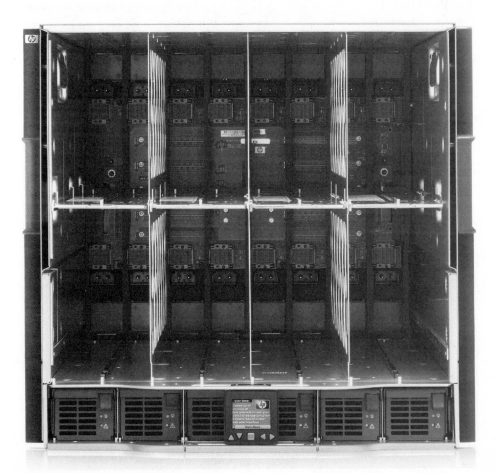

Figure 4.5: Open blade chassis
Source: Hewlett-Packard

Most midplanes are split to disassociate the power distribution from the I/O distribution. This split is to reduce the interference and costs associated with routing power and I/O. In addition, splitting the midplane airflow from the front to the rear of the chassis significantly reduces the cooling required for the highly dense, high-thermal blades.

Server Blades

The blade server is the central computing element of the blade system. Figure 4.6 shows an example of a blade. A blade server typically has either one or two CPUs (also called one-way or two-way blades). Four-way blades are also available but may take up two slots in the chassis, depending on the vendor. Each CPU processor can be single-core or multicore, adding more horsepower per socket. In addition to the processors, each blade has a variable amount of memory and a minimum of one network connection (Ethernet by default). There also may be an I/O card (daughter or mezzanine card on the blade motherboard), which provides additional network connections, typically with redundant configurations (dual ports). The blade servers can communicate with multiple network fabrics in addition to the management network. These include Ethernet, Fibre Channel, and InfiniBand.

Figure 4.6: An individual blade
Source: Courtesy of Dell Inc.

Depending on the vendor, each blade may be capable of local storage, configured with up to two hard-disk drives (HDDs). If HDDs are on the blade, they are placed on the front side of the blade in most designs, and are hot-pluggable. Originally, these drives were ATA-class drives but were changed to SCSI drives for higher reliability. Some vendors (such as Egenera) do not include drives on the blade at all (called *diskless* or *anonymous* blades). In this scenario, the blade server communicates to external storage on a NAS device or a SAN. Most vendors offer their blades with or without disk drives, leaving the choice to the user. Considerations for using anonymous blades will be discussed more in Chapter 7, "Blades and Storage."

I/O Modules

A blade chassis generally has two or three *switch modules* (also called switch blades or blade switches) to communicate between the blades and various external networks (both data networks and storage networks). These switch modules are typically redundant, as are the I/O options supported on the blade server. Two types of switch modules are available for blades: switch modules and pass-through modules.

Switch modules are typically switches that provide aggregation of all I/O connectivity to the blades. In other words, each blade talks to the switch module, which provides standard network switching for all the blades in the chassis.

Pass-through modules, on the other hand, provide one-to-one access from an external switch to the I/O connectivity on each server blade. In essence, this provides a pass-through cabling function from each blade to an external switch. In order for the blades to communicate with each other or to an external network, at least one switch module or pass-through module must be present in the chassis.

Supported switches for blade communications include Gigabit Ethernet, 10Gb Ethernet, Fibre Channel (2Gb and 4Gb), and InfiniBand. Switch modules for these networks are built by the same vendors that build stand-alone switches for rack servers. In general, most of the major vendor's switches (such as Cisco, Brocade, and McData/QLogic) are available for each of the major system vendor's chassis (including IBM, HP, and Dell). Some of the smaller blade manufacturers may not have switch blade options for all the switch vendors.

Management Modules

Many of the blade chassis designs incorporate a *management module* that is responsible for controlling and managing the various components in the blade chassis, including the power supplies, the fans, the switches, and the blades. The management module is also responsible for powering up the blade system and its individual components, configuring the switches and the blades, and monitoring the operations of all the various components in the blade chassis. The management module can communicate directly with each blade and each switch in the chassis via an out-of-band, direct connection.

Other Shared Modules

The final components of a blade system include the media or device bay and the KVM module. These components were used initially in blade systems, primarily as shared diagnostics devices, connecting to one blade server at a time. In the early blade system chassis, the device bay was typically a floppy/CD-ROM device, used for boot purposes and/or diagnostics. With the advent of USB-based boot media support, KVM modules can be equipped with USB ports that provide another means to boot the blade server. Advances in KVM over IP now allow the KVM functions to be handled by the management module using standard IP protocol. Because of these types of advances, the trend is toward elimination of these components, allowing more space for other blade components.

Conclusion

The architecture of blade server systems accomplishes a number of objectives that makes them highly attractive for IT organizations to implement, both within the data center and in remote locations. In addition to putting more computer power into a smaller footprint, blade systems also simplify the connectivity between servers, network switches, and storage switches, eliminating the cabling nightmare and expense of predecessor rack servers. Blade systems also benefit from the sharing of various components within the chassis, including redundant power and cooling systems and diagnostics devices such as KVM switches. The built-in design of the management module allows full systems management of the blade chassis and all components within, both locally and from a remote location. Together, these architectural features deliver a new level of modularity and simplicity for integrating all the elements of computing and provide increased levels of manageability, availability, and serviceability while reducing both CapEx and OpEx.

This chapter has provided a look at the physical architecture of blade server systems, how the components work together, and some of the benefits that blade systems architectures can offer. The next chapter extends this view to cover how blade technologies can be used to bring many of these benefits beyond servers to include user workstations through PC blades and thin client technology.

PC Blades

Blade servers are generally what come to mind during discussions of blade technology. In addition, most of the market buzz and analyst statistics focus on blade servers. However, interesting opportunities also exist with blade technologies and PCs. In particular, PC blades offer benefits in centralizing management, increasing security, and addressing specific environmental requirements.

PC Blade Architecture

PC blades take the basic concept of the blade architecture and apply it to desktop computing. Instead of having a user's PC on/under the desktop, with the keyboard, video monitor, and mouse (KVM) user-interface components located next to it, the PC blade architecture consists of taking the guts of the PC (what traditionally resided inside the tower), and putting it on a blade, which is then inserted into a chassis, typically located within the data center (see Figures 5.1 and 5.2).

Figure 5.1: ClearCube PC blade
Source: ClearCube Technology

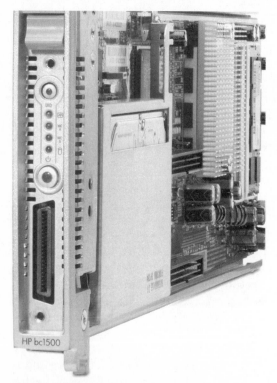

Figure 5.2: HP BladeSystem blade PC
Source: Hewlett-Packard

The keyboard, monitor, and mouse remain at the user's location/workplace, and communicate to the PC blade via a KVM interface device, which enables the "remoting" of the KVM functions between the PC blade and the user location. The interface device may be attached to the PC blade locally, or connected remotely over IP. Figure 5.3 shows how these components operate together. In both of these cases (remote and local), there is a 1 to 1 ratio — one PC blade to one user.

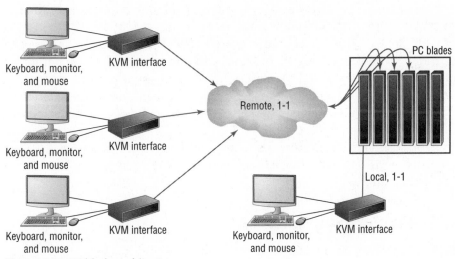

Figure 5.3: PC blade architecture

Source: Focus Consulting

Although PC blades use a bladed form factor, they differ from blade-server systems in several ways:

- They fit into their own chassis, and are not part of a blade server chassis.

- They do not share components (networking, power, cooling, and so on) like blade server systems do.

- Each PC blade is its own stand-alone entity, and although it is hot-pluggable into the chassis, it can run on its own.

The PC blade architecture allows all of the PC blades to be centrally located, secured, and managed. Significant security benefits can be achieved by keeping the PC blades within a locked data center, minimizing the possibility of the PCs (and the data stored on them) being stolen. As an example, North American Aerospace Defense Command (NORAD), which controls air security for the United States and Canada from Cheyenne Mountain in Colorado, has implemented PC blades as part of its increased security. PC blades are all within locked and highly secured facilities, with only a monitor, keyboard, mouse, and a small PC KVM interface device located at each user station.

Removing the PC blades from the user location also offers environmental advantages in certain situations. Hospital operating rooms and medical examination rooms can include a user station without introducing all the unsanitary components of a PC into the room. In addition, eliminating the PC offers additional security, in accordance with HIPPA regulations. Manufacturing environments, where conditions are less than optimal for computer operations, can also benefit from PC blades by keeping the PC blades in a clean, ventilated data center rather than out on the manufacturing floor.

Having the PC blades all centrally located offers productivity advantages to the IT staff as well, since all the blades are in one location and are not in the middle of heavily trafficked user areas (such as hospital rooms and trading floors). Updating software, for example, becomes much simpler. In addition, if a PC blade fails, it is easy to switch the user of the failing PC over to another PC blade with minimal disruption.

Vendors use various approaches to accomplish the separation of the user interface from the PC blade. Methods include KVM user-port solutions and thin client solutions.

KVM User-Port Solutions

This first approach, used by ClearCube Technology, who has been the leader in the PC blade market, involves a KVM interface device, also called a user port, which resides at the user's location. The keyboard, video monitor, and mouse devices plug into the user port, using standard keyboard, video, and mouse cables. The user port may also support additional USB ports for other types of user-oriented devices. The user port then connects to the PC blade located in the data center. This connection can be local using either Cat 5 cable (up to 200 meters) or copper fiber (up to 500 meters), or remote using an Ethernet network. Figures 5.4 and 5.5 show local and remote user ports.

Although in some cases the combined cost of all the hardware components may exceed the cost of a standard PC, the security, management, and environmental benefits plus the cost savings in OpEx can, in many cases, justify the up-front CapEx. OpEx savings come largely from reductions in ongoing management costs. In addition, user downtime will be reduced in the event of a blade failure, because the user can be switched to another blade automatically.

Figure 5.4: ClearCube local user C/port (containing connectors for KVM and optional additional devices)

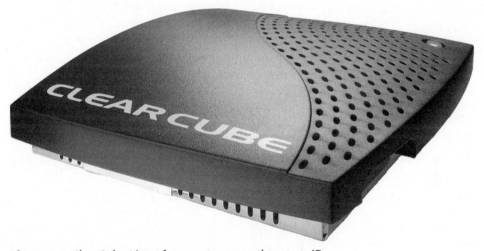

Figure 5.5: ClearCube I/port for remote connections over IP
Source: ClearCube Technology

Thin Client Solutions

A thin client may also be used to communicate with the PC blade. This is the approach taken by HP with its Consolidated Client Infrastructure (CCI) and the HP BladeSystem PC blade (see Figure 5.6).

Figure 5.6: HP thin client used to communicate with the HP BladeSystem PC blade
Source: Hewlett-Packard

Instead of a KVM user port, this approach uses a specialized hardware/software combination called a thin client, located at the user work area. Thin clients contain only the client code necessary to manage the user interface and communicate the information to and from the PC blade. Thin clients have been used for years in other ways as well, for communicating to terminal services such as Citrix and Windows Terminal Services.

Dedicated or Dynamic PC Blades?

Although PC blade approaches separate the user interface (and the user) from the PC blade and offer a number of advantages, they still maintain a one-to-one relationship between the user and a PC blade (a dedicated blade). As a result, many PC blades, like traditional PCs, sit idle for much of the time (when the user isn't at work, or is in meetings, and so on). Low utilization also happens with servers, but is even more pronounced with PCs, which are used by only one user.

As a result, the trend for PC blade solutions is moving toward offering a variation for desktops that eliminates the requirement for a dedicated blade for each user. This dynamic blade environment allows multiple users to run on a single blade through the use of virtualization software. This approach improves the utilization of the blades and reduces the number of blades needed to support the PC user base.

A *dynamic blade environment*, also sometimes called a virtual desktop or virtual client infrastructure, can be implemented using virtualization software on PC blades or on server blades. Virtualization on server blades will allow more users to run per blade, but virtualizing PC blades can offer a lower cost per seat. Both virtual solutions offer a many to 1 ratio — many users to one blade. See Figure 5.7.

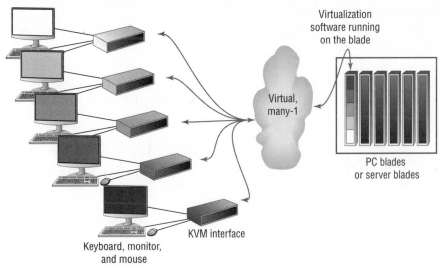

Figure 5.7: Virtual PC blade implementation

Source: Focus Consulting

A number of vendors offer this type of dynamic blade solution. ClearCube offers a dynamic blade solution using ClearCube's PC blades, I/ports, Sentral management software and connection broker, and third-party server virtualization software from VMware or Microsoft.

IBM's Virtual Client offering (which evolved from their Virtual Hosted Client Infrastructure, VHCI) is an example of a virtual desktop solution that runs on a blade server system. It consists of server virtualization software from VMware running on IBM BladeCenter; a connection broker from Leostream; and thin clients from Neoware, Wyse, or Devon IT. (IBM has also been offering a dedicated PC blade solution through their relationship with ClearCube).

VMware's Virtual Desktop Infrastructure and the Citrix Dynamic Desktop Initiative also fit in this virtual desktop space. They offer varying combinations of thin clients, server virtualization software, connection brokers, and terminal services (also known as shared services or published desktops).

Conclusion

Applying blade technology to individual user PCs offers a variety of benefits in security, manageability, and environmental options. Centralizing the computing portion of PC functions allows the PC (blades) to be locked in a central, secure facility and managed more easily by IT. The simplicity and modularity of blade technology makes the software deployment and management for the PC blades far easier. Adding a virtualization layer on top of the PC blade approach yields even greater benefits by allowing multiple users to run on a single blade (either PC blade or server blade), increasing utilization, and reducing the number of blades needed to support the user base. Although the PC blade market has traditionally not been included in industry-analyst statistics, a significant number of users are operating on PC blades. The benefits of blade technology, coupled with the advances in virtualization in this area, make desktops a large growth opportunity, particularly with the evolution of the virtual desktop.

This chapter completes the architectural look at the computing portion of blade technology. The next two chapters examine the I/O aspects of blade server systems and take a closer look at architectural issues and considerations for networking and storage in a blade environment.

Networking and Related Technologies

Networking is a critical aspect of blade server systems, involving both the ability to communicate between blades within a chassis and to connect to networks outside the chassis. This includes network connections to external local area networks (LANs), wide area networks (WANs), metropolitan area networks (MANs), and potentially storage area networks (SANs).

Blade server systems support three types of open networking protocols and additional related technologies:

- IP/Ethernet/Gigabit Ethernet (GbE)/10Gb Ethernet (10GbE)
- Fibre Channel (FC)
- InfiniBand (IB)
- Remote Direct Memory Access (RDMA)

A blade server chassis may contain multiple switch modules. Typically, the first two switch modules are Gigabit Ethernet, and the others can be either Fibre Channel or InfiniBand. Each blade has the ability to communicate with multiple types of networks: GbE (which comes standard on a basic blade) and one or more of the others (through a daughter card talking to its counterpart switch module).

This chapter will discuss each of these types of networks, along with their required components and how they can be integrated into blade server systems. Since many of the concepts and functions exist across all types of networks, it is useful first to discuss basic networking concepts.

Networking Concepts

In a blade environment, basic elements of computing are modularized into scalable components. Processing power is delivered on server blades, with increasing ability to process application and system functions in shorter and shorter time periods. This includes the ability to perform many functions simultaneously through multiple (co-) processors, multicore processors, and symmetric multiprocessing. Network components are also modularized and shared inside the chassis, providing connectivity within the chassis as well as outside the chassis. At the same time, I/O storage devices of many types and capabilities exist outside of the chassis, ranging from disk to tape devices with the ability to store and retrieve data on platforms that range in capacity and performance.

Tying systems and I/O together is the role of the network. Ideally, every piece of information that a blade would ever need would be resident immediately in memory as a function of that blade. Networks are simply a way to get data into memory for applications to use. This requires a transport and storage system that comes as close as possible to just-in-time information access and processing.

Requirements for Networks

To provide this information-delivery function, networks must meet the following basic requirements of a transport system: error-free delivery, high-speed movement, flexibility in quality of service, flexible media and signals, pathway virtualization, and high availability.

Error-Free Delivery

With most information flows, it is important to preserve 100% integrity of the information in transit between the server and the I/O or between servers. Although some information flows do not require this, most do. For example, with audio and video, it may not matter that one frame of video has a pixel color slightly distorted, or the pitch of a second of sound is raised due to a bit shift caused by interference. However, in a remote medical imaging application with doctors making a diagnosis based on a speck that shows up on the heart, it is critical to ensure that the data is transmitted accurately. In fact, in this situation data integrity is worth the trade-off in time versus quality, and it is important not only to detect the error, but to retry the delivery until correct data is received.

High-Speed Movement

Networks today can operate at gigabit rates through their transceiver send/ receive functions implemented in hardware. For various technologies, these rates include 1, 2, 4, 8, 10, 16, and 20 gigabits per second. Gigabit rates allow networks to represent a bit of information in much less time from server to server and server to storage. High-speed options are available in various forms with GbE, Fibre Channel, and InfiniBand, with varying configurations and adapters continuing to come into the marketplace over time.

Flexibility in Quality of Service

Network technologies today provide the capability to build infrastructures that can be shared among many server and storage components. When sharing, it becomes important to have mechanisms that enable information-flow requirements to be stated and acted on. This capability is called many things, including type of service, class of service, and quality of service (QOS). In this way, requests can be prioritized by systems and applications to give very high-speed service to application transaction requests, medium service to background attended file transfers, and slow (but acceptable) service to bulk email flow, for example.

Flexible Media and Signals

Networks must also allow for choices in the selection of transport media and transport signals to represent the information. For example, single-mode fiber and very high-nanometer-generating lasers can be used to move light impulses over very long distances at very high rates where performance needs outweigh price considerations. On the other hand, copper cable, electrical voltage levels, and small connectors may suffice.

Pathway Virtualization

By creating flexible "cloudlike" infrastructures of hubs, bridges, switches, routers, gateways, and the functions these components provide, networks can be implemented using multiple technologies that meet varied information-flow requirements. Pathway virtualization creates the *appearance of media* to allow end nodes to communicate with each other regardless of the protocols and paths that may be used to move the data. For example, as discussed later, iSCSI encapsulates SCSI (small computer system interface) commands and data over an IP pathway, unbeknownst to the SCSI initiator and target. Likewise, an InfiniBand to Fibre Channel gateway allows a host to communicate via InfiniBand to native Fibre Channel storage devices. Pathway virtualization is supported in all of the network technologies used in blade environments, including Ethernet, Fibre Channel, and InfiniBand.

High Availability

A variety of development techniques can be used to provide high availability within networks. With fault-free or fault-tolerant systems, components never fail — or at least never appear to fail. Redundant components are built within the system, and automatic failover occurs.

In networks as well as systems, critical components must be redundant. I/O adapter cards can be (and generally are) dual-ported, and individual blades can have dual adapters. The blade chassis typically includes two of each type of network switch module. In Serial Attached SCSI (SAS) networks and InfiniBand networks, a port can have multiple transceivers. This enables a port to continue to function if the transceiver (or more likely the switch it connects to) fails.

As far as the network goes, this dual approach enables redundancy for failure, but also redundancy for parallel processing and improved throughput. In SAS, all transceivers of a port can act as the end of a virtual cable going to storage, and all can be active at the same time. In InfiniBand and some 10Gb Fibre Channel implementations, information is striped across multiple transceivers, with each transceiver transmitting a byte from a sequence of bytes in a stream. With Infini-Band, it is possible to aggregate individual links. For example, twelve 4Gb links can be aggregated to create a stream of 48Gb flow. (Picture a fire hose moving back and forth sending a wide swath of water down several pipes.)

Types of Networks

Networks, because of their inherently redundant and flexible nature, are used in many different aspects of computing, including system-to-system communications, server-to-storage communications, and processor-to-processor communications.

System-to-System Communication Networks: LAN, MAN, WAN

Local area networks (LANs), metropolitan area networks (MANs), and wide area networks (WANs) represent various levels of geographically distributed networks. (See Figure 6.1). A LAN enables multiple systems and storage to access each other over a smaller geography. This can be extended to larger geographies with the concept of virtual LANs (VLAN), using switches and connectivity over MANs and WANs. These traditional geographic boundaries blur when the same performance characteristics can be exhibited regardless of geography. MANs and WANs relate to larger and larger geography. However, in most cases the networks are all providing an *appearance of media,* which is a virtual path that connects one system to another, such that geography is immaterial and the data structure that is built to move information from one system to another (called a *frame*) is addressed from one port to the other.

LAN, MAN, WAN

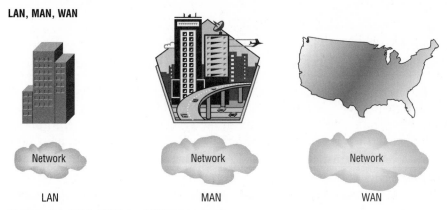

Figure 6.1: LAN, MAN, and WAN topologies
Source: Howard Goldstein Associates, Inc.

The connectivity used for NAS and SAN storage, whether a single cable or a network cloud, could be over LAN, MAN, or WAN.

System-to-Storage Networks: DAS, NAS, SAN

Direct-attached storage (DAS), network-attached storage (NAS), and storage area networks (SAN) represent three ways of connecting storage and servers, by introducing a network component at a different point in the pathway (see Figure 6.2).

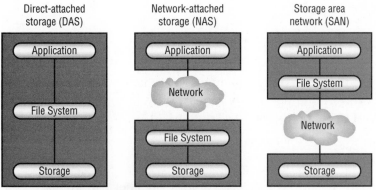

Figure 6.2: Basic storage networking technologies
Source: Howard Goldstein Associates, Inc.

With DAS, the application, the file system, and the storage are usually resident on or physically connected to the same system. Examples include the following:

- A laptop computer with a serial ATA connection to an internal hard drive
- An Ethernet or USB cable to a connected storage device
- A server blade with an SAS or SATA drive on the blade itself

With NAS, the file system and storage components are distributed over a network infrastructure, enabling file sharing amongst multiple systems. NAS allows heterogeneous shared access to a common file system. In a blade environment, this NAS function is typically implemented outside the blade server system, with a network connection, usually GbE, between the blades and the NAS.

With a SAN network, the file-system component remains in the server, and only the storage function is distributed over the network, enabling block-level access to storage devices over the network. The SAN enables access to a common set of storage space, configured into logical units of free space. Both GbE and FC are used for SAN networks.

Interprocessor Communication Networks: BAN, PAN, CAN

Blade area networks (BANs), processor area networks (PANs), and cluster area networks (CANs) are new terms in the blade and networking arena. These types of networks are used to connect and aggregate or pool processors for utility and grid processing models. These networks require very high speed and efficient networks for interprocessor communications. Both 10GbE and InfiniBand are often used for this aggregate type of network.

Common Protocols

Through the history of computing, network protocols (the rules for transmitting data) have evolved to better serve the different types of network connections. These protocols include varying amounts of reliability, redundancy, and security — with corresponding amounts of overhead, both at the protocol level and in regard to the protocol's effect on the CPU.

Ethernet

Ethernet today is the most prevalent type of local area networking used with PCs, workstations, and open-systems computing. It is virtually ubiquitous, replacing all other LAN standards such as token ring and ARCNET. Invented in the 1970s at Xerox to connect peer computers, it defines wiring and signaling (how the bits move across the wire) used by the physical layer, and frame format and protocols for the data link (Media Access Control, MAC) layer of the network. It has become standardized to the IEEE 802.3 specification. Despite changes over the years in the physical characteristics, making it continually less expensive (for example the move from coaxial cable to twisted-pair RJ-45 connectors), it remains the same from a programming point of view.

At either end of the Ethernet cable (network) are computer systems requiring an Ethernet interface. The interface card located in the system is called a network interface card (NIC). The NIC accepts the bit stream from the wire and begins to organize it back into the information that was originally transmitted. From the physical layer, the NIC passes the bits on to the data-link layer (MAC and Logical Link Control — LLC), up to the network layer (IP), and on to the transport layer (TCP); an architecture commonly called *TCP/IP over Ethernet* (see Figure 6.3). Intelligent NICs, which offload various types of functions and processing from the host, are also available. Examples include TCP offload, iSCSI initiators, RDMA, and security tasks such as SSL encryption/decryption.

	Internet Protocol Suite		OSI Model
Host Layers			Application layer
			Presentation layer
			Session layer
	Transmission Control Protocol (TCP)		Transport layer
Media Layers	*Internet Protocol (IP)*		Network layer
	Ethernet		Data link layer
			Physical layer

Figure 6.3: The OSI model and Internet Protocol suite (TCP/IP over Ethernet)
Source: Focus Consulting

Ethernet in Blade Server Systems

TCP/IP and Ethernet are, in essence, the default LAN communications used in blade server systems. Blade servers communicate using TCP/IP over Ethernet to either the network switch modules or pass-through modules then outside the chassis. The processor on the blade communicates over the PCI (Peripheral

Component Interconnect) bus to an I/O adapter called an onboard NIC, which then connects to the switch module(s). Most basic blades come with dual-ported 1Gb Ethernet NICs that, by default, communicate with redundant GbE switch modules in the chassis. For applications requiring additional ports, an I/O expansion card can be added to provide two additional NICs for that blade, which can be GbE or 10GbE for high performance. (Higher-speed systems offer 10GbE switches as well.)

As mentioned, by default most blade chassis come with redundant GbE switch modules on the back side of the midplane. This can be an issue for customers who have, for simplicity and manageability, already chosen a specific Ethernet switch provider for their entire network operation. Switch modules for the blade chassis may not be available from the preferred provider. To remedy this situation, blade vendors created pass-through modules to be used in place of switch modules. Pass-though modules simply extend the "wire" from the midplane to the back side of the chassis, where network cables could then connect to external switches. Pass-through modules can be used in place of Ethernet switch modules, Fibre Channel switch modules, or InfiniBand switch modules.

If a blade needs to communicate with storage over Ethernet through an iSCSI SAN, an iSCSI initiator is required, along with a NIC. This can be implemented with a software initiator (usually free) and the standard GbE NIC, with a software initiator and a NIC (usually higher-speed) daughter card, or a hardware initiator implemented on the daughter card NIC. The latter typically offers a TCP offload engine (TOE) to offload the TCP processing from the CPU and improve performance. Ethernet and iSCSI SAN configurations are discussed further in the Chapter 7, "Blades and Storage."

Fibre Channel

Although the idea of a network technology for connecting servers to storage has existed for many years in the mainframe world through Enterprise Systems Connectivity (ESCON), the ESCON technology is a proprietary storage-network protocol. Fibre Channel, on the other hand, is an ANSI standard protocol that addresses the needs of all systems, including open system environments such as Windows, Linux, Unix, and AIX. Fibre Channel is the first technology to combine the connectivity of networks with the speed and reliability of traditional I/O channel architectures. It has many features that make it attractive for supporting storage access protocols, in particular the SCSI protocol, including the following:

■ **Bandwidth** — Fibre Channel transceivers operate at many bit rates, including 1Gbps, 2Gbps, 4Gbps, and 10Gbps. At these rates, the bandwidth meets and exceeds the traditional parallel SCSI Bus Ultra 1, 2, 3, 4, and beyond. These rates range from full-speed Fibre Channel at 100 MBps (megabytes per second) to 1,200 MBps. These higher rates are implemented as a backbone Interswitch Link (ISL) connecting Fibre Channel switches.

- **Low error rates** — Fibre Channel standards require a minimum error rate of 10^{-12} and most implementations yield orders of magnitude beyond that.

- **Flexible topologies** — Fibre Channel is a technology that supports loop, point-to-point, and fabric topologies. Low-cost Arbitrated Loop connectivity is used today in conjunction with loop switches internally in the highest performing RAID controllers. Point-to-point and fabric topologies provide the ability to connect large numbers of servers and storage through switches. The Fibre Channel architecture allows for 239 switches connected through ISLs to appear as one fabric distributed across a large geographic environment. This connectivity can be direct or through bridges and gateways that leverage other longer-distance technologies, such as TCP/IP networks.

- **Long distance** — Fibre Channel supports both copper cabling and various fiber-optic media, including single-mode and multimode fiber. This enables low-cost connectivity through copper cabling or printed circuits in the blade environment, along with distance extension from 500 meters to 100 kilometers, point to point.

- **Firmware and hardware** — Much of the Fibre Channel function at the adapter card level occurs through firmware and hardware. All of the port functions implementing traditional transport, network, data link, and physical-layer function is done in high-speed hardware. This leverages the hardware offload function used in I/O and unburdens the host processor from wasting expensive CPU cycles.

- **Multiple-protocol support** — Fibre Channel has the ability to support many protocols simultaneously. It is used primarily today to support the connection of SCSI and ESCON storage protocols; however, it can also support real-time audio/video, IP packet transfer, and virtual interface capability in support of large memory-to-memory remote transfer in RDMA.

- **High availability** — Fibre Channel adapters are often dual-ported, and/or systems and storage can have multiple adapters for high availability. This, coupled with redundant switch infrastructures, makes Fibre Channel ideal for supporting the enterprise environment.

Fibre Channel SANs provide an excellent option for high-speed, reliable storage networks that can be shared across multiple servers, including blade servers. If FC SANs are within an organization, connecting servers (blade or otherwise) to those SANs requires specific hardware and software.

Fibre Channel Components

Fibre Channel networks require specific components both on the server side and on the storage side, in addition to the FC switches within the network. On the server side, Fibre Channel is implemented through a host bus adapter (HBA) card. The server software functions as though it is using the file system local to the host and writing to a SCSI drive. The SCSI commands and data are then encapsulated within the Fibre Channel Protocol (FCP) on the HBA and then sent across the Fibre Channel network through a point-to-point connection over a series of Fibre Channel switches. On the storage side, the reverse function takes place through a Fibre Channel storage adapter, which connects the switch port to the storage node.

Fibre Channel in Blade Server Systems

If a blade within the chassis needs to communicate to a Fibre Channel SAN, it requires an HBA, just like any other server. For blades, the HBA is implemented as an I/O expansion (daughter) card to the blade. The HBA then communicates to a Fibre Channel switch, either internal or external to the blade chassis.

If only a few blades within the chassis need to communicate via Fibre Channel, those blades can utilize a pass-through module to communicate to an external switch. The pass-through module essentially allows the HBA on the blade to have an external connection on the backplane, to connect a cable to the external Fibre Channel switch. These can be either copper or optical. In either case, there is an external connection (N-port) on the backplane for each pass-through module. For a low number of connections, using pass-through is a lower-cost implementation from the blade system perspective, since it does not require a Fibre Channel switch module in the chassis.

If most of the blades in the chassis need Fibre Channel access, it makes sense to aggregate those ports on a Fibre Channel switch module in the chassis. In this case, the HBAs communicate directly to the Fibre Channel switch module, which then has E-ports (ISL connections) on the backplane to connect to external switches.

There are currently blade implementations of Fibre Channel at both 2Gb and 4Gb with advanced features also available, such as ISL trunking for improved performance, advanced performance monitoring for optimizing SAN performance, and secure fabric for increased security in the SAN. Options vary by blade system and switch vendor. In general, most features that are implemented in standard Fibre Channel switches are being implemented in blade switch modules; however, there may be some lag time before the blade version is available.

InfiniBand

As processors and I/O devices have increased in speed, they have outgrown the capabilities of the PCI bus used in PCs since the 1990s. Two alternatives initially were investigated as a replacement for PCI. These included Future I/O and NGIO (Next-Generation I/O). The two architectures and supporting vendors argued the merits of each technology, and much time and energy was wasted. In August 1999 the two proposed technologies finally combined into something upon which both groups could agree: InfiniBand. The name InfiniBand was taken from the phrase "infinite bandwidth."

Seven of the computing industry's leaders — Compaq, Dell, Hewlett-Packard, IBM, Intel, Microsoft, and Sun Microsystems — joined together in an independent industry body called the InfiniBand Trade Association. The focus of the association is to work toward a new common I/O specification to deliver a channel-based, switched fabric technology that the entire industry can adopt.

Why a New I/O Interconnect?

Existing interconnect technologies have failed to keep pace with computer evolution, specifically processor speeds, and the increased burden imposed on data servers, application processing, and enterprise computing created by the success of the Internet. High-end computing concepts such as clustering, fault tolerance, and 24/7 availability demand greater capacity to move data between processing nodes as well as between a processor node and I/O devices.

These trends require higher bandwidth and lower latencies, as they are pushing more functionality down to the I/O device, and demanding greater protection, higher isolation, deterministic behavior, and a higher quality of service than currently available.

IB architecture can support bandwidths that are anticipated to remain an order of magnitude greater than prevailing I/O media (SCSI, Fibre Channel, and Ethernet). This enables its role as a common interconnect using these technologies. With InfiniBand, the network cloud rises a layer to replace the last big bottleneck in performance.

In addition, the IB design includes native support for advanced features such as remote direct memory access (RDMA) and Internet Protocol version 6 (IPv6) headers (for efficient transport over IP infrastructures), which make it a strong platform for the future.

Features and Advantages of InfiniBand

InfiniBand offers a number of advanced features and benefits, particularly for high-availability and high-speed interconnect applications:

- Scalable point-to-point switched-fabric technology

- High reliability, availability, and serviceability (RAS)
  - Redundant paths and/or fabrics
  - In-band/out-of-band management
  - Layered error management
- High performance
  - Direct application communication via Remote DMA
  - Virtual Lanes (VL) allow for independent data flow within a port
  - CPU-offloaded hardware support
  - 10Gbps and increasing
- Previously, network implementations required a separate fabric for each network type (Ethernet, Fibre Channel, SCSI). InfiniBand offers one integrated fabric for all types of communication, including inter-process communication (IPC), storage I/O, and network I/O.
- I/O is moving outside the box for greater connectivity and accessibility, particularly in the blade environment.
- Applications require considerable IPC in which high-speed communications are particularly important.
- Architecture for low-latency clustering with improved IPC using blade-to-blade communications via RDMA.

InfiniBand Architecture and Components

The InfiniBand architecture is a relatively new interconnect technology that defines a fabric switched interconnect based upon three primary components. The first is the InfiniBand switch. Connected to the switch are host channel adapters (HCAs) and target channel adapters (TCAs). The HCA typically resides in the server. The TCA is used to connect to other technologies, including Fibre Channel storage and Gigabit Ethernet networking. Figure 6.4 is a conceptual diagram of the InfiniBand architecture.

An IB system can support a single processor and a few storage devices to a massively scaled computing system with hundreds of processors and thousands of devices. The Internet Protocol–friendly nature of IB allows IPv6 addressing in bridging to Internet and intranet networks. The IB architecture also capitalizes on current I/O technology by allowing bridging to installed storage architectures. Figure 6.5 demonstrates a large-scale computing environment with an Internet connection and a bridge to Fibre Channel and SCSI storage.

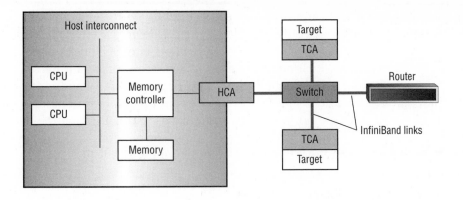

Figure 6.4: InfiniBand architecture

Source: Howard Goldstein Associates, Inc.

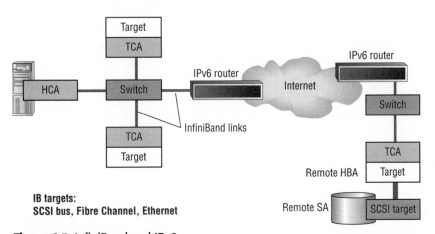

Figure 6.5: InfiniBand and IPv6

Source: Howard Goldstein Associates, Inc.

At a high level, IB serves as an interconnect for end-nodes. Each end-node can be a processor node, an I/O unit, and/or a router to another network. The IB network is subdivided into subnets that are interconnected by routers. End-nodes can attach to a single subnet or multiple subnets, and a subnet is composed of nodes, switches, routers, and a subnet manager. Each IB device may attach to a single switch or multiple switches and/or directly with each other. Multiple links can exist between any two IB devices.

IB is designed around a point-to-point, switched I/O fabric, whereby end-node devices are interconnected by cascaded switched devices. Each node can range from a very inexpensive I/O device (like a single chip SCSI or Ethernet adapter) to very complex host computers. Switched communication allows many devices to communicate concurrently and provides high bandwidth, low latency, and a protected remotely managed environment. End-nodes can communicate over multiple ports and can use multiple paths through the IB fabric. The multiplicity of IB ports and paths through the network is exploited for both fault tolerance and increased data-transfer bandwidth.

InfiniBand in Blade Server Systems

The InfiniBand specification defines modules, form factors, connectors, LED placement, ejector latches, vents, and every physical aspect of hardware design, including implementations on blade systems. However, there are still variations in implementation. Many of the InfiniBand implementations used in blade systems are based on the IB silicon chips produced by Mellanox. Initial blade implementations of IB still use the PCI Express bus, although this may change over time. The key advantages offered in this implementation focus on two areas: improving interprocessor communications (blade to blade) over IB and converging various types of network traffic over IB.

Some implementations include only an HCA with a pass-through option to an external IB switch. Other implementations include an IB switch module in the chassis. Initial implementations of IB in blade systems have not yet replaced the PCI bus, but instead use an InfiniBand HCA adapter card attached to a switched version of the PCI bus called PCI-E (see Chapter 7 for more information on PCI-E). The HCA then communicates to one of the two IB switch modules in the backplane. For interprocessor communications, the switch then communicates with the second blade at high speed, with the added advantage of using RDMA (which is described in the following section).

When using IB for the advantages of IPC communications, the IB switch could also be used for high-speed connectivity to storage. Until more native IB storage devices are available, it is necessary to communicate to FC storage devices using an FC-IB gateway and a protocol called SRP (SCSI RDMA Protocol) over IB. To do this, the operating system communicates via SRP to the HCA and then to the IB switch in the chassis (see Figure 6.6). The switch then communicates (potentially across other switches) to an FC-IB gateway (that essentially implements a TCA in the gateway), which then talks to the FC storage.

Although it is possible to also send IP traffic over IB (IPoIB), most users will prefer to route their LAN traffic through the Ethernet switch, as blades come with NICs and chassis include Ethernet switches by default.

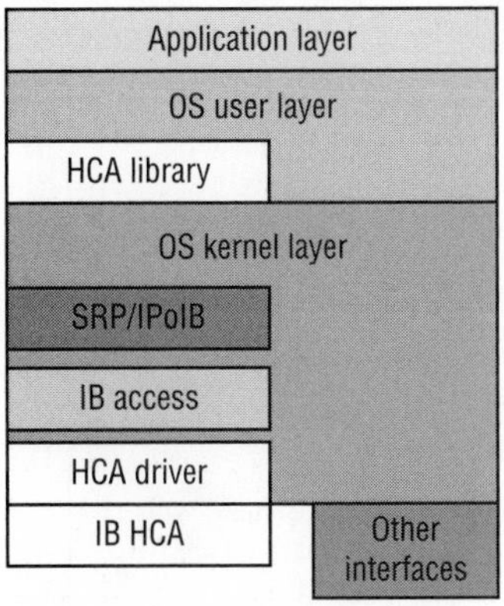

Figure 6.6: InfiniBand OS stack
Source: Focus Consulting

As more functionality is implemented in IB for blades, more advanced features will become available. For example, it is possible to allocate bandwidth within the HCA to specific virtual lanes. As this feature becomes accessible to virtualization software (see Chapter 8, "Virtualization") this will allow for QOS functionality within virtualized environments.

RDMA

Remote direct memory access (RDMA) is a distributed mechanism that enables a remote processor to access another system's local memory as if it were local memory. Within a single system, direct memory access (DMA) occurs when one application's buffers are placed in a shared memory location that another application can access through DMA. As shown in Figure 6.7, the local process includes a local copy mechanism where information is copied into memory and a DMA engine can then copy that information from the source address to a destination address in another application's memory space.

In a traditional technology such as Ethernet or Fibre Channel, when the adapter card is signaled via I/O interrupt to begin processing a request for movement, it reaches into local memory through the DMA process. This process makes it unnecessary to interrupt the CPU until that transfer is complete.

As shown in Figure 6.8, the RDMA process is designed to transfer information from the memory space of one computer (src address) to the memory space of another (dst address), regardless of size and location. Additionally, no intermediate I/O interrupts are required on long and large transfers until the entire operation is completed, freeing up CPU cycles on both systems.

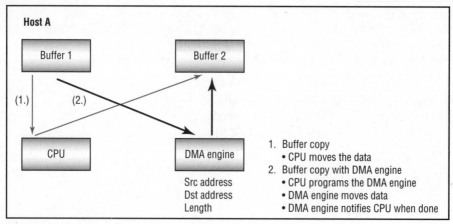

Figure 6.7: Direct memory access (DMA) processing
Source: Howard Goldstein Associates, Inc.

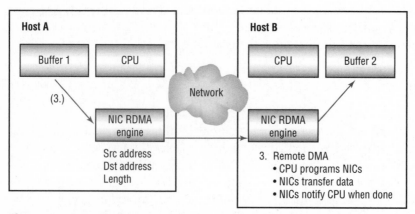

Figure 6.8: Remote direct memory access (RDMA) between two hosts
Source: Howard Goldstein Associates, Inc.

RDMA also delivers content to and from server and storage memory at very high speeds with no CPU intervention. There are several examples of RDMA and storage. iSER is iSCSI extensions for RDMA, and allows the data movement and placement functions to be offloaded for more-efficient data transfers. iSER eliminates the need for TCP/IP software and Ethernet NICs for iSCSI and replaces the TCP/IP offload-engine approach with an RDMA-style solution (delivering a similar CPU offload). NFS/RDMA handles NFS file requests and resulting file movement across remote systems.

Since RDMA is movement from local to remote memory as quickly and as unencumbered as possible, many transport technologies can be used for RDMA.

PCI Express provides a switched interface from an adapter into local memory and eliminates the bottleneck of the PCI bus. It also protects local memory from a rogue adapter from overlaying another process's memory. InfiniBand does the same but goes further in that it uses IPv6 and multiple interconnected subnets to go from a remote InfiniBand device HCA to a local HCA. This would be RDMA over InfiniBand. It is also possible to do RDMA over VI/FC since Virtual Interface allows a large payload transfer over FC frames. (Picture a payload of megabytes in one transfer [rather than SCSI blocks] for large files and backups.)

Conclusion

Connecting blades to each other and to the world outside of the blade server system chassis is a critical piece of blade system implementation. Blades and blade chassis come with 1Gbps Ethernet connections, allowing basic LAN connectivity by default. High-speed connectivity can be implemented in addition, either through 10GbE, Fibre Channel, and/or InfiniBand, depending on the systems you need to connect to within your environment. Most networking and switch features are available for blade systems, but it is important to check with your networking vendor for the latest information on feature availability and compatibilities.

This chapter has covered the basic information needed for understanding networking concepts and implementation considerations. Chapter 7 builds on this information, adding the concepts and considerations for blade storage — both on-blade storage (if appropriate) and connecting to various types of network storage (NAS and SAN).

Blades and Storage

In many ways, the options for storage and storage connectivity with blades are the same as with standard servers. A blade, after all, is a server in a different form. However, given that some of the appeal of blades is simplicity of management and the ability to move seamlessly to another blade in the event of a failure, some implementation choices for storage should be considered. This chapter reviews the way that storage is accessed in a traditional server platform and contrasts it to storage options in blade-server systems. Storage implementation and access alternatives are discussed, along with typical business reasons for making various implementation decisions.

I/O Architectures and Buses

Since the early 1990s when the PCI bus was introduced, most servers and PCs have relied on it as the I/O bus of choice. For the most part, this bus architecture has not changed. In the past 10–15 years, the increase in speed of the processors has significantly outpaced the performance of the PCI bus, leading to data-starved CPUs.

In an attempt to keep up, the PCI-X specification was created, which essentially took PCI from a 32-bit bus to a 64-bit bus. This increase basically doubled

PCI's address space, increasing its parallel transmission capabilities. The PCI-X specification also increased the clock rate from 66MHz to 133MHz, allowing for 1Gbps bandwidth. Since then, additional upgrades have been made to the PCI-X specification, primarily to increase bandwidth; however, these changes still have not been enough to keep up with the changing CPUs.

As discussed in Chapter 6, in an attempt to remedy this situation, in the late 1990s two competing interconnect standards for converged networking were developed — the Future I/O (FIO) and the Next-Generation I/O standards. Knowing that only one would win out in the markets, the two standards were merged and became InfiniBand.

The InfiniBand I/O specification has met with some success, but people like to stick with what they already know. Hence, a next-generation PCI architecture based on a point-to-point switched approach was developed, called PCI Express (PCI-E). This latest specification offers many of the same benefits as InfiniBand, but only for local devices. Although InfiniBand solutions are available for switch modules and blade InfiniBand adapters (for blades to communicate with other blades in the chassis as well as devices outside the chassis), PCI Express has become the onboard I/O interconnect of choice for blade systems. With the PCI-E specification, the programming interface remained primarily the same, making upgrading to the newest specification much easier than changing I/O architectures altogether.

PCI-E provides scalable bandwidth of 16Gb per second. It is a general-purpose serial I/O interconnect (providing bandwidth and scalability advantages over the previous parallel interfaces of PCI and PCI-X), with the benefit of compatibility with previous PCI programming models. All other interconnect technologies within the blade chassis (GbE Ethernet, Fibre Channel [FC], and InfiniBand [IB]), as well as any other local devices such as hard-disk drives (HDD), connect into the onboard PCI Express as shown in Figure 7.1.

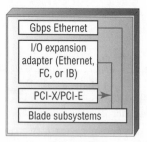

Server blade

Figure 7.1: Blade I/O diagram

Source: Focus Consulting

InfiniBand is primarily used in clustered environments or other applications where very high-speed/low-latency interprocessor communication is required. (In the blade environment, the IB switch module can provide this function for intrachassis blade communications as well as for connecting blades in multiple chassis or traditional servers outside the chassis.) Blade server systems with IB switch modules may also use InfiniBand to Ethernet and/or FC gateways for converged LAN and SAN connectivity.

There has been talk about replacing PCI-E with InfiniBand because IB is inherently a high-speed switched environment that also provides RDMA capabilities and extends to remote devices.

Blades and Storage Connections

All blades come standard with (at minimum) a 1Gbps Ethernet connection (NIC) to communicate with the standard Ethernet switch modules in the backplane. Some blades come standard with dual ports for redundancy. If your applications need either additional NICs or faster Ethernet bandwidth (10GbE NICs are available), a daughter/mezzanine card can be attached onto the I/O expansion adapter on the blade. Depending on the blade vendor, up to two additional expansion cards can be supported.

If the blades within the chassis need to connect to a Fibre Channel SAN, you can also add a Fibre Channel adapter (HBA daughter card) to each blade requiring access. The HBA then communicates to one or two shared Fibre Channel switch modules in the backplane. If instead you require the high-bandwidth/low-latency converged interconnect offered by InfiniBand, you can add an InfiniBand adapter card onto the appropriate blades to communicate with a shared IB switch module. Blade chassis generally support Ethernet switch modules and one type of high-speed switching in the backplane, either IB or FC (see Figure 7.2).

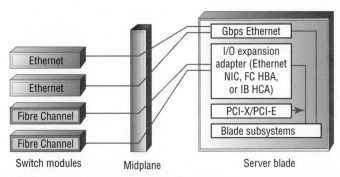

Figure 7.2: Sample chassis I/O diagram

Source: Focus Consulting

Any blade within the chassis can access any switch module through the midplane, thereby building in redundant paths within the chassis. However, if you prefer not to use a switch module in the chassis (if you have enough available ports on an existing external switch; if you are using advanced features on your external switch that are not available on the equivalent blade switch; if you just don't want yet another, possibly unknown switch type in your environment; and so on), you can implement pass-through modules that allow you to connect the adapter on the blade out to the backplane for connection to an external switch (see Figure 7.3). Pass-through modules do simply that — pass the traffic through without any processing. They can be thought of as a straight wire to the outside of the chassis.

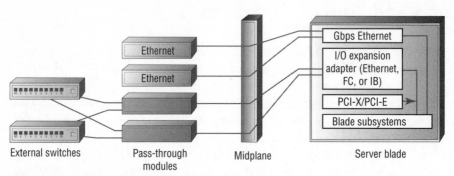

Figure 7.3: Using pass-through modules

Source: Focus Consulting

Storage Options with Blade Servers

At a high level, there are three ways to implement storage with blades, as with any server: *onboard* storage, *external* storage, and a combination of the two. More often that not, with traditional servers, businesses implement a combination of onboard storage to be used for system functions and external storage, either network-attached storage (NAS) or storage area network (SAN), for business-application data storage.

Onboard Storage

The area inside a blade chassis is tight, so space is always a consideration. Most vendors allow up to two small form factor (SFF) 2.5-inch disk drives on their blades. A number of disk drive options are available in this form factor. The most frequently used onboard drives include SFF serial-attached SCSI

(SAS) drives and SFF Serial ATA (SATA) drives, which are both hot-pluggable. The hot-pluggable feature is important because the disk drive is the only moving part on the blade and is more prone to failure. To minimize downtime due to disk failure, blade companies have started providing RAID (redundant arrays of independent disk) controllers that will *stripe* (for performance) and *mirror* (for redundancy) the data across the two disks.

Many vendors also offer blade storage expansion units, which take up another blade slot that support a number of 3.5-inch HDDs as well as adapters for additional I/O daughter cards.

External Storage

External storage comes in a variety of configurations with a number of different protocols used for access. The two primary methods used are network attached storage (NAS) and storage area Nntworks (SAN).

Network Attached Storage (NAS)

With the standard Ethernet connectivity available on the blade, storage can be accessed using NAS protocols over IP. If the operating system running on the blade is Microsoft Windows, the CIFS protocol is generally used. Both Linux and UNIX operating systems use the NFS protocol. Of course, third-party software is available for each operating system to allow both file protocols in either environment. Through the NAS protocols, the blade can access, and even share, any files other systems have made available. More often than not, a special NAS storage solution is used for this purpose rather than an off-the-shelf server with attached storage. In a NAS storage solution, the server component has been both stripped down and enhanced to excel at file-serving; its sole purpose is to send and receive files across the network.

Storage Area Network (SAN)

Since the late 1990s, SANs have gained vast acceptance and have been widely deployed to meet customer requirements for reliability, flexibility, scalability and availability of their data. SANs have allowed businesses to better manage and utilize their storage resources, providing consolidation of disk and tape storage into resource pools that can be shared by multiple servers. Rather than having storage connected to and managed independently by each blade, an entire chassis of blades, multiple chassis, or both chassis and traditional servers can share a pool of tape and disk storage, thereby consolidating and simplifying storage as well as servers.

Fibre Channel SAN

Historically, the most common and widely deployed SAN has been the Fibre Channel SAN. For blade servers, attaching to an FC SAN requires the addition of a Fibre Channel host bus adapter (HBA) I/O expansion adapter (daughter card) on each blade that will access the SAN. Most of these FC I/O expansion adapters contain two ports for redundancy. These cards come in performance levels of 1Gbps, 2Gbps, and most recently 4 Gbps. Then, on the back side of the blade chassis, either Fibre Channel switch modules or pass-through modules (copper or optical) will be needed (see Figure 7.3) to complete the connection from the blade to the external SAN.

iSCSI SAN

As discussed previously, with the standard Ethernet connectivity and a software initiator (usually free), customers can configure and access iSCSI SAN storage using the iSCSI protocol, also called an IP-SAN. The iSCSI protocol is the SCSI protocol, which is typically used to access storage, encapsulated into IP packets so it can be transmitted to storage via a LAN, or even a WAN, over TCP/IP. On the storage side, there must be either a bridge or iSCSI storage that knows how to extract the SCSI commands from the IP packets and perform the tasks.

Enhancing Storage Access over TCP/IP

With the availability of 10Gbps Ethernet, users are questioning the need to implement yet another network for their storage, especially if they are moving to blade systems. Why not just use Ethernet? This is a question worth exploring.

Several storage protocols use TCP/IP over Ethernet. Two that are addressed in this book are the NAS (NFS and CIFS) and iSCSI protocols. The arguments against using TCP/IP as a storage network protocol involve guaranteeing reliable performance using this "chatty" network protocol, especially if your applications require a great deal of I/O.

What if your TCP/IP network becomes overloaded and I/O requests can't be serviced? Most applications do not deal with I/O timeouts or dropped requests very well, even with the advent of SANs. One typical way to get around this is to isolate your storage network from your communications network — something you would be doing by default if you were to implement a Fibre Channel SAN.

Another aspect of TCP/IP that is less than optimal is that it is most often processed in software as part of the operating system. It is not unheard of for an I/O-intensive application to consume as much as 80% of the CPU in TCP/IP processing only. Obviously, it would be better to have the CPU working on business-related activities rather than OS activities. To address this, TCP Offload Engines (TOEs) implement the TCP/IP protocol in hardware and are placed on NICs. This makes for very efficient and fast processing of all network traffic, including NAS and iSCSI storage traffic.

In a blade environment, TOEs are implemented as daughter cards and can be added just as another NIC would be, by connecting it to the I/O expansion adapter on the blade.

If you plan to connect blades to an existing SAN, either FC or iSCSI, or if you choose to implement your SAN using specific switches and storage, it is important for you to check with your vendors to verify that the blade I/O expansion adapters and switch modules are interoperable with their hardware.

Storage Implementation Considerations

The best way to implement storage with one or many blade systems is highly dependent upon your business goals. This section explains the trade-offs in many of the implementation decisions you will face.

Disk or No Disk

It's not often you will find a traditional server with no onboard storage, even if it is used only to boot the system. However, with blade servers, there are a number of arguments for using *diskless* (also called *anonymous* or *stateless*) blades:

- Cooling and power issues
- Reliability and maintainability
- Management and provisioning

Cooling and Power

As mentioned previously, the area within a blade chassis is efficiently used. The tight quarters mean airflow and cooling need to be highly effective, or the blade processors will overheat and start to fail. Although all the blade chassis have been through rigorous environmental tests with disks attached to the blades, the disks add heat. Removing any additional sources of heat can only be of benefit to the chassis environment. Disks also draw quite a bit of power. In an environment where cooling and power are shared by all the components, the power used by the disks could otherwise be allocated to faster processors.

Reliability and Maintainability

Disks are the only moving components on the blade. Therefore, they're the components most likely to fail. Granted, for many implementations the data is mirrored to minimize impact in the event of a single disk failure. Even though many of the disks used are hot-swappable, pragmatically one would pull the entire blade rather than hot-swapping a disk on a blade. Still, if there are no disks on the blade, this would not be an issue.

Management and Provisioning

If simplicity of management is a goal, having all blades boot from one disk image on SAN-attached storage simplifies ongoing management. This will reduce the chance of blade failure due to disks and eliminate the need to synchronize updates to software located on each blade disk. In many cases, booting from SAN can provide better performance and fault tolerance than local disks. Most blade vendors support booting from SAN-attached storage using PXE (Preboot Execution Environment). PXE was introduced by Intel as part of their Wired for Management framework. It allows the computer to be booted from the network rather than local disk. Check with your vendor to verify support for diskless booting and specific configuration support.

In addition, one of the big advantages to the modularity and standardization of blades is that they simplify the process of provisioning and reprovisioning servers to different applications and workloads. Separating the server from the storage that various applications need to access simplifies this provisioning process. With anonymous blades, when it is time to provision a server to run a specific application with specific data, you simply point the server to the appropriate boot image, with access to the appropriate storage. There is no need to worry about what is stored on a particular server's local disk.

Finally, when implementing a virtualized server environment, which will be discussed in Chapter 8, "Virtualization," the flexibility of the blade is crucial to gaining the high utilization rates desired for these systems. Using anonymous blades in this environment is essential.

SAS or SATA

If you have decided you need disk-on-blade configurations, what type of local disk would better suit your needs: SFF Serial Attached SCSI (SAS) disk or SFF Serial ATA (SATA or S-ATA) disk? These drives hold many of the same considerations as their predecessors, parallel SCSI and parallel ATA (IDE) drives. SAS drives provide multiple connections where SATA drives do not. SAS drives are more reliable than SATA drives; however, SAS drives are more expensive than SATA drives.

As a guideline, if you are running mission-critical or disk-intensive applications (scale-up), with higher performance requirements, SAS drives are generally recommended. If you are running non–mission-critical applications where minimal downtime is acceptable or applications that are not disk-intensive (scale-out), you can use SATA drives at a lower cost.

SAN or NAS

If you already have NAS and/or SAN storage in your environment, your blade server systems can access them using similar connectivity to what your traditional servers are already using. Considerations for which of these two types of storage to use are not specific to blade technology.

If you have not yet implemented either one, the primary key to deciding whether to implement SAN or NAS (or both) lies in the answer to the question, "Do you need to share *data* or do you need to share *storage*?" If you need to share data, your storage implementation has to have a shared file system structure. SANs are based on block-level access rather than file-level access, and do not provide a shared file view, so for file sharing across blades, you will need NAS storage. That being said, software is available that will create a distributed file system (DFS) across a cluster of systems at the operating system level. A SAN can be used as the storage infrastructure for this type of shared environment.

iSCSI or FC SAN

FC SANs and their benefits became widely accepted in the late 1990s. At that time, Fibre Channel boasted significantly faster speeds than Ethernet. It wasn't long before Ethernet vendors caught on, and the race between Fibre Channel and Ethernet for dominance in the SAN began.

In 2002, the first iSCSI devices started showing up, and the iSCSI standard was ratified by the IETF (Internet Engineering Task Force) in early 2003. By this time, many of the enterprise companies who required the benefits of a SAN had already implemented an FC SAN. Due to the Fibre Channel stronghold along with the arguments against IP-based storage networks discussed earlier, iSCSI has had a difficult time in the enterprise market. iSCSI SANs did capture a larger share of the small-medium business (SMB) space. The SMBs required the flexibility and reliability of a SAN but often didn't like the price tag that came with FC SANs, and the performance of the iSCSI SAN fit within their business objectives.

All that said, with the advent of 10Gbps Ethernet, and TOE technology, many arguments for FC have since been refuted, and iSCSI has gotten a toehold in the industry. Especially in a blade environment, many businesses are choosing to use an iSCSI SAN for simplicity of the solution. All blades come with a standard 1Gbps NIC with 10Gbps adapters available as well as TOEs. For businesses that are deploying blade chassis to remote locations with little to no onsite systems management personnel, implementing a consistent interface to all networks makes sense. However, it is recommended that, even in these environments, the communications and storage networks be separated to reduce the amount of excess traffic interfering with storage processing.

Businesses that are deploying blade systems into an environment where there is already a large FC infrastructure will most likely want to simply add the new blade servers onto the existing FC storage — gaining greater value from their storage consolidation.

As with most considerations, often good reasons can be found for both options, local disk or no local disk, SAS or SATA, NAS or SAN, iSCSI or FC. It all comes down to what makes the most sense for reaching your business objectives.

Conclusion

Blades are not much different from other servers when it comes to the storage choices available; they have many of the same options. However, the lack of space within the blade chassis does present some interesting challenges, as do the application environments where blades are being deployed. In addition, the inclusion of Ethernet, Fibre Channel, or InfiniBand switch modules in the chassis, along with the flexibility and provisioning benefits of anonymous blades, are compelling reasons for connecting diskless blades to NAS and/or SAN storage. Much like standard servers, however, the decision criteria come down to the usual suspects: capital expenses, operational expenses, and meeting the business objective as effectively as possible.

This chapter reviewed the different storage and storage networking options available to blade servers and discussed some of the options that need to be considered when deploying blade server storage. Chapter 8, "Virtualization," discusses virtualization technologies and some of the pros and cons of various approaches.

Virtualization

Now that we have examined the architecture of blade systems, it is time to drill down into virtualization. So far, we have covered a basic description and history of virtualization. This chapter discusses the various types and implementations of virtualization and delves more deeply into server virtualization. It also examines the key issues of managing virtual server environments.

The overall goal of virtualization is to create a logical abstraction of physical assets. *Wikipedia*, in 2006, further defines virtualization as follows:

"Virtualization is the process of presenting a logical grouping or subset of computing resources so that they can be accessed in ways that give benefits over the original configuration. This new virtual view of the resources is not restricted by the implementation, geographic location, or the physical configuration of underlying resources."

What this means as it relates to blade servers is that virtualization of blade servers allows them to be both grouped together as well as subdivided into virtual servers to provide a variety of benefits. Virtual servers may or may not be tied to the physical configuration of the physical server(s) on which they reside. In addition to server virtualization, other types of virtualization are highly involved with blades servers, including storage, network, and I/O virtualization.

Definitions

In discussing *virtualization*, a number of terms (that are often misused) are helpful to define. Although these are not exhaustive definitions, they will explain how these terms are used within the context of this book. Terminology, especially when talking about both physical and virtualized resources, can get quite muddled.

Aggregation

When virtualization of physical resources involves combining multiple servers to act as one system, it is also known as *aggregation*. Clustering (discussed further in Chapter 9, "Clustering and Blades") is a way of aggregating systems. Some blade system vendors offer solutions that are specifically designed to aggregate blades and allow them to act as a single entity, with proprietary tools (for example, from Egenera and PANTA Systems) designed to help manage this process.

Disaggregation/Server Virtualization

Disaggregation of servers allows multiple independent instances of an operating environment to run on a single server (dividing one physical server into multiple virtual servers). This is the typical usage of the term *server virtualization*. This type of virtualization allows for the consolidation of multiple, underutilized, physical servers onto one server with higher system utilization — reducing management overhead, floor space, power, and cooling requirements.

Server virtualization can be implemented in a variety of ways, with pros and cons associated with each. Implementation approaches include *emulation*, *paravirtualization, hypervisors, hosted approach* and *OS virtualization*, which are described later in this chapter. For clarity, in this book, when referring to physical hosts, the term *server* will be used. When referring to virtual servers, the term *virtual machine* or *VM* will be used.

Storage Virtualization

Storage virtualization applies an abstraction to the storage systems within the enterprise and is often a key component used with blade systems. Virtualizing the storage allows virtual disks to be defined to components running on the server and separates the physical management and sometimes connection of those disks from the application software on the server. Storage virtualization can be implemented within the server (host-based), within the storage area network (network- or fabric-based), or within the storage subsystem (a RAID arrays). These solutions may take an in-band approach, in which device that does the virtualization is in the data path, or an out-of-b approach, in which the device that performs the virtualization is not in data path.

Network Virtualization

As with other virtualization forms discussed, an abstraction layer is applied to the networking components to provide better service, availability, and security to the physical servers and their applications. Depending on the implementation, the virtualization layer can be placed in the network at the switch level, on the host within the networking hardware (NIC), or in software. For example, a VLAN creates a virtual network, abstracted from the physical network, that provides isolation and security. *Network virtualization* is often done within switches, at the different layers of the OSI stack, to create an abstraction of an IP address such that the sender may not know the actual IP address of the final destination. Common applications of network virtualization include load balancing, secure connection, and state monitoring and transparent failover.

I/O Virtualization on Blades

Blade vendors are taking virtualization to the next step to make managing the blade environment simpler. The basis of blade I/O virtualization is similar to network virtualization; it abstracts the I/O interface away from the blade. For example, Egenera virtualizes I/O such that processor blades (pBlades) consist of processors and memory only and have no I/O adapters (such as NICs or HBAs). All the I/O interfaces are located on the control blades (cBlades), and shared virtually by the pBlades. This allows the processor blades to be stateless and easily interchangeable. HP offers a software example, in which even though the I/O adapters (that is, HBAs) are on the individual blades, they share a virtual pool of worldwide names, simplifying software configuration management.

Server Virtualization Implementations

Server virtualization can be implemented in a variety of ways. Multiple virtual environments can be implemented using techniques including emulation, hard partitioning, OS virtualization, hosted mode, and hypervisors. All of these methods control access to host physical resources including processors, memory, network resources, storage, KVM, and local USB and/or serial port connections. One of the benefits of server virtualization is that many of these implementations can support multiple different operating environments running at the same time, including Windows, Linux, BSD, and Solaris.

Emulation

Software emulation is the easiest to implement and the least efficient of the types of virtualization listed. It allows an operating system to run, unmodified, "on top of" or as a guest of an alternate platform or operating system. Emulators re-create an entire environment, including all CPU instructions and I/O devices, using software. This allows emulation of a different CPU environment, such as Windows software running on a non-Intel Mac. Emulators come with significant overhead, since every instruction must be translated and executed through the emulation process. Emulators are most often used when performance is not an issue — for example, a Windows emulator running on a UNIX system. This provides the UNIX users the ability to run Microsoft Office applications on their desktop, enabling them to read (or write) Word documents attached to email messages. Their high overhead makes them cumbersome for operational environments. Many emulators are available on the market, often via open source channels — for example, QEMU.

Paravirtualization/Enlightened Operating Systems

With this approach, the guest operating systems are modified to know they are running in a virtual environment. The guest operating system uses a special API to communicate with the virtualization layer and interface more directly with the hardware — for example, the I/O subsystems. The guest operating system is modified to be aware that it is running virtualized, and performance can be significantly improved. The performance benefits, however, must be weighed against the need to modify the guest operating system.

Partitioning

Partitioning of the system resources, either through hardware or software, is another approach for disaggregation within a single system. Either partitioning method creates multiple isolated servers, or partitions. Each partition is allocated one or more CPUs, a physical memory block, and specific I/O paths, and runs its own instance of the operating system. Resources are owned by the partition, without any sharing across partitions. Depending on the implementation, there may be the ability to have dynamic partitioning such that resources may be added to, moved to, and removed from a partition. Partitioning assumes all partitions run the same OS.

OS Virtualization

Operating system virtualization, such as Sun's Solaris Containers and SWsoft's Virtuozzo, is a complete virtualization at the OS layer and creates multiple virtual environments of the operating system. The instances have their own run-time environment while sharing both the system resources (which have been virtualized) and a base kernel. Since all virtual environments are sharing a single virtualized OS, rather than each virtual environment loading its own OS copy, overhead is minimal. OS support is limited to a single operating system — for example, Solaris for Solaris Containers and either Linux or Windows (not both at the same time) for Virtuozzo. Through management interfaces, quality of service can be adjusted by allocating amounts of memory, CPU, and network bandwidth to specific virtual environments.

Hosted Approach

The *hosted approach* is a melding of emulation and OS virtualization in that there is a base operating system that runs under the virtualized environment. Hosted virtualization utilizes a layer that sits between the native operating system and the virtualized servers, allowing for multiple isolated virtual operating environments of *different types* to be run simultaneously (see Figure 8.1). The underlying operating system provides broad device support natively. However, since all I/O operations must pass through three levels of software (the virtual OS; the hosted virtualization layer in which the request is translated into something the host OS will understand; and the native OS), it is not a great option for I/O-intensive applications. Examples of hosted virtualization are Microsoft's Virtual Server and VMware Server (formerly VMware GSX).

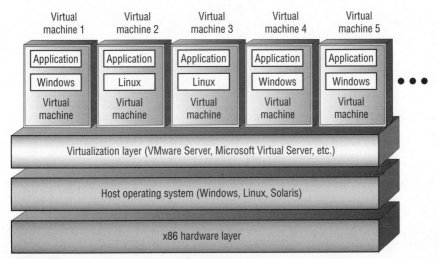

Figure 8.1: Hosted approach for virtual servers

Source: Focus Consulting

It is important to note that resources must be divided between not only each of the emulated operating systems but also the resident host operating system.

Hypervisor/Bare Metal Approach

A hypervisor is a thin, guest OS–independent virtualization layer that is loaded onto bare metal, which interacts with the hardware directly and creates virtual machines in which operating systems, either enlightened or not, can run. The hypervisor virtualizes hardware resources, such as memory and CPUs, for the different virtual machines (VMs) and their guest operating systems.

As shown in Figure 8.2, the hypervisor model is more streamlined and efficient than the hosted model. Examples of hypervisor virtualization products include VMware ESX, Xen 3.0, Microsoft Windows Server Virtualization (Viridian, which will be released in 2008) along with the traditional mainframe virtualization software (derivatives of VM/370).

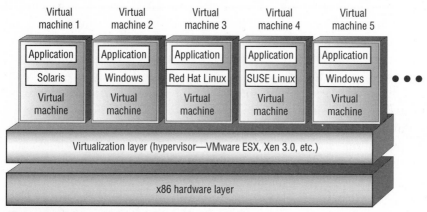

Figure 8.2: Hypervisor model for virtual servers
Source: Focus Consulting

Virtualization Hardware-Assist

The x86 operating environment was never designed to be a shared environment, making it difficult to create an optimized hypervisor that can efficiently allocate hardware resources and manage multiple virtual machines and their operating systems. An x86 processor has four privilege levels, commonly referred to as rings 0–3. An operating system, such as Windows or Linux, assumes that it will be running with access to the highest privilege level, or be run in ring 0, and its applications will run in ring 3. Virtualization, however, presents a problem since a hypervisor must also occupy ring 0.

Without hardware assistance from the processor, the typical solution to this scenario is to run the hypervisor in ring 0, the guest OS in ring 1, and the guest applications in ring 3 (0/1/3 model). Alternatively, some implementations run both the guest OS and guest applications in ring 3 (0/3/3 model). Both of these models require the hypervisor to perform occasional binary patching of the guest OS's running kernel whenever it attempts to perform an operation restricted to ring 0, such as a *push* operation.

To solve this problem, both AMD and Intel implemented chip-assisted virtualization, which introduced a new privilege level called ring –1 (read as "ring minus 1"). The hypervisor runs in ring –1, the control OS (for example, Red Hat Enterprise Linux or RHEL for VMware) runs in ring 0, and the control OS's applications (for example, the vmware -cmd utility function) runs in ring 3 (see Figure 8.3). The virtual machines are run in *virtual* ring sets so that each guest OS in a VM believes that it is running in ring 0. This way the hypervisor no longer has to fool the guest OS into thinking that it is running in ring 0.

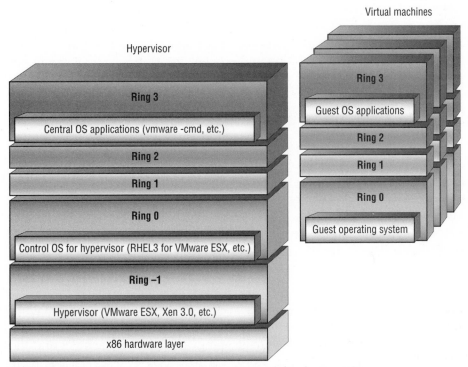

Figure 8.3: Hypervisor model for virtual servers with hardware assist

Source: Andrew Kutz

The Intel Virtualization Technology (Intel VT) extensions, code named Vanderpool (x86) and Silvervale (IA-64), have been supported in some of their CPUs since late 2005. AMD's virtualization technology, codenamed Pacifica and released as AMD Virtualization (AMD-V), has been available in some of their CPUs since mid 2006. The battle over advanced virtualization functions in the chipsets continues to be key competitive ground between the two chip manufacturers. To determine the current level of virtualization extensions supported by each CPU chipset (used by various blade servers), check the blade and chip vendors' websites.

Managing Virtual Server Environments

Consolidation of servers to blades and the use of server virtualization can significantly reduce the number of physical systems to be managed. However, it is equally important to use best practices in managing your virtual environment. This is especially true due to the ease with which one can provision a virtual server, leading to virtual server sprawl and increasing management workload rather than reducing it.

Server management tools and features are useful in managing virtual environments. These include virtual resource managers, physical resource monitor and management tools, migration and movement utilities, virtual symmetric multiprocessing features, and virtual clustering.

Resource Monitoring and Management

Resource monitoring and management of both the virtual and physical environment are especially critical because the resources are shared. The first step in being able to properly balance the virtual environment within the physical limitations of number of processors, CPU speed, memory size, and so on, is to know how much resource is being used. The second step is being able to add or remove resources from a virtual environment, preferably while it's running (called *hot add* or *hot remove*). These capabilities allow one to either manually or automatically provision virtual and physical resources to the virtual environment.

Moving Running VMs

In conjunction with resource monitoring and management, the ability to move active VMs from one system to another with minimal disruption is an important tool. It is required for balancing the workloads across multiple blades or systems. It is also a very handy tool for moving virtual environments off of hardware for a period of time to perform maintenance without application downtime.

Some vendors allow for uninterrupted movement of running VMs, and others require the VM to be *quiesced* (meaning to quiet all activity) and restarted. Some vendors do not allow for movement of VMs at all.

Migration Utilities

Migration utilities help transition from one environment to another. The most common migration tool is physical-to-virtual migration (P2V). These tools take a snapshot of the physical system environment and migrate that snapshot onto a virtual environment. Another equally important tool is virtual-to-physical migration (V2P). Not all applications are well-suited to virtualization, but you may not know until you try. V2P tools become your backout plan, in case you need to move an application environment running virtual back to a physical system. Physical-to-physical (P2P) and virtual-to-virtual (V2V) tools can help in both a bladed and virtual environment and are especially helpful in a testing scenario. Migration utilities are available from both the virtualization vendors themselves, as well as from third-party vendors.

Virtual SMP

Virtual SMP allows a single virtual environment to run symmetrically across multiple processors — that is, the workload is shared equally across all processors, with shared memory capabilities between the processors. This capability allows you to further define and manage the virtual environment in which your applications are running.

Virtual Clustering

Virtual clustering is the ability to cluster virtual environments for high availability (HA) or for high performance computing clustering. This is usually done across physical systems rather than on the same system to prevent hardware failures from taking down your application environment. Clustering of virtual servers can also be done within a virtualized environment, using clustering software that operates with guest operating systems, such as Microsoft Cluster Services. Some environments allow these clustered guest-OS environments to span multiple physical servers.

Policy-Based Management

Just when you think both the physical and virtual environments are balanced and running smoothly, a spike will hit, and everything will come to a grinding halt. This is when policy-based management comes into play. It allows for automatic provisioning, reprovisioning, or movement of resources and/or environments given utilization thresholds — all without getting you up in the middle of the night.

Virtual Desktops and Applications

Many of the concepts of virtualization that have been discussed in this chapter can also be applied to desktops and applications (on desktops and servers). These types of virtualization implementations bring similar benefits as other types of virtualization, separating the logical work being done from the physical resources.

Virtual Desktops

Virtual desktops combine the concepts of virtual machines and thin clients. This approach allows a user running any PC, PC blade, or thin client to access a centrally managed virtual machine or service. Virtual desktops leverage the Remote Desktop Protocol (RDP), Microsoft Windows Terminal Services, and Citrix Presentation Server models to allow a PC to connect into a remote desktop and run its applications. Newer implementations (introduced with Windows Vista and Windows Server Longhorn) will include additional features, including the ability to remote a single application instead of an entire desktop.

Application Virtualization

The final step to a truly on-demand, utility computing environment is application virtualization. At a high level, application virtualization decouples the application environment completely from the runtime (system) environment such that the business application can be provisioned onto any system at any time without causing the application to fail. This is more than simply application management and provisioning. Not only can an application be virtualized and run on any remote system (desktop or server), but running applications can be moved in real time from one desktop/server to another, much like live movement of virtual machines.

True application virtualization requires an environment in which applications are dynamically reassembled in real time and support automatic stateful migration. This allows the application to stop processing, save all state and data information, move to another (possibly heterogeneous) platform, and continue processing from where it left off. This has interesting ramifications for blade servers running as application servers, where application load balancing could be automated by moving virtualized applications across servers as needed.

Conclusion

As with all major changes to an IT infrastructure, numerous implementation aspects should be thought through prior to purchasing and implementing a virtualization solution. A few of these considerations have been touched upon in this chapter, such as whether to implement a hosted environment or a hypervisor. These and other considerations will be discussed in detail in Chapter 14, "System Software Considerations."

A virtualization strategy, in conjunction with a blade system implementation, brings substantial additional benefits in simplifying and improving the data center. Server virtualization reduces the number of physical servers required, while maximizing resource utilization and increasing manageability, thereby reducing cost. Blade systems reduce the number of racks, the amount of power and cooling required per server, the number of network and storage network switches, and the number of cables required. Together, these technologies offer simplicity in provisioning, reprovisioning, and managing the data center, while delivering high availability and increased flexibility.

This chapter has covered virtualization from a *disaggregation* perspective. Chapter 9, "Clustering and Blades," will address server *aggregation* methodologies and products, defining clustering terminology and discussing various clustering implementations.

Clustering and Blades

The term *server clustering* has become so broad that when it's used in conversation, it is difficult to know exactly what is meant. *Wikipedia* defines clustering as "a group of loosely coupled computers that work together closely so that in many respects they can be viewed as though they are a single computer." Cluster computing is closely related to multprocessor computing. The difference lies in where the interprocessor communications are performed. Multiprocessing is defined as interprocessor communications inside the computer via an internal communications bus/network (for example, on the blade). Clustering is defined as interprocessor communications outside the computer (for example, off the blade) using commodity (or proprietary) networks.

Four primary types of clustering are discussed in this chapter:

- High-availability (HA) clusters
- Load-balancing clusters
- High-performance computing (HPC) clusters
- Grid/utility computing clusters

Each type of cluster solution was developed to solve specific business issues.

Clustering and blades are well-matched technologies as clustering is based on a group of computers sharing an infrastructure, and blade servers inherently share an infrastructure within a chassis. In addition, blade solutions' built-in redundancy, hot-swap capabilities, and high-speed interprocessor communication abilities make blade servers particularly ideal for HA and HPC clusters.

Short History of Clustering

Informal clusters have been around for probably as long as computers have been in use. Businesses have always had the need to keep the business running and to use every possible resource available. In 1967, Gene Amdahl of IBM (and later founder of Amdahl Corporation) published the definitive paper on parallel processing. This paper describes the performance increases that can be expected from parallelizing a task versus performing the task serially. This became the basis for both multiprocessor and cluster computing.

The very nature of clusters includes networks; hence, the rise of clusters closely followed the rise of networking through the 1970s and 1980s. ARCnet by Datapoint was the first commercially available clustering solution, released in 1977. Clustering didn't really take off, however, until the mid 1980s, when DEC released VAXcluster for the VAX/VMS operating system.

In 1989, the parallel virtual machine (PVM) software was developed based on TCP/IP communications and made available as open source. PVM and the introduction of low-cost PCs led NASA to build a supercomputer out of commodity hardware in the early 1990s. This project was called the Beowulf Project, and it was an attempt at building a cost-effective alternative to a supercomputer out of commodity components. Beowulf clusters continue to be their own genre within HPC clustering.

Work in clustering eventually raised the question, "If we can draw on the resources of many locally networked computers to increase computational performance, can we also use remote computing resources?" These advances in clustering lead to the development of grid computing — based on clustering across local and remote networks.

It is interesting to note how terminology around multiprocessing and clusters has changed over time. As discussed in Chapter 2, "Evolution of Computing Technology — Setting the Stage," the terms *loosely coupled multiprocessing* (LCMP) and *tightly coupled multiprocessing* (TCMP) originated in the 1970s for describing types of multiprocessing. These terms are still used today; however, their definitions have evolved. Tightly coupled multiprocessing is used to describe an environment in which the processors are interdependent. Loosely coupled multiprocessing is when the processors function fairly independently. HA clusters and high performance clusters are often tightly coupled; grid and load-balancing clusters are often loosely coupled.

Another term that is used in describing multiprocessing is SMP or *symmetric multiprocessing*. SMP is considered a form of tightly coupled multiprocessing. SMP environments are made up of two or more identical processors that share main memory. Another way to say it is that any task can run on any processor no matter where the data is located in memory.

Clustering Concepts

Why create a cluster? Three primary reasons exist for creating clusters in your business environment: increased availability through redundancy, increased workload capacity/software performance, and reduced management complexity. HA clusters address redundancy with automatic failover capabilities. Load balancing clusters, HPCC, and grid clusters address increased workload capacity, and high performance computing increases the performance of individual cluster-aware software programs. All clusters (except perhaps grid clusters) are managed as a single entity, reducing management complexity.

Regardless of the type of clustered solution being implemented, all clustering solutions share several characteristics:

▪ Multiple computing nodes or systems (either physical or virtual)

▪ Some form of interconnect or network connecting the systems

▪ Either access to shared data (as in a shared-everything clustering model) or isolated nodes (as in a shared-nothing clustering model)

▪ Clustering software

Multiple Computing Nodes

In the past, clustered solutions were composed of homogeneous computing nodes. They used identical processor, memory, and OS configurations on each of the nodes. This is still prevalent, especially in HPC clusters. With HA clusters, it is a requirement. The homogeneous environment makes managing the environment as a single entity much easier, especially when HPC clusters grow to support more than four nodes (there are HPC clusters supporting over 1,000 nodes).

Load balancing clusters are also often homogeneous, especially when the cluster is performing many iterations of the same task. More recently, however, with the concept of on-demand computing, much of the load-balancing software can pair tasks with appropriate node configurations.

Grid clusters are more frequently heterogeneous, performing a multitude of independent tasks.

With the advent of virtual machines (as described in Chapter 8, "Virtualization"), virtual clusters can be created within a single blade or across blades.

Interconnect/Network

The network or interconnect allows communications between the cluster nodes to take place. Often Ethernet, using TCP/IP, is used as the network because of its broad availability. More recently, low-latency interconnects have been developed and used, including a proprietary communications protocol called Myrinet and the InfiniBand open specification. For very low-latency interconnect between blades, hypertransport can be used. Hypertransport is an extremely fast point-to-point interconnect technology that provides very low-latency chip-to-chip communications on a blade (or board) and/or blade-to-blade (board-to-board) links within a chassis.

Data and Storage Access

Depending on the type of cluster solution, data will need to be accessed by all the nodes in the cluster, commonly called a *share-everything cluster model*, or the nodes will work in isolation, called a *share-nothing cluster model*. Typically, HA clusters and HPC clusters are built around the share-everything model. Load balancing clusters can either share data or not, and grid clusters are typically built using the share-nothing model.

In a share-everything cluster model, data can be shared by the compute nodes in a number of ways, depending on the application(s) running on the cluster. Data sharing either must be controlled by the application itself, as with Oracle 10g RAC, or the operating system on each node has to have an understanding of the shared environment. Shared file systems such as network file systems (NFS or CIFS), Global File Systems (GFS), and Cluster File Systems (CFS) — which are part of or can be added to an operating system — are common methods for sharing data. Data replication from one node to another is an additional method and is often used to allow read-only access to files from multiple nodes, enabling the cluster to share the workload without modifying the data (for example, clustered nodes serving up web pages). Many implementations use network attached storage (NAS) for file-level data sharing and/or storage area networks (SANs) to provide access to the storage and/or data, at a block level, for all the nodes in the cluster.

Clustering Software

Clustering software, in addition to the base operating system, is the final requirement. This software provides the protocol for communications between the nodes in the cluster. Often, the clustering software is specific to the type of cluster being implemented. For example, Linux-HA is an open source high availability clustering solution that provides the software to enable redundancy between nodes. Microsoft Cluster Server (MSCS) can be configured to provide redundancy (HA clusters) and load balancing (load balancing clusters). Sun Cluster can be configured for HA clusters, Sun Cluster Advanced Edition for Oracle RAC supports HPC clusters, and Sun Cluster Geographic Edition or Platform Enterprise Grid Orchestrator (EGO) supports enterprise grid clusters. For HPC clusters, the applications must be HPC-aware — that is, developed specifically to run in the HPC environment.

The MPI (message passing interface) libraries provide a programmatic interface to implement interprocess communications between the nodes in the cluster. Parallelizing compilers also are available to help develop these kinds of applications.

Blade server systems offer close proximity of many computing nodes within a single chassis, coupled with low-latency networking capabilities and shared efficient access to data, making blade solutions excellent candidates for a clustered configuration.

Types of Clustering Solutions

The following are descriptions of four types of clustering solutions, designed to solve specific business issues.

High-Availability Clusters

The most common clusters are HA clusters. These are used to ensure that business computations continue, with little to no interruption, in the event of a failure, regardless of what caused the failure (hardware, software, nature or human, planned or unplanned). HA clusters implement redundant infrastructure, including networks, network routes, storage, and compute nodes, to eliminate any single point of failure. In the event of a failure, the redundant infrastructure, together with the failover logic of the HA software, provide the capability to restart services on healthy systems within the cluster. The most common implementation of HA clusters uses two computing nodes, although larger node HA clusters are becoming more widespread.

HA can be implemented in a number of different ways in the blade environment. Traditional solutions monitor the *heartbeat* (health) of the other nodes through either Ethernet or InfiniBand networks, as shown in Figure 9.1. When there is a failure on one of the blades, the processing is restarted on the blade with which it is clustered.

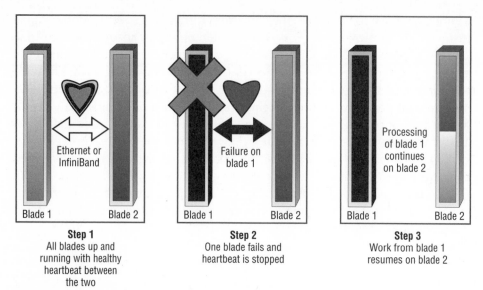

Figure 9.1: Simple HA cluster within a blade chassis

Source: Focus Consulting

Within the blade chassis environment, as described in Chapter 8, there is another way HA clustering can be implemented. The increasingly popular virtual machine approach from companies such as VMware offers the ability to provide failover capabilities to other VMs running on a blade, as well as to other physical blades. In this environment, when a VM fails, the virtualization software (which monitors the state of each VM) restarts both the VM and the process. When a blade fails, the entire virtual environment is moved to another blade.

HA clusters typically require shared data sets between the systems. SANs, shared files via NFS and/or CIFS, and replication are three frequently used storage architectures underlying HA cluster configurations. Replication between storage nodes ensures that the storage subsystem does not become a single point of failure.

It is important to note that not all cluster software includes HA capabilities. Even when the HA modules are included, they often require additional configuration.

Load Balancing Clusters

Load balancing clusters offer a way for a group of servers to share a large workload in a way that is transparent to the users accessing the service. This approach is used to balance the computational resources with the workload required to improve both application performance and resource utilization.

These clusters are usually implemented by having the workload *load balanced* through a set of head nodes that allocate the processing task to a suitable computing configuration. Large deployments of this type of cluster are often called *server farms*. Applications that can take advantage of this type of infrastructure are often called scale-out applications. Web services (HTTP) and application middleware tiers are commonly configured in a load balanced configuration. In addition, load balanced clusters typically do not require shared data access across systems.

As shown in Figure 9.2, within a blade chassis there easily can be one blade running the load balancing software, distributing the workload among the other blades within the chassis. Another implementation might have load balancing servers/appliances running external to the blade chassis, distributing the work across multiple blade chassis.

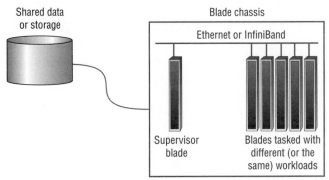

Figure 9.2: Load balancing blades within a single chassis
Source: Focus Consulting

Many commercial load balancing products are available in the market today for Windows, Linux, and UNIX. An example of a blade-specific solution that supports several cluster types, including load balancing clusters, is Egenera's PAN Manager. In addition, virtualization software from Xen, Virtual Iron, VMware, Qlusters, Microsoft, and others automate virtual server provisioning and workload balancing within and among blade chassis.

High-Performance Computing (HPC) Clusters

HPC implementations distribute a single computational task across multiple cluster nodes for increased performance. HPC, as mentioned briefly earlier, came about when researchers required more processing power but could not afford the very expensive mainframes. After adding custom-built resource managers and schedulers, they were able to leverage their commodity PCs (which were sitting idle and/or underutilized) by interconnecting them in a makeshift distributed fashion. This configuration allowed the computational workload to be subdivided across the collection of systems. HPC clusters (HPCCs) are now optimized for high-speed communications between the cluster nodes when interprocessor communications are required during computations. The compute capabilities of HPCCs coupled with high-speed networking and low-latency implementations such as RDMA (as described in Chapter 6, "Networking and Related Technologies") have been shown to meet and even exceed the speeds of supercomputers.

Most applications designed to exploit HPCCs through parallelism are custom and computationally intensive. These applications often can be run on symmetric multiprocessing systems as well. Industries such as EDA (electronic design automation), CAE (computer-aided engineering), and oil and gas commonly require applications of this sort.

Blade solutions can be extremely effective for HPCCs because of the support for multiple processors on each blade, as well as the high-speed interconnect (GbE, 10GbE, and InfiniBand) networking technologies available. As Figure 9.3 shows, multiple types of HPCC environments can be accommodated easily with a blade solution. With the switch modules located within the blade chassis, or rack, distances and hops through a network are minimized, reducing latency. Many blade solutions come preconfigured for HPCC environments.

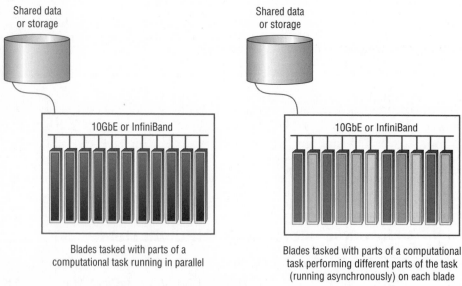

Figure 9.3: HPC clusters within a blade chassis

Source: Focus Consulting

Grid Clusters

Grid clusters (used for grid computing) are much like the other clusters described in this chapter. The primary difference is that grid clusters are made up of computers that typically have no working knowledge of other systems in the cluster. They, therefore, tend to perform work independent of the other computers in the grid with minimal data sharing. Also, the computers in a grid will often consist of heterogeneous platforms rather than the homogenous environments supported in traditional clusters. Grid clustering requires asynchronous processing in which intermediate results of one task do not affect the other tasks allocated to the other nodes on the grid.

One application of grid clusters that is gaining popularity is enterprise grids (see Figure 9.4). Enterprise grids allow multiple departments within the company to share resources across an enterprise or campus. With an enterprise grid, the security and policy management issues are well contained and easier to implement.

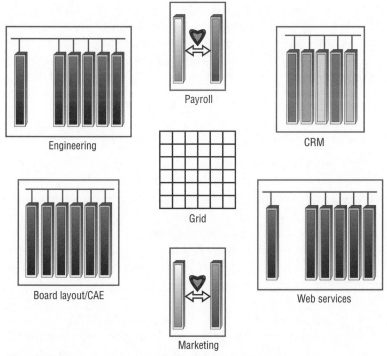

Figure 9.4: Blade clusters as part of an enterprise grid
Source: Focus Consulting

Companies with global reach are also implementing global grids made up of collections of smaller grids and clusters within the company, sometimes referred to as departmental clusters. This is often the case in environments where work is being done 24/7, such as sales, customer support centers, and global engineering departments.

As companies consolidate servers and storage, blades often become part of an enterprise grid in which computing and storage resources are shared. The modularity of blades, along with their ease of provisioning and reprovisioning, makes them an excellent platform for grid computing.

Other Forms of Multiprocessing with Blades

Many blade vendors offer multiple processors on each blade (often referred to as multisocket or multi-CPU configurations). If the operating system running on the blade supports SMP, such as Linux (2.0 or higher), Solaris, or Windows XP Professional, parallel applications can take advantage of SMP capabilities.

Several blade vendors have implemented hypertransport technology on their blades. Implementing hypertransport on blades has enabled companies like PANTA Systems and Fujitsu Siemens to aggregate blades into SMP clusters. For example, PANTA Systems can configure, on the fly, two contiguous four-socket, dual-core blades into a single eight-socket (16 core) SMP cluster.

Conclusion

Blade solutions are ideal for creating any type of clustered environment. A cluster can be created within a blade chassis using only two blades, for high availability of the processes running on those blades. Another option is to have entire chassis of blades configured as one cluster, or multiple chassis can be combined to create a larger cluster or an enterprise grid. With support for high-speed networking (GbE, 10GbE, InfiniBand, Hypertransport) native on blades or accessible with a daughter card, and switch modules located within the chassis, cluster traffic can stay entirely within the chassis for improved cluster performance.

This chapter has reviewed different types of clusters and how blade servers can be used in clustered environments. It has also touched on virtualization relative to clustering. Chapter 10, "Managing Blade Systems," continues the look at software related to blades as it explores blade and blade systems management.

Managing Blade Systems

Reducing the total cost of ownership (TCO) is one of the key benefits of blades. Much of this reduction comes from hardware modularity and standardization, reduced complexities over previous rack server implementations, and overall improved manageability. This chapter discusses the state of systems management in the enterprise environment — both in general, and specifically as it relates to blades. It also reviews the standard ISO management model, which categorizes the various types of management functions needed. It then discusses various technologies and types of tools available for managing blade server systems as part of the enterprise.

State of Systems Management and Blades

Systems management technology and tools cover a broad range of management functions and continue to evolve in the enterprise, improving overall manageability. The advent of blade systems has contributed to the evolution by offering modular and flexible configurations, as well as sharing redundant components (including management modules) — ultimately reducing complexity and improving the reliability and availability of the systems to be managed. However, these shared resources — including power supplies, networking infrastructure, and heat-management facilities — also create some unique management requirements.

One significant improvement offered by blade systems via the blade management module is the use of out-of-band management for all the components within the blade chassis. This allows a remote management system to monitor and control all components of the blade system without requiring the use of the host operating system and regardless of the current power state of the system. This capability, which will be discussed further later in this chapter, also allows blade systems to share the management module infrastructure among all the blades and other modules in a chassis, thereby reducing the per-blade cost of management.

Traditionally, both out-of-band and in-band management (via the operating system) are often performed by developing scripts to automate a variety of management tasks through the use of various command-line protocols that have emerged. A new standard called Systems Management Architecture for Server Hardware (SMASH) has defined a command-line protocol (CLP) that is beginning to provide a common interface for automation scripting. This standard has been developed by one of the key industry standards organizations focused on management issues, the DMTF (see Chapter 11, "Industry Organizations and Related Standards," for more information).

Many of the tools that were developed to manage nonbladed systems have been adapted to manage blade environments. Although this gives a good logical view, it doesn't always provide a true picture of the physical aspects of the blade systems, leaving this function to tools that are provided by the individual blade manufacturers.

Since blade servers do not involve a user interface for their standard operation, the use of a remote keyboard, video, and mouse (referred to as KVM) provides a shared vehicle for these functions, as well as a method to remotely manage, diagnose, and configure these systems. Newer technologies use Ethernet connectivity (KVM over IP), which allows the KVM to be used remotely over the existing network infrastructure. This approach provides the ability to access the console of the blade system as if the system were local. However, this one-to-one approach does not scale well for providing system-level management to thousands of systems, leaving the one-to-many type of advanced management to other more sophisticated tools (for example, software distribution, policy-based management, and others).

For years, Simple Network Management Protocol (SNMP) has been the predominant technology to manage remote components. This has served the IT community well and will be around for years to come. However, SNMP was also designed to be a single component-based management approach and does not scale to manage the large numbers of distributed systems that continue to be deployed.

Another key emerging standard developed by the DMTF is the Common Information Model (CIM) (pronounced "sim"). CIM's role is to define the known universe of managed elements to allow the centralized management of all components in the enterprise. CIM is an object-oriented information model that defines not only a common set of objects, but also their properties, methods, and associations. This allows management systems to have a common set of objects to manage using a well-understood set of semantics.

The CIM model is leveraged by a number of initiatives, including SMASH, the Web-Based Enterprise Management (WBEM) initiative of the DMTF, and the Storage Management Initiative Specification (SMI-S) of the Storage Networking Industry Association (SNIA). These technologies and initiatives have been implemented in products and systems since 1998 and have been increasing in both number and functionality.

New web services-based technologies are being implemented that will employ the service-oriented architecture (SOA) tools and standards that are prevalent today. One such protocol, WS-Management, provides a web services management protocol to manage CIM-based systems and devices using state-of-the-art technologies such as SOAP (Simple Object Access Protocol), XML (Extensible Markup Language), and WSDL (Web Services Description Language).

Tools that are available for all types of blade systems management are too numerous to cover in this chapter. The discussion here will address the various technologies, topologies, and approaches that these tools use with regard to managing blade servers.

Management Model

Management functions span a variety of functionality that can be broken down into categories. The ISO model FCAPS is a good way to organize these categories. FCAPS is an acronym for five management functions — Fault, Configuration, Accounting, Performance, and Security Management (see Figure 10.1). It is valuable to look at each of these categories to understand the breadth of capabilities needed in order to manage blade systems.

Fault Management	Configuration Management	Accounting Management	Performance Management	Security Management
Fault detection isolation correlation	Resource initialization	Track service and/or resource usage	Utilization and error rates	Selective resource access
Diagnostic test	Network provisioning	Cost for services	Consistent performance levels	Enable NE functions
Network recovery	Backup and restore	Combine costs for multiple resources	Performance reports	Security events reporting
Error logging and recovery	Copy configuration and software distribution		Maintaining and examining historic logs	Security-related information distribution
Clear correlation	Software license audit			Security audit and trail log

Figure 10.1: ISO management model, FCAPS

Fault Management

Fault management is the process associated with managing failures or faults. This would include anything from sending alerts for power or thermal sensor indications, to logging software errors or other types of exceptions. Alerts are delivered via asynchronous messages or stored locally as information that is collected at a later time. Fault management is typically handled by the firmware and software of the managed system and by systems, network, and enterprise management software used by the organization, including such products as IBM Director, HP Insight Manager, and Dell Open Manage at the systems level, and IBM Tivoli, HP OpenView, and CA Unicenter at the enterprise level.

As mentioned previously, fault monitoring and management is a huge strength for blades. Blade-specific tools are available from the blade vendors, with full remote capabilities to handle everything short of physically swapping out a failing blade. (In addition, blade swapping is so simple, it can be done by a nontechnical person; it involves simply looking for the light indicators on the failing blade, popping out that blade, and inserting a new one. All other tasks to bring that blade online can be done remotely through the management software.) More details on this, as well as a couple of screen images, are provided later in this chapter.

Configuration Management

Configuration management is the process of discovering, monitoring, tracking, and updating the configuration of managed resources. This process includes tracking versions of the hardware configuration, and often more importantly, the software and firmware elements installed on the resources as well as software licenses. In the case of blade server systems, the configuration of all components in the chassis or rack will be defined, monitored, and if needed, updated — including the redundant and shared components as well as the individual blades. Configuration management is an area in which products utilizing the CIM model can contribute greatly, allowing management of all resources via use of CIM information. IBM, HP, Dell, Sun, Microsoft, Oracle, Symantec/Veritas, and others have CIM support (to varying degrees), both in their managed resources and in their management tools.

Configuration management also includes the functions required for provisioning and reprovisioning blades, as discussed later in this chapter.

Accounting Management

Accounting management involves gathering usage statistics about a managed resource. A wide range of information about processor, disk, memory, network, and other I/O utilization is collected and analyzed. This information is often used for billing or charge-back systems on a per-user or per-application basis or to calculate ROI. Although blade systems provide the means for storing this information, the tools that provide these management functions are general-purpose server-management tools and are not specific to blades.

Performance Management

Performance management considers the managed resource utilization to optimize the overall performance. This is accomplished by monitoring application runtimes, workload throughput, and response times to make changes to configurations in order to provide the best bang for the buck. A wide variety of tools is available for server performance management and storage resource management (SRM). Again, the tools used here are not blade-specific.

Security Management

Security management controls access to managed resources. It includes functions such as authorization, authentication, revocation (of access or certificates), and non-repudiation (guaranteed secured message delivery). These functions are critical not only to the security of the managed resource but also to the entire management infrastructure. Security management for blades must fit into the overall enterprise security scheme, but blade-specific security issues also need to be considered. For example, out-of-band management provides separation of transaction data from management data, offering improved security. In addition, access to blade management functions includes total control, including power-off capabilities. Also, if KVM over IP is used for remote console functions, security on the IP connection is an important issue. Furthermore, merging or separating transaction traffic and storage traffic (if both are using IP) has security ramifications. All of these functions raise associated security management issues of access control, including authorization and authentication.

CIM and Blade Server Systems

CIM is a conceptual information model for describing computing and business entities associated with Internet, enterprise, and service-provider environments (see Figure 10.2). It provides a consistent definition and structure of data, using object-oriented techniques. CIM provides a way to define common elements, describe them and their associations with other elements, and define what actions (methods) apply to them (in CIM terminology, these definitions include object classes, properties, methods, and associations). These definitions are then used by management applications.

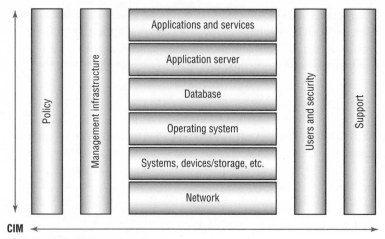

Figure 10.2: CIM coverage

Source: Distributed Management Task Force, Inc.

CIM offers standardization that allows any CIM-enabled management application to manage any component that uses the CIM model. As CIM implementations progress, this standardization offers users more choices while requiring less (proprietary) work on the part of the vendors.

Physical versus Logical

CIM categorizes managed elements into two main types: logical and physical elements. Physical elements occupy space and conform to the elementary laws of physics. The physical-element class represents any component of a system that has a physical identity; it can be touched or seen. Logical elements represent abstractions used to manage, configure, and coordinate aspects of the physical or software environment. Logical elements typically represent systems themselves, system components, system capabilities, and software.

Blades and CIM

Blade servers within CIM are no different from traditional systems, when viewed as a logical system or element. However, when modeling the physical aspects of a bladed system, the differences become apparent. The relationships (or *associations*, as they are called within CIM) show the connections between components in a chassis, including associations between blades and the shared components, such as power supplies, cooling fans, and physical network connections. There are also relationships between a blade and the chassis and slot where the device is physically located.

The relationship between physical and logical systems becomes especially important in fault and configuration management, when dealing with a failing blade or other component. Management tools are available that provide the ability to power off the failing blade, reprovision the tasks that were running on that blade to another blade, and when the failing blade has been swapped, to bring the new blade online. (If the blades are running within a virtualized environment, virtualization software functions allow the new blade to be added into a pool of blades, simplifying the reprovisioning process.)

Provisioning and Bare Metal

As an extension to configuration management, *bare metal provisioning* is a way to take a new blade without any software previously installed, load operating system and application software, and then configure the blade to an operational level. The technique generally used is called a pre-boot execution environment (PXE — pronounced "pixie") boot. With the PXE, the blade is booted from a disk on the network. The PXE capability was designed to provide a way to boot a system without having to know anything about its operating environment. This gives the ability to automate software installation and system configuration, reducing associated costs and minimizing/eliminating human errors.

PXE boot was created as part of a bigger initiative from Intel called Wired for Management (WfM), introduced in 1998, to improve the manageability of desktop, mobile, and server systems. Intel's goal was to enhance manageability, thereby decreasing the TCO of business computing. Wired for Management is being upgraded to a new initiative with even higher levels of capability called Intel Active Management Technology (AMT). This will be a major industry initiative and will provide additional features beyond bare metal provisioning, including virus detection and asset tracking (another major aspect of configuration management).

In the blade environment, more and more systems are being implemented using anonymous (diskless) blades that boot from the network, greatly simplifying configuration, software management, provisioning, and reprovisioning. A wide variety of products is available to aid in the deployment process of new systems, operating systems, and virtual machines. Products include some from the systems vendors themselves — such as HP's Integrated Lights-Out (iLO) remote management software, HP Control Tower, HP Insight Manager, and IBM Director and IBM Remote Deployment Manager — as well as from third-party management software vendors such as Altiris, Cyclades, and BladeLogic.

In-Band versus Out-of-Band Management

Two well-defined modes of management exist within the industry. These two modes are called in-band and out-of band; the difference is mainly in the path that the management takes to provide the monitoring and control of the managed system.

In-Band Management

In-band management is the traditional method of management, in which management access and processing is done by the host system. This means that management requests, functions, and responses are carried out by the operating system and over the data network on which the target system is located. This has the advantages that no additional hardware, network, or processing environment is required. One big disadvantage is that if the network or targeted platform is not operational, then no remote management will be available either. The other disadvantage is that if the intent is to measure performance or resource utilization, using in-band techniques will impact the results as the processing and network activity associated with the test will impact the measurement. It is also possible that in-band management could have a negative impact on the system itself, using resources that may already be over utilized.

Out-of-Band Management

Out-of-band infrastructure (OOBI) management offers the ability to provide management functions using completely separate processes, networks, and hardware. Phone companies have used this tecnnique for years in their network management, providing a control plane within the infrastructure that is completely separate from the voice network.

Blade systems provide some unique opportunities for creating management architectures using shared out-of-band processors and networks. Several different levels of out-of-band approaches are used in blades and other systems.

Baseboard Management Controllers

The least expensive approach is to use a baseboard management controller (BMC) — a fairly low-cost controller that can generate various alerts and allows for system restarts when the operating system is hung. Within most blade chassis, blades include a NIC and share the data network for communicating between the blades and the management plane. However, the management interface has a different IP address and a separate path from the NIC, known as a sideband interface. The sideband interface communicates to the

BMC via a separate hardware path. This provides the ability to perform power-state management for each blade in the chassis. Via this interface, it is possible to turn on a powered-off blade. The BMC and the NIC can operate in what is called flea-power mode, allowing machines to be brought online and offline without physically having to go to the system.

Management Service Processors (Management Modules)

A more elaborate and capable approach taken by newer blade server systems is the use of a management service processor, also called a management module. A management module is a complete (shared) management system with its own separate management processor, its own memory, and its own NIC. The service processor in the management module communicates with service processors on each blade via its own internal bus. The management module can perform all of the functions listed previously under BMCs, as well as providing other capabilities and protocols such as IPMI (see the next section) and KVM switching (these functions vary by vendor and product). The management module stores all event and error information and is the focal point for any troubleshooting, monitoring or active management of components within the chassis. It is known externally by its IP address and is accessible via a web browser.

Intelligent Platform Management Interface (IPMI)

Many systems today use capabilities defined in the Intelligent Platform Management Interface (IPMI). This set of specifications, created by a consortium of platform vendors including Intel and Sun, provides a set of low-level protocols and data records used to provide out-of-band manageability and access to hardware management information via a set of in-band application programming interfaces (APIs).

Shared Management Resources in Blade Systems

In addition to shared management service processors, blade systems support other shared management resources, which can reduce the cost of the management overhead per system. By sharing service processors and management NICs across all the blades in the chassis, the number of ports and processors can be reduced while still providing all of the out-of-band capability mentioned previously.

KVMs

Because there is generally no reason to have a separate KVM for each server within a rack, KVM switches have been used for some time to manage rack servers. With a KVM switch, it is possible to connect through the KVM switch to any system in the rack, and that system's KVM connection would be enabled so that local display and input could be performed.

Most blade chassis today have an embedded KVM switch, providing a single keyboard, video, and mouse port for the entire chassis of blades.

KVM over IP

Another new approach is to allow remote console access over the network. This approach, known as KVM over IP, converts the keyboard, monitor, and mouse commands to IP packets that can be sent over the IP network. This can be implemented using the existing network or can be routed on a completely separate network (alleviating security concerns). This gives managers in remote locations the ability to see and control the remote system console without having to be at the physical system location.

Virtual Media

Many vendors provide the capability for blades within the chassis to share a removable media device, using a similar approach to the one used for KVM functions. This approach, called *virtual media*, allows various types of media (for example, CD-ROMs, diskettes, or USB-attached devices) to be attached to a shared interface (or even connected over the network) and makes them accessible from the local management console. This allows remote administrators to apply patches and fixes to servers without having to go to the physical server or system. Virtual media interfaces also can be integrated into the KVM interface, allowing for simpler cabling and the use of a common infrastructure.

Management Software

Management of blade server systems requires a combination of hardware components and software. Some of the software management functions are included as part of various operating systems (for example, many of the CIM components are included in the OS); some are functions of virtualization hypervisors; and some are implemented as stand-alone management tools.

Virtual Machine Management

As discussed in Chapter 8, "Virtualization," an emerging use of blade servers is to run several server operating environments on a single physical server. Virtualized environments require the management system not only to manage the operating systems, application services, and hardware, but to interact with the virtualization software (that is, hypervisor) to manage the virtual machine environments as well. This creates some additional complexity, but such complexity is generally offset by the reduction in the number of physical servers and their associated complexity. In addition, some virtualization products offer certain management benefits, such as allowing the creation of a virtual pool of resources, which can then simplify the provisioning process.

Aggregation Management

Although a great deal of focus has been on virtualization, which provides the ability to slice a physical server into multiple virtual servers (dis-aggregation), it can also be useful to combine servers to work together as a larger unit (aggregation). Clustering offers a way to provide this aggregation function (see Chapter 9, "Clustering and Blades"). Egenera, PANTA Systems, and Fujitsu Siemens, for example, have developed software for managing a blade-specific clustering environment.

Blade Management Tools

Management tools used for blade server systems include point products as well as full management suites, offering a broad array of capabilities. These tools (and the vendors delivering them) are changing rapidly and continuously, making it impractical to cover them here in any detail. It is possible, however, to provide examples of the types of functionality available. Many tools make it possible to monitor servers in real time to detect problems, and to check the status of each blade in the chassis (see Figure 10.3 for HP Insight Manager's Enclosure View). Like most management tools, these tools typically allow *drill-down* — clicking on an individual blade to see a more detailed status report and description of any problems. The level of detail may vary by vendor, along with the available options for remote management (executing commands or functions on the remote system).

Some tools allow blades to be grouped together (for example, by department), allowing an administrator to perform a task on an entire group of blades with one mouse click. This grouping could be used for upgrading firmware on multiple blades simultaneously (see Figure 10.4 for a sample screen from IBM's Director). Additional functions provided by management tools allow you to monitor and provision storage resources, scan for security vulnerabilities, and even remotely deploy new operating systems or virtual machines.

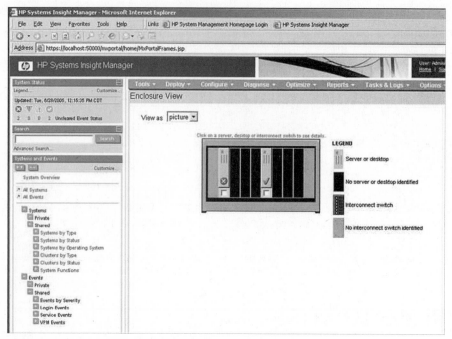

Figure 10.3: HP Systems Insight Manager Enclosure View

Source: Hewlett-Packard

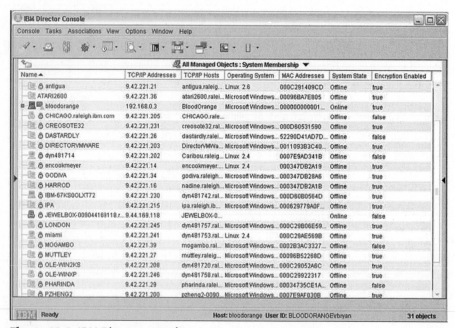

Figure 10.4: IBM Director console

Source: IBM

Conclusion

Management is one of the critical aspects of implementing and operating blade systems. Simplified management is one of the key benefits of blades, due to such features as shared management modules, sharing of other components within a chassis, prewired connections of blades to shared components, the use of anonymous blades, and more. Although managing blades utilizes many of the same tools as managing other systems, these additional features contribute to a higher level of manageability with blades, resulting in a lower TCO and higher server-to-administrator ratio.

In addition to discussing the state of management for blades and the types of management tools needed/available, this chapter also discussed the role of standards in improving the manageability of blades. Chapter 11, "Industry Organizations and Related Standards," continues the standards discussion and looks at the industry organizations related to blade systems.

Industry Organizations and Related Standards

Numerous organizations and consortiums are developing various standards that pertain to blades and blade management. Some of these organizations are focused solely on blade server systems. Other organizations are working on standards that are broader in scope than just blades (for example, systems management, including blades as well as conventional servers). Some of the standards discussed here have been around for years and are simply being modified to support blade environments.

This chapter highlights activities and key industry standards to be aware of when making implementation decisions involving blade systems. Appendix B, "Standards and Specifications," has more detailed information on the various specifications. However, many of these are still in the process of being developed and refined. Web sites of the various organizations and standards are listed here and are the best source of up-to-date information.

Blade-Specific Work

Several organizations have contributed specifically to blade standards in various ways. The Blade Systems Alliance was created to focus on the overall advancement of blade systems. The PCI Industrial Computer Manufacturers Group (PICMG) developed the Advanced Telecom Computing Architecture (AdvancedTCA) specification for blade standardization in the telecom space.

The organization known as Blade.org began as a joint IBM and Intel effort (as opposed to being an industry-wide standards group), but to date offers the only open specification for blade servers outside of the telecom space.

Blade Systems Alliance

Blade Systems Alliance (BladeS) is an independent, not-for-profit organization of server blade manufacturers, software suppliers, system integrators, analysts, consultants, end users, and other interested parties. Its focus is to serve as a clearinghouse for information about blade systems, provide a means for extending and improving standards, and promote their use in enterprise applications. More information can be found at http://www.bladesystems.org.

PCI Industrial Computer Manufacturers Group

The PCI Industrial Computer Manufacturers Group (PICMG), founded in 1994, is a consortium of more than 450 companies that collaboratively develops open specifications for high-performance telecommunications and industrial computing applications. PICMG's original mission was to extend the PCI standard for use in nontraditional computer markets such as industrial automation, medical, military, and telecom. PICMG specs have continued to evolve, resulting in a series of specifications that include CompactPCI, AdvancedTCA or ATCA, and CompactPCI Express.

The ATCA specification includes a definition of standardization for blade systems in the telecommunications space and is the only standardization that has been accomplished relative to standardizing blades and blade chassis. The ATCA specification has had more than 100 companies participating, including telecommunications equipment manufacturers, board- and system-level vendors, computer OEMs, software companies and chassis, and connector and power-supply vendors. ATCA includes standardization of the telco blade system form factor, addressing features such as NEBS (Network Equipment-Building System) compliance and DC power, which are required for telco environments.

More information about the PICMG ATCA standards and activities can be found at http://www.advancedtca.org.

Blade.org

Blade.org differs from other organizations described here in that it was created by IBM and Intel to focus exclusively on delivering IBM BladeCenter solutions. The reason it is listed here is that IBM has been the only server vendor to open a blade specification to other vendors. Unless and until a standard specification for blades outside of the telco space is developed, the open specification for BladeCenter is the only open specification that exists.

Blade.org was launched in February 2006 as a collaborative developer community focused on accelerating the development of blade solutions. By June 2006, it had more than 75 members, ranging from hardware and component providers to application developers and distribution partners. The program has had significant success, with a large number of integrated horizontal and vertical solutions being delivered. Examples of BladeCenter products and initiatives include the *Virtualized Hosted Client Infrastructure*, where IBM, VMware, and Citrix collaborated to deliver a hosted client offering with full desktop functionality, and *Systems Solutions for Branch Banking*, a solution for financial services and banking customers.

For more information on Blade.org, refer to `http://www.blade.org`. For access to the current IBM BladeCenter open specifications, refer to `http://www-03.ibm.com/systems/bladecenter/open_specs.html`.

General Standards Organizations

Much of the information presented here is from a cross-industry effort to share information about standards between various standards-setting organizations. Such information is maintained online in shared forums (on wikis that allows visitors to edit the content, such as *Wikipedia*) to allow it to be updated constantly by various representatives and experts participating in these organizations. This collaborative process was started within the Global Grid Forum by the working group known as the Standards Development Organization Collaboration on Networked Resources Management (SCRM-WG at `https://forge.gridforum.org/projects/scrm`) as a repository of relevant standards. This effort includes work by leading industry bodies including the Distributed Management Task Force (DMTF), Global Grid Forum (GGF), the TeleManagement Forum (TMF), the Internet Engineering Task Force (IETF), the International Telecommunication Union — Telecommunication Standardization Sector (ITU-T), the Organization for the Advancement of Structured Information Standards (OASIS), the Storage Networking Industry Association (SNIA), and the World Wide Web Consortium (W3C). Many of these are discussed on the following pages.

Distributed Management Task Force

The Distributed Management Task Force (DMTF) is the industry organization leading the development of management standards and the promotion of interoperability for enterprise and Internet environments. DMTF standards define common management infrastructure components for instrumentation (making an object manageable), control, and communication in a platform-independent and technology-neutral way.

DMTF Standards

DMTF standards include the Common Information Model (CIM), communication/control protocols like Web-Based Enterprise Management (WBEM) and Web Services for Management (WS-Management), and the Systems Management Architecture for Server Hardware (SMASH) initiative. More information about DMTF's standards and activities can be found in Appendix B and at http://www.dmtf.org.

Common Information Model

The DMTF Common Information Model (CIM) infrastructure defines a standardized approach to the management of systems and networks, based on an object-oriented paradigm. The CIM schema is a conceptual information model for describing computing and business entities in Internet, enterprise, and service-provider environments. CIM provides a consistent definition and structure of data. CIM has been adopted in varying degrees by most systems and network vendors, allowing systems and network elements to be managed by any management software product that supports CIM.

Open Grid Forum

The Open Grid Forum (OGF) was created in 2006 from a merger of the Global Grid Forum (GGF) and the Enterprise Grid Alliance (EGA) to bring the entire grid community together. OGF will focus on accelerating the adoption of grid technology.

Prior to the merger, the GGF had established a community of users, developers, and vendors leading the global standardization effort for grid computing. The GGF community included thousands of individuals in industry and research, representing more than 400 organizations in more than 50 countries. GGF's focus was primarily on the grid requirements of IT vendors, and the EGA's emphasis was on meeting the needs of enterprise users.

The combined OGF will also focus on such things as how grids integrate with virtualization, SOAs (service-oriented architectures), and automated systems. OGF hopes to help overcome obstacles to adopting grid computing by including issues involving people, processes, and technology. Information about OGF's standards and activities can be found at http://www.ogf.org.

Internet Engineering Task Force

The Internet Engineering Task Force (IETF) is a large open international community of network designers, operators, vendors, and researchers concerned with the evolution of the Internet architecture and the smooth operation of the Internet. The IETF is responsible for maintaining the standard for SNMP (Simple Network Management Protocol), one of the major contributions to network management. SNMP is the protocol used for network management over IP networks. In addition to SNMP, key IETF standards include the Structure of Management Information (SMI), which addresses the management information base (MIB), and the NETCONF configuration protocol, which defines mechanisms to install, manipulate, and delete the configuration of network devices. More information about IETF's standards and activities can be found in Appendix B and at http://www.ietf.org.

International Telecommunication Union

The ITU, headquartered in Geneva, Switzerland, is an international organization in which governments and the private sector coordinate global telecom networks and services. ITU specifications include recommendations for a security framework (Security for the Management Plane) for telecom networks and next-generation networks (NGN), and recommendations for management principles, requirements, and architecture for managing NGNs (Principles for the Management of Next Generation Networks). More information about the ITU's standards and activities can be found in Appendix B and at http://www.itu.int.

Organization for the Advancement of Structured Information Standards

OASIS (Organization for the Advancement of Structured Information Standards) is a not-for-profit, international consortium that drives the development, convergence, and adoption of e-business standards. The consortium produces open standards for web services, security, e-business, and standardization efforts in the public sector and for application-specific markets. Founded in 1993, OASIS has more than 5,000 participants representing more than 600 organizations and individual members in 100 countries. Related OASIS standards include Web Services Distributed Management (WSDM) Management Using Web Service (MUWS), which defines a web-service interface for management providers; Management of Web Services (MOWS), for the case where the managed resource is a web service; and Solution Deployment Descriptor (SDD), an XML schema that describes the characteristics of an installable unit (IU) of software. More information can be found in Appendix B and at `http://www.oasis-open.org`.

Storage Networking Industry Association

The Storage Networking Industry Association (SNIA) is a not-for-profit global organization made up of more than 460 member companies and close to 7,000 active individuals spanning virtually the entire storage industry. The association's goal is to advance the adoption of storage networks as complete and trusted solutions. SNIA is active in delivering standards, education, and services. One of its main accomplishments is the ongoing development and adoption of the Storage Management Initiative Specification (SMI-S), which defines a standard for interoperability in managing storage networking resources.

More information can be found in Appendix B and at `http://www.snia.org`.

What's Missing in Standards

Many standards are involved in blade systems and systems management, and some are still emerging. Over time, there will be a greater emphasis on web services standards as some of the underlying technologies and tools mature. Many of the standards mentioned here provide standardization that applies to more than just blade technology, but most of them have been extended to support and take advantage of blade systems.

However, one of the biggest disappointments is the lack of any standards around the blade form factor itself (outside of the telco space). Many users would like to have the ability for blades from different vendors to be interchangeable within racks. Unfortunately, as of early 2007 this has yet to materialize. This is probably explained by the fact that the chassis infrastructure implemented by vendors has a great deal of uniqueness, offering competitive advantages and claims of specific added value, such as redundant hot-swappable power and cooling subsystems, and unique management infrastructure. In any case, standardized chassis and blades have yet to appear.

Conclusion

Although much work is being done to standardize the management infrastructure, much work remains. Competing standards will eventually result in a de facto winner as the decisions are ultimately made by the customers with their purchasing power. Although it appears that many standards exist, increased efforts are being made to have better coordination of standards efforts, with the end goal of providing the customer with increased choice, reduced cost, and improved interoperability.

This chapter reviewed some of the work being done in the industry to advance the uses and overall adoption of blade systems. It completes Part II of this book. Part III, "Hardware, Facilities, and Software Considerations," moves on to discuss hardware, software, and data-center facilities considerations, both for choosing products and for planning and implementing those products.

Hardware, Facilities, and Software Considerations

CHAPTER 12

Assessing Your Needs — Blade System Hardware Considerations

This chapter focuses on assessing your hardware requirements. It poses questions to ask as you make decisions on whether and where blade systems are right for you. It also offers tips for your consideration during your product selection and implementation processes.

Blade System Considerations

The first step is to assess your current hardware environment, including both current and future requirements, and consider how these relate to the benefits and limitations of blade systems. Although initial blade systems were limited to low-speed processor blades, current offerings range from low-power CPUs to very high-end, dual-core (soon to be quad-core), high-memory blades with high-speed, low-latency interconnect options. Blade systems, with some specific exceptions, can be used anywhere that rack servers were used in the past. Those exceptions center mostly on specific hardware issues, raising the following questions:

Q Do you have requirements for a large number of network connections per server (more than eight)?

Q   Do you have requirements for specific chipsets for unique processing or graphics applications, which may not be available in a blade form factor for your chassis?

Q   Do you require a very large number of local hard drives for each server?

Q   Are you addressing environments with four or fewer physical servers in one location?

Q   Is your data center reaching the power and cooling limitations of the facility? If so, would the blade servers augment or replace the existing legacy server hardware (through consolidation — either physical, virtual, or both)?

If the answer to all these questions is no, then nothing should be stopping you from gaining the many benefits of blade systems. Blades have evolved to offer the full variety of rack servers while bringing the additional benefits of modularity, shared components, prewiring, and ultrahigh density that brings substantially more computing power per physical footprint. Even if you are at your limits for power and cooling, blades, if properly implemented, can help rather than hurt your power and cooling situation.

If you are currently committed to one or two systems (server) vendors, for purchasing reasons or other approved-vendor-status reasons, then your blade vendor decision may have already been made. (For example, users who currently buy only IBM or HP rack servers will most likely move to buying only IBM or HP blades.)

If you are not locked in to a specific server vendor, then reviewing the pros and cons of the various architectures will be a key part of your decision process.

Product selection and criteria are discussed further in Chapter 15, "Differentiating and Selecting Products." Inasmuch as they apply to implementation considerations, this chapter will discuss some of these issues as well. Examples include interconnect speeds (ranging from GbE, 10GbE, ATM, and IB), added layers of virtualization (for example, in overall design as with Egenera, or in virtualized I/O options such as HP, Sun, and others), and shared component options (for example, switch modules versus pass-through connections to external switches).

CPU Considerations

After you have decided to use blades, sizing the CPUs is not much different than it is with traditional servers. Understanding your application requirements is the key to success for CPU sizing, as well as for memory and I/O connections. These become even more important if you are consolidating physical servers into multiple virtual machines on a blade. (This is discussed further in Chapter 14, "System Software Considerations.")

Q What operating systems will you be running on the blade? Are they supported by the blade vendor?

If you are running virtualization software that requires virtualization hardware assist such as Intel VT or AMD-V, this must be your starting point.

TIPS

Check all your systems and application software for any requirements for specific chips, including the following:

- Requirements for hardware virtualization assists (such as with Xen and Windows Server Virtualization)

- Architectural requirements for special chips or chipsets (for example, some applications may require a particular chip that is available from only one vendor)

- Requirements for multithreading (SMP)

Q How CPU-intensive are the applications that will be running on each blade?

Q What is the current utilization (CPU, memory, I/O)?

Q Will a faster processor improve your performance, or is there a memory or I/O bottleneck?

 As CPUs on blades continue to evolve, blades are increasingly going to two or four sockets, and dual core (soon to be multicore). This can cause confusion in terminology — the number of CPUs versus number of cores versus number of sockets.

TIPS

- Be clear when discussing CPUs, cores, and sockets. The total number of cores per blade is calculated by the number of sockets times the number of cores per socket. This can be especially important for software licensing, as some vendors may license by CPU or cores, and some by the number of physical sockets on the blade.

Continued

TIPS (CONTINUED)

- Aim high on processor power, especially if you are consolidating through virtualization.

- Consider purchasing high-end blades with efficient power and cooling built in. Evaluate the cooling requirements of the processor-chip options you are considering (that is, evaluate comparable options from multiple vendors, including AMD and Intel).

- If you are using different classes of blades (for example, some low-end and some higher-end), you might consider grouping them by frame for manageability. However, if your high-end blades produce excessive heat output, consider mixing them within the frames to spread the heat, and managing them as a group of resources.

- If necessary for proper cooling, it's OK to leave some empty space in your chassis or racks. Even if you don't fully populate your chassis or racks due to power or cooling issues, blades still offer more computing power per footprint than traditional servers.

- If you are using or planning to use server virtualization, the tools for moving running virtual machines may allow movement only within matching processor groups. This may also be true for image deployment and server failover. Consistency in memory size may also be helpful. Keep this in mind as you make your blade-purchasing decisions. (This is one of the reasons that virtualization goes well with blades, because blades are typically bought as a group.)

Memory

Many of the considerations listed for CPUs also apply to memory. Understanding your applications and their runtime characteristics is the best way to determine requirements when moving to blades.

Q   What are the memory requirements of the applications that will run on the blades, including all tiers of the application infrastructure?

 For example, in a three-tiered architecture, with a web front end, middleware, and a back-end database, it is important to understand the needs of each tier as well as how they communicate.

Databases may be CPU-heavy and require a lot of memory for efficient database record handling. In this case, the database back end should be run on a more powerful blade with lots of memory. If the middleware is I/O-intensive, don't stack all the middleware blades within the same chassis (spread them across chassis so you don't saturate the I/O connections).

TIPS

- **Aim high on memory as well as speed, especially when virtualizing.**

- **Understand how each application utilizes memory and CPU resources. If possible, use a performance-monitoring tool to baseline the current application performance parameters.**

- **If possible, use a test lab to size the hardware and to test the effects of higher-speed processors and/or more memory. Does adding more power make a difference, or is the bottleneck in I/O?**

- **Keep in mind that applications such as database engines or heavy crunchers like SAS will perform better the more resources they have (both higher processing speed and more memory).**

I/O

I/O issues need to be considered at various levels of blade selection and implementation. Chassis backplanes vary considerably in terms of types and speeds of interconnects and I/O-card options. There is also significant diversity in both the approach to blade I/O and in speeds of switch modules. In addition, some vendors offer pass-through options as well as switch modules, and others offer only pass-through.

Q Do any of your applications have requirements for special add-on cards (for example, SSL encryption accelerators)? Are these available in a blade form factor as blade mezzanine/daughter cards, or only as PCI cards?

 Some blade chassis support add-on cards only as daughter or mezzanine cards to their blades. Some vendors/chassis have standard slots for PCI Express cards for installing special cards to be allocated to a specific blade, or in some cases, shared across blades.

TIP

- If you have special requirements for cards not available as mezzanine cards and your chassis does not support PCI-E cards, you may not be able to run that application on a blade.

Q Will you be running I/O-intensive applications with requirements for a lot of bandwidth?

Q Is the communication mostly between blades in the chassis or from the blades to other servers/storage outside the chassis?

Q How many blades will be I/O-heavy?

Q How many network interfaces or NICS are required per application/ blade?

If you have need for high-speed I/O interconnects, it is important to identify this as a key blade-selection criterion. Some vendors specialize in high-speed interconnects, some offer them as an option, and some may not have competitive high-speed offerings. Also, chassis vary in the number of NICs supported per blade.

TIPS

- Evaluate all of your I/O requirements before deciding on a chassis. If you plan to run applications with low I/O requirements, there may be lower-speed options that are more cost-effective. If, however, you will need high speed now or down the road, implementing a chassis with a high-speed backplane/midplane will allow the blades in the chassis that do need the speed to leverage that backplane.

- Investigate your current environment for the number of NICs that are used per server. Ensure that the chassis is not limited to less than the number needed per blade.

- Consider the I/O speed needed per blade for your LAN connections. If you are running Ethernet, will GbE be enough, or will you need to upgrade to 10GbE within the next five years?

- After you have looked at individual blade requirements, remember to consider the possibility of saturation at the aggregated level (that is, the switch), especially if you are consolidating through virtualization.

Continued

TIPS (CONTINUED)

- When deciding between switch modules and pass-through connections to external switches, investigate whether you have any special features on your current switches that may not be available in the switch module that runs in your chassis. Also check for compatibility between switch vendors (of switch modules and your existing external switches).

Storage

For I/O to storage devices, most blade chassis offer the option to use on-blade storage and/or to connect to a SAN or NAS. Diskless blades were introduced by Egenera in the very early days of blades and now are being implemented more frequently across all blade-vendor chassis.

Q   Do you have a requirement for local disk storage on each/all blade(s), or can you configure your blades to have shared access to storage on a SAN?

 With the boot-from-SAN option, using diskless (also known as anonymous) blades eliminates state from the blade, allowing simpler provisioning/reprovisioning since you don't have to worry about how to access (or back up) the information on the on-blade storage.

TIPS

- If you are connecting to a SAN, does your environment support boot from SAN, also known as PXE boot (Preboot Execution Environment)? This option is generally supported for all Fibre Channel connections and, more recently, for most iSCSI SANs as well (depending on which iSCSI initiator is used). Check with your SAN vendor to confirm any configuration requirements for SAN boot (for example, OS levels, firmware, and so on).
- If you are connecting to a SAN and don't have a strong requirement for local disk storage on each blade, consider going diskless to simplify reprovisioning and management.
- Understand bandwidth requirements for your SAN connections. Fibre Channel HBAs are available for most blades in 2Gb and 4Gb options. If you are using iSCSI, would your performance benefit from a TCP Offload Engine (TOE) option on your IP NIC, if one is available?

Q Does your chassis support embedded switch modules for your SAN?

Q Will you be using an embedded switch module or passing through to an external SAN switch?

 Most blade vendors support embedded SAN switch modules from most major SAN switch vendors (McData, Brocade, QLogic, and Cisco). If your chassis does not, it will require you to use a pass-through connection option to your external SAN switch.

TIPS

- **If your chassis supports switch modules from your SAN-switch vendor, it is important to verify that there are no special features configured on your external switch that are required but not available on their blade switch module.**

- **Understand your aggregated bandwidth requirements. Remember to verify not only that you have enough bandwidth at the blade level, but also at the aggregated level. If, for example, you are running 14 blades connected to an embedded switch module, will I/O become a bottleneck? This can become an even bigger issue if you are consolidating/virtualizing multiple virtual servers with high I/O requirements onto single blades. If this becomes a problem, it may be necessary to use the pass-through option rather than switch modules for certain applications.**

Q If you do require local disk storage, how much capacity do you need?

Q What type of drives do you want to use?

Q How important is high availability (HA) of those drives?

 Most blade vendors offer a variety of local HDD options, including SCSI, SATA, and SAS drives, with varying levels of redundancy and hot-swap capability. Some also offer storage-expansion options.

Since the HDD is generally the only component on the blade that has moving parts, it may be at the highest risk of failure. For many users, if a problem occurs with a blade HDD, they will (at least initially) simply swap out the blade. Some vendors offer mirroring of the local disks for HA, but if performance is an issue, make sure that it's hardware mirroring rather than software mirroring.

> **TIPS**
>
> - If you require local HDD support, look for redundancy and hot-swap capability to help minimize disruption due to disk failures.
> - If a particular server application requires a large number of direct-connect HDDs (for example, 10), blades may not be the right choice.

Conclusion

Blade system chassis, modules, and the blades themselves come in many different flavors. Choosing the right vendor, the right chassis, and the right blades requires a thorough assessment of your needs, as well as careful planning. This chapter offered a variety of questions to ask yourself and your potential vendors about various blade system options and how they address your unique environment and requirements. It also provided considerations and tips to help with your blade implementation.

The next chapter, "Power and Cooling," moves from hardware considerations to facilities and environmental factors — chief among these are power and cooling. Chapter 13 offers an introduction to power and cooling issues, and offers suggestions for tackling these all-important matters.

Power and Cooling

This chapter discusses power and cooling requirements and considerations for implementing blade systems. It also offers tips on how to prepare your data center for a smoother implementation.

According to an IDC study of end-user perspectives, power was the top-ranked issue facing user data centers (see Figure 13.1). Why is power such a pressing concern? Data-center electricity costs are greater than $3 billion per year, and IDC predicts that the number of servers in the United States will grow 50% over the next four years. Furthermore, businesses paid 20% more for electricity in 2005 than they did in 2004, with rates in some areas jumping more than 40%. According to Robert Frances Group, power, cooling, and electricity together comprise 25–40% of a data center's annual operating cost.

To understand power and cooling discussions, it is helpful to review basic terms such as volts, amps, watts, and BTUs, and clarify them with an analogy. Voltage (volts) can be viewed as the size of the pipe bringing in the power. Amperage (amps) is the flow rate within the pipe, or how fast the power flows. Wattage, then, (measured here mostly in kilowatts, or kW) is the total amount of power delivered, calculated as voltage times amps. This is how power requirements for blade chassis and racks are typically given.

Since power also equates to heat, wattage in equals wattage out (for example, if the power requirement is 30 kW, the heat generated is also 30 kW. Cooling can then be estimated in BTUs (British Thermal Units) as wattage times 3.41. Cooling requirements are often quoted in BTUs.

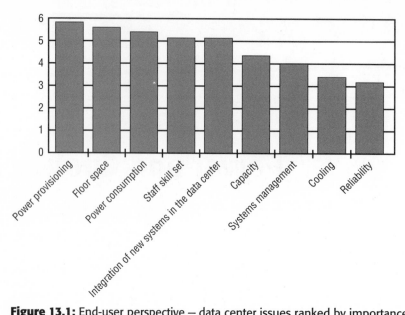

Figure 13.1: End-user perspective — data center issues ranked by importance
Source: IDC, End User Perspectives on Server Blade Adoption, Doc #TB20060525, May 2006

In a Data Center Users' Group survey in fall 2005, 67% of the data centers surveyed were already using high-density servers, with an average peak load per rack of 9 kW of power. (As of 2007 blade power requirements are more like 30 kW per rack and increasing.) The average wattage was 55 watts per square foot. Most (94%) had generator power, with less than half having any DC power.

In terms of cooling issues, as more power is required to run the system, more heat is generated. This translates into paying once to power the servers and paying again to cool them. A rack that uses 24 kW of power requires about 78,000–81,000 BTUs of cooling capacity.

Airflow is another key aspect of cooling servers, measured in cubic feet per minute (cfm). According to power and cooling vendor APC (American Power Conversion), blade server systems need 120 cfm of cool air per kW of power. Most data centers to date provide 200–300 cfm of cool air per rack location, which is about 10% of what's required. If no additional cooling is used, this would limit rack power to less than 2 kW per rack, and blades would not be an option.

The ultrahigh density of blade systems has raised power and cooling issues to a new level. However, contrary to what many people believe initially, the problem with blades is not power and cooling, but rather the distribution of power and cooling to the places where they are most needed.

Power and Cooling Improvements

Although power is an important factor, cooling tends to be the more common barrier listed by users in moving to a blade architecture. Therefore, we will focus on the various approaches, features, and tips for addressing cooling concerns, and will address power issues as they apply.

Server Consolidation and Virtualization

Every server, whether tower, rack, or blade, generates heat. More servers generate more heat; fewer servers generate less heat. Consolidation of physical servers reduces the number of physical servers within the data center, which not only reduces the amount of heat generated, and thus the amount of cooling required, but also reduces the floor space required.

Consolidating servers can be accomplished in multiple ways. First, for applications that play nicely together on a single operating system, it is possible to consolidate applications that previously have been spread across physical servers, by *stacking* them together on a single server. Server virtualization goes the next step by consolidating entire servers as virtual servers onto a single physical server.

When consolidation and virtualization are implemented together with blades, the reduction in cooling and floor-space requirements can and should be highly beneficial and carefully considered in your data-center planning.

Blade System Cooling Features

From the outset, the high density of blade systems created a higher heat output per footprint than rack servers. In addition, as blade systems began to use higher-speed processor chips, the heat (and, thus, the cooling issues) intensified. Fortunately, during this same evolution, a number of other features were introduced at the chip level, the blade and chassis level, and even in related software.

Chip Features (Multicore and Power Management)

First and foremost, while blades were taking advantage of higher processor speeds, the chip manufacturers found a number of ways to reduce heat output. The most significant of these has been the move from a single-core chip that fits into a socket on the blade, to a dual-core chip that fits into the same socket. These dual-core chips place two processing engines within the same silicon area but operating at a slightly reduced clock speed. This reduction in speed generates less heat overall, but nearly doubles the processing power. Dual-core chips are available from both Intel and AMD, with quad-core chips expected in 2007 from both vendors. (Multicore already exists outside the x86 world with Sun's UltraSPARC). With these advances, multicore chips offer significant improvement in performance per watt, which has become a key metric for evaluating competitive chips. In addition, some chips are now offered in a variety of heat grades, running at different watt levels. This allows users to choose between pure performance and performance per watt. (Intel predicts its Woodcrest processors will reduce thermal power by 40% over single-core designs, and AMD claims 60% faster performance over their single-core chips within the same power envelope.)

The other improvement in heat at the chip level comes from the mobile technology that was first used in laptop computers. For quite some time, laptops have had the ability to adjust their processors to enter a low-frequency mode, originally to conserve power while running on battery power. This power-management capability has now been extended to other environments — such as blades, to allow a server blade to adjust its processor state on demand based on CPU utilization. This allows the CPU to reduce its power at idle (as much as 75%, according to AMD), conserving power and generating significantly less heat.

> **TIP**
>
> Consider power and cooling features carefully when making decisions on chips used in your server blades.

Blade Server and Chassis Features

In addition to the advances at the chip level, blade system vendors have also made great strides in power and cooling. One of the major sources of heat within servers has been due to inefficiencies of power supplies. For example, according to IBM, their 1U rack server power supply operated at 65% efficiency. This means that only 65% of the power that comes from the wall is converted into usable power by the server. The remaining 35% goes into the room in the form of heat. So for every 1 kW from the power provider, 650 W go to the server, and 350 W go into the room as heat. IBM's second generation of blade systems improved their power supplies to run at 91% efficiency, which translates to losing only 90 W as heat into the room. Similar advances in efficiency have come from others, such as HP, helping to make heat within the chassis less of an issue with newer blade server systems.

Another area of improvement within the chassis comes from improved airflow within the chassis. One of the primary ways to improve cooling is to eliminate heat as close to the source as possible. If you remove heat from the rack before it reaches the room, the cooling is more efficient. Features within the chassis/rack, such as heat exchangers and filler panels (which prevent hot air in the back from going to the front), help by removing the heat within the chassis/rack.

Power and cooling management have been addressed through software as well. Power-management software has been introduced by multiple blade system vendors to help in monitoring, managing, and automating management relative to power and cooling. At the lowest level, some blades include circuitry that communicates with the management module to allow control of power management (for example, reducing clock speed if power is low). Monitoring software tracks power consumption, measures voltages, and reports both at a given point in time, as well as over time. More-advanced software allows policy-management functionality, such as capping power at a specified amount.

TIP

Consider features such as power-supply efficiency, air flow, and power-management software when making decisions on blade system vendors.

Data Center/Facilities Planning

Many aspects of power and cooling challenges have been and continue to be addressed by the various chip and blade vendors, helping to mitigate the barriers to blade adoption. However, these features and improvements can only go so far. The final and critical element in dealing with power and cooling is in data-center facilities planning and management. This section discusses these planning issues and offers tips to help you prepare your data center for high-density computing.

Hot Aisle/Cold Aisle

The concept of alternating hot aisles and cold aisles was created by Robert Sullivan (now of the Uptime Institute) in 1992 while he was at IBM. The idea is simple: Instead of having all the data-center equipment facing the same direction, so that heat comes out of the back of each row and into the front of the next row, equipment is installed in rows that face each other.

Cold aisles, the aisles in which the equipment racks are facing each other, are created with vented floor tiles that allow cool air to come up from under the raised floor, so the cool air goes into the front of the racks and out the back into the hot aisles. Hot aisles are those in the back of the racks, and the floor tiles are not vented. This separates the cool air source in front from the hot air that is sent out into the room. Hot-aisle tiles are not vented, because vented tiles in the hot aisle would mix hot and cold air. In order for the cooling units to be at their most efficient, you want the air that returns to the cooling units to be hot.

TIPS

- Check to ensure there are no vented tiles in the hot aisles.
- Increase cold aisles to two tiles wide if possible.
- Use unloaded racks with blanking panels between blade racks to prevent hot air from going around the sides to the intake area.
- Place CRACs (computer room air conditioners) perpendicular to hot aisles for maximum efficiency.
- Place the hottest (highest-kW) racks in the center of the row (hot aisle).
- If possible, move the UPS (uninterruptible power supply) outside of the room to keep out the heat.
- If the blade solution you are implementing uses something other than front-to-back cooling (for example, Verari Systems cools their blade solutions from bottom to top), check with that vendor for specific recommendations on the data-center layout best suited to cooling their blade systems.

Bypass Airflow

After a data center has been implemented using the hot aisle/cold aisle concept, one of the most common problems is bypass airflow. This means that the cool air is not getting to the air intakes of the computer equipment, but is instead bypassing the intended route through leaks, cable cutouts, holes under cabinets, or improperly placed vented tiles.

Bypass airflow can be avoided easily, through the following tips as recommended by experts such as the Uptime Institute, APC, and Liebert:

TIPS

- Seal all the holes in the computer-room perimeter.
- Seal all openings in the raised floor to prevent bypass cold-air flow (cable cutouts, PDUs [power-distribution units] and cooling units, floor edges, cutouts for pipes, and so on).
- Install blanking plates in all unused spaces in equipment racks and cabinets to prevent recirculation of hot air.

Continued

TIPS *(CONTINUED)*

- Use empty racks with blanking panels between blade racks to prevent hot air from going around the sides to the intake area.

- Ensure that there are no vented/perforated tiles in the hot aisles.

- The problem is air flow, not air temperature. Do not try to compensate by lowering the temperature setting in the CRACs; it can worsen the situation.

Ceilings and Floors

Another area that contributes greatly to the efficiency or inefficiency of cooling your data center is the room itself. Think of the floor as one of the chief means of delivering cooling to the equipment, and the ceiling as the path to removing the heat.

Several factors are important to consider relative to raised floor. First, the higher the floor, the more airflow there is. However, the higher the floor, the less weight it can hold. With the high density of blades, it is critical to also pay attention to floor weight load. Typical raised-floor height in data centers is 30 inches, with a minimum of two feet recommended. Second, the height of the floor is irrelevant if the cabling, pipes, and other obstructions under the floor don't allow air to pass through. Note that raised-floor cooling is limited to cooling 5–8 kW, due to the power it takes to push the air through.

There are three ways to return the heat to the cooling system: through the room, through a duct system, or through a ceiling-return air plenum. If the data center is height-constrained, heat removal presents special difficulties that may require you to seek outside help (for example, from your blade system vendor(s) or from power and cooling vendors such as Emerson Network Power, Liebert, or APC).

TIPS

- Improve air flow to the room by reducing obstructions under the floor.

- Watch for floor-weight restrictions.

- Check for good return air flow.

- Allow three feet of clearance between the tops of racks and the top of the return air path to cooling units.

- Get help from your vendors to assess your environment in general, and to identify cooling leaks in particular.

Supplemental Cooling

When the methods listed thus far do not offer enough cooling to meet your needs, it may be necessary to consider supplemental cooling at the rack or room level, adding 10 kW or more of cooling per enclosure. Two types of fluids are used in supplemental cooling — chilled water (CW) at 45 degrees, and refrigerant (which is pumped at low pressure). Each has its pros and cons; many blade vendors offer one or the other. For example, IBM and HP offer rack-level attachment options with water cooling. The HP panel attaches to the side, and the IBM offering fits on the back. Egenera has partnered with Liebert, offering a pumped-refrigerant option.

Although some users are resistant to the idea of liquid cooling, it is worth noting that water cooling has been used in mainframe data centers since the 1970s. According to the Data Center Users' Group survey, in fall 2005, 47% of the users were open to refrigerant cooling and 39% were open to water cooling. (Leaks, toxicity, and regulations made up 57% of users' concerns about refrigerant, and leaks and equipment damage made up 67% of users' concerns about water.) Overall, 19% of the users said they would never use any form of liquid cooling. (Anecdotally, a large number of those had used water cooling in their mainframe data center previously.)

> **TIP**
>
> If ceilings and floors are too low or there is not enough air cooling, consider liquid-cooling options.

Physical Location

In addition to everything discussed so far, here are several options to consider, relative to the physical layout of the data center, when implementing high-density computing:

- Spread the load. One way to help dissipate heat is to spread the hot blade racks across the data center and not create a single hot area.

- Create a high-density area or row. Create a single heat-producing area with 10–30 kW per rack, but with sufficient additional cooling to address the heat output.

- Create a high-density room. If necessary, create the high-density area as its own room, with its own increased cooling.

For any of these options, here are a few final tips:

TIPS

- **Don't use the nameplate to estimate your requirements. The numbers on the equipment and/or spec sheets are conservative numbers in specific environments. If at all possible, use your own environment to test power and cooling requirements, and then plan your data center accordingly.**

- **Wherever possible, shorten the distance from the heat source to the cooling source.**

Additional Power Issues

A number of power issues have already been discussed as they relate to cooling requirements. In addition, there are a few issues related to power availability.

Insufficient Power

Check to ensure that you have sufficient power availability into the facility overall, as well as power distribution to where it's needed.

TIPS

Always plan for more outlets and more watts than you think you will need. Additionally, check for insufficient power distribution in each of the following areas:

- **Not enough wiring under floor or overhead**
- **Insufficient PDU capacity**
- **Insufficient UPS capacity**
- **Not enough breaker positions**

Power Supply Features

As part of your hardware decision and planning process, don't forget the power supplies.

> **TIPS**
>
> - Pay attention to the total wattage, redundancy, and hot-pluggable features.
> - Remember; the larger the module (UPS or battery), the lower the cost per kVA (kilovolt-amp)

DC Power

DC power is the type of power generally used internally by the components within servers, with the power supply converting the external data-center power (AC) to internal power to the components (DC). It also has been used externally in the telecommunications business for years, ensuring power availability for telco switching in far-flung regions. More recently, there has been some movement toward using DC power for enterprise data centers as well. There is still debate among many as to the potential savings in switching to DC power for the data center, with estimates ranging from 10–25%. IBM, HP, and Sun all have available offerings using DC power.

> **TIP**
>
> If you are considering DC power, check with your current and prospective vendors for product availability.

Conclusion

Since the introduction of blade server systems and their ultrahigh-density implementation, power and cooling have been a topic of conversation both as a problem of blades and a potential benefit of blades. The density of blade systems creates a higher requirement for power and a higher heat output per physical footprint, yet the shared components and innovations in design have improved both power and cooling efficiencies over what traditional servers offer.

This chapter described both the issues and the improved efficiencies in power and cooling for blade systems. It offered tips for evaluating and implementing blade systems in terms of power and cooling, and for planning and preparing your data center for high-density computing. The next chapter moves on to system-software considerations, focusing on server virtualization.

CHAPTER 14

System Software Considerations

When implementing a new infrastructure there are always things to consider in terms of system software. Architectural issues, application compatibility, hardware and software requirements/compatibility, and the transition from current environment and processes are a few of the important factors to think about prior to making a choice. This chapter poses questions to ask before making implementation choices and offers tips for consideration during implementation.

Virtualization

To virtualize or not to virtualize; that is the question. Chapter 8, "Virtualization," discusses many reasons to implement server virtualization, including higher processor utilization levels. If you are implementing server virtualization, here are a few things to think about.

Q   What changes in systems configuration are required to support many virtual machines (VMs) and/or OS environments? What type of virtualization architecture will you use?

> Inherently, the virtual environment is a shared environment. Even though virtualization software encapsulates the application environment so the different virtual machines don't step on each other, there are still limited CPU, memory, and I/O resources available on any system.

TIPS

Here are some tips for planning your implementation:

- Understand your application environments — is one application CPU-intensive with minimal I/O activity? Does another require large amounts of memory? Is CPU utilization low, but the application takes 80% of the I/O bandwidth?

- Perform capacity planning for the application environments to make sure that resources can be used effectively.

- Plan which application environments you intend to run on the same blade, considering all resources required by the applications.

System Requirements in a Virtualized Environment

Traditional distributed server architectures have one application on one system, regardless of whether the application utilizes the resources on that system to their fullest. Virtualization supports many applications running on a single system to better utilize all system resources and localize management of those applications to one system.

Q   How much memory do your application and your operating environment need in a single-server configuration? Is memory utilization fairly consistent throughout the process execution or are there spikes?

> Understanding the memory requirements and usage patterns of each application environment will enable you to configure your blades with sufficient memory to support multiple application environments on virtual machines. Overburdened memory is the primary reason for virtualization failures. The secondary reason is often overburdened disk I/O bandwidth — too many applications vying for the same disk resource.

Q   Is your application environment CPU-bound? I/O bound? What is your combined disk and network traffic going to be?

Memory and CPU utilization are only part of an application's resource utilization profile. Tracking utilization patterns for all aspects of your application environments allows you to configure complementary application environments on a single blade, thereby creating balanced utilization of all resources.

TIPS

- Don't skimp on memory — add 20% to your estimated memory requirement to allow for application growth.
- Don't forget to allocate memory for the virtualization software itself.
- When choosing a CPU, consider factors such as whether you need to run with 64-bit support or only 32-bit support, or both; whether your virtualization software requires virtualization hardware-assist (Intel VT or AMD-V); and how fast the processor(s) runs. All of these factors will determine which CPU features you will require. If you plan to implement virtualization, it's wise to choose the fastest CPU you can. The number of VMs that can be supported will coincide with whether your CPU can keep up.
- Most blades come with 1 Gbps Ethernet NICs standard. Multiple VMs supporting applications that require high network bandwidth may require an additional 1 Gbps or even 10 Gbps Ethernet network adapters.

Applications in a Virtualized Environment

The application drives the business decision. Understanding your application environment, as well as your existing infrastructure, is crucial to defining and creating a successful virtualized environment. This applies to sizing of resources as well as deciding which application environments fit well together on one blade and whether some applications are best left outside the virtual environment for now. For most applications, the move to a virtual environment is trivial. However, there are a number of things to consider prior to a move.

Q   Are all the applications that are intended for the virtual environment mission critical? If so, are there peak timeframes associated with these applications?

 The amount of resources required by the multiple application environments is only part of the equation. The other part is when the resources are needed, especially with mission critical applications.

Understanding resource requirements over the application execution cycle (time) will allow you to better match applications to be run concurrently within the virtual environment on a single blade.

Q   Do your applications rely heavily on disk accesses?

> Applications with heavy disk access requirements, such as some databases, may not be the best candidates for a virtual environment until the virtual I/O performance issues are addressed (see "Choosing a Virtualization Architecture" later in this chapter).

Q   Do your applications require 64-bit support?

> Many processors support a 64-bit architecture for extended memory addressing, though few applications take advantage of this. If you have an application that does use the 64-bit architecture, be sure the virtual environment also supports 64 bits.

Q   Do your applications require multicore or multiple processors — symmetric multiprocessing (SMP)?

> With multicore processing available on a single blade, there are several blade and virtual software vendors that support both physical and virtual SMP environments. Vendors that support physical SMP tie two or more adjacent blades together via high-speed transports to aggregate processors.

Virtual SMP is done at a software level through a form of clustering. If your application can (or will) take advantage of either a physical or virtual SMP environment, consider the options.

Q   Are your applications supported in a virtual environment?

> For most applications, the move to a virtual environment will be trivial. However, if something fails, the application vendor may ask for testing in a nonvirtual environment to verify the problem is with the software rather than the environment.

TIPS

- In a virtual environment, put applications that have complementary peak workload times together on the same blade. For example, an application that will primarily be performing network accesses during the day and background processing at night would fit well with an application that is compute-intensive during the day and doesn't run at night.

- If you need to run both 32-bit and 64-bit operating systems concurrently in your virtual environment, be sure you choose a virtualization software vendor whose implementation supports this.

- Check with your application vendors to determine if their solutions have been tested and are supported in a virtual environment.

Choosing a Virtualization Architecture

Chapter 8 defined the different virtualization architectures. Choosing which architecture will best fit with your environment requires an understanding of what your application environment needs, as well as what the long-term (five-year) goals are for the infrastructure. Choosing which virtualization architecture to proceed with will require thoughtful consideration of the trade-offs, and depend on what your long-term IT strategy encompasses.

Q   Do you want/need to run multiple OS environments (for example, Windows and Linux) on the same blade or do you typically run in one OS environment?

 The ability to run multiple concurrent, differing, operating systems in a virtualized environment on one blade provides great flexibility to the blade environment. This comes, however, with the cost of process overhead.

The hypervisor architecture provides the broadest OS support if you need to run multiple concurrent (differing) operating systems. If you have standardized on one OS environment for all applications, OS virtualization is worth considering as it has less overhead than a hypervisor and provides access to the greatest number of resources.

Q   How many virtual environments do you need to run per physical server?

The scalability of the virtualization solution may be limited by the virtualization software. It is important to understand what your scalability requirements are when choosing a virtualization solution.

Q   Do you need broad device support?

 If your application environment requires access to a number of different devices, the architectures that have broad device support inherently may be the best.

The Hosted and OS Virtualization architectures both have a mature resident operating system underlying the virtual environment and, therefore, come with the broad device support of that operating system. The device drivers for hypervisors were developed more recently, for and with those hypervisors, and therefore there may not be support for nonstandard devices.

Q   Will you be purchasing new blades to implement virtualization, or using older blades?

 The latest chips from AMD and Intel have hardware-assist for virtualization, leveraged by the newer virtualization software products — for example, those based on Xen 3.0.

Some of the newer hypervisors have been limited to working only with the new chips. (Xen 3.0 can work with the older chipsets but requires the OS to be enlightened/paravirtualized — for example, Linux, BSD, and Solaris — thus limiting the array of supported operating systems.) Conversely, some of the older virtualization solutions can work on both the old and new chips but may not take advantage of the hardware-assist.

Q   Do you require very fast I/O access?

 I/O-intensive applications may not be the best applications to use in a virtual environment. There are two reasons for this. Most virtualization architectures create overhead that reduces I/O performance (I/O calls go through multiple software layers before getting out to the bus). Of the architectures, a single OS virtualization architecture is the best option for high I/O performance. The hypervisors that take advantage of the virtualization-assist chips (Intel VT and AMD-V) can get near-native performance. The hardware-assist is designed to make I/O in the virtual machines more efficient by changing the way the I/O interrupts are handled.

Actual performance improvements depend on the efficiency of the device firmware, as well as the efficiency of the hypervisor. In addition, the concept of sharing I/O devices, to the level that virtualization requires, even at the bus level, is either nonexistent or not used in the open systems world. However, work is being done to reduce I/O overhead in all virtualization solutions and work must be done at the I/O hardware and protocol levels to incorporate the concept of true device sharing.

TIPS

- **Hypervisors give the broadest flexibility of guest OS support if you need to run multiple concurrent operating systems. Some hosted architectures can also support multiple concurrent operating systems, and OS partitioning is limited to running multiple partitions of the native OS.**

- **Some partitioning implementations do fixed hardware partitioning, which gives excellent isolation of environments but can be inflexible when service spikes require dynamic resource allocation. Be sure that you understand how the partitioning is implemented.**

- **Hypervisor architectures were designed as a "thin" virtual machine manager and will require fewer CPU and memory resources than the standard hosted environment, which uses an unmodified native OS to manage the virtual environment.**

- **Some virtualization solutions have a hard-coded maximum number of virtual environments they support per physical server; others are limited by performance only.**

- **If you are planning to run on older blades, make sure that your virtualization vendor supports the processors.**

Management Tools

As the server virtualization market matures, many of the management challenges will be overcome. However, if the virtualization solution you choose today does not include at least a basic set of management tools, your investment will soon become your burden.

Regardless of whether you choose to implement virtualization, it is imperative that you understand what management tools are available for and compatible with your blade solution. When personal computers were first available, there was a proliferation of small, unmanaged systems. Can you imagine what the unbridled proliferation of blades and VMs would mean to your operations without proper management products and processes?

Like so many other technologies, comprehensive management software lags behind technology releases, and blades and virtualization are no exception.

However, the delta between what is available and what is desired is fairly small. At press time, well-developed server and virtualization management suites exist, but many don't tie the two together and don't provide for automation. When dealing with thousands of virtual servers, automation is what keeps your OpEx from getting out of control. When evaluating management software, make sure that it has the ability to integrate with your blades and your virtual environment.

Provisioning/Change Control

One of the greatest benefits of blade systems is the ease of management over standard rack or stand-alone server environments. The higher density of blades combined with the ease of proliferation of virtual environments makes automated provisioning and change control essential to lowering operating expenses.

Q   What management tools are there for managing/provisioning/reprovisioning the blade systems you are implementing? And management tools for VMs within the virtualized environment? And tools for migrating physical environments to virtual environments (P2V) and virtual-to-virtual (V2V)?

> **Ease of provisioning and reprovisioning is a strong benefit for the management of both blade and virtual environments. Most vendors sell software to provide these functions at various levels. You need to know how their management software interfaces with your current management software, or if your current software has add-ons that will allow you to manage the blade and virtual environments much as you have been managing your server and rack environments.**

Q   Does your management tool include a change-control capability that will track what versions and patch levels of which operating environment, application software, and so on you're using and where they are located?

> **If you are thinking of implementing one or two chassis with a total of 20 blades, you may not think configuration-control management of this environment is much of an issue. However, when you also consider that each of those blades could support several virtual environments (let's say five to be conservative), you now are managing 100 server environments. It doesn't take a great stretch of the imagination to see how quickly managing a growing virtual environment can get out of hand. Therefore, if you don't currently have change-control capabilities within your server management environment, you should consider acquiring them.**

Q   Can a single console manage any/multiple blades and/or VMs across the entire blade environment, or only for one chassis?

 To reference the previous example, with only two chassis, more than 100 servers can be created. Having a single console to manage those environments will increase the number of servers a single admin can support.

TIPS

- Find out whether your management software vendor can provide add-on modules for support of blade and/or virtual environments so your people don't have to (potentially) interface to multiple management consoles and learn a completely different management interface.

- With the higher density of blades and with multiple virtual machines on top of that, change control can quickly become a nightmare. See whether your current change-control software also supports blades and virtual machines.

- Look for management tools that provide a broad view of both the entire blade infrastructure and the virtual environment, and also can drill down at the component level. This will give you the most flexibility and allow administrators to manage more entities.

Resource Management

In a traditional server environment, there is a one-to-one relationship between the application and the systems resources. In a virtualized environment, this is not the case. To effectively and efficiently manage resource allocation, you must, at the very least, have tools that monitor resource utilization so that you can move applications and/or resources around if you need to. The number-one reason, but not the only one, for application performance decreasing in a virtualized environment is too little memory. Remember that CPU utilization is only part of the calculation — a server running at 10% CPU utilization could have an I/O bottleneck.

Q   Does the management system provide the ability to monitor resource utilization?

 Monitoring resource utilization, especially in a virtual environment, is imperative and can be tricky. Without this capability, application environments can easily clash for resources, bringing all applications to a grinding halt.

Monitoring the VMs themselves is extremely important, but be careful where you look for utilization information. The OS inside a virtual machine may report utilizing 80% of its memory when the virtual machine may only show 25% utilization because of some of the advanced resource-management techniques that virtualization software employs.

Q   Does your management system automate load balancing of VMs across or within a group of physical servers based on utilization and/ or other criteria? How much granularity is there? Can you define policies for automation, or is the definition purely percentage-based?

 If you plan to propagate hundreds of virtual machines, tweaking each virtual environment will become overwhelming for administrators.

TIP

Investigate what advanced management features are included in or offered by the various virtualization environments you are considering. Examples include the ability to move running virtual machines to other host servers, automate load balancing, set policies for dynamic resource management, and automate intelligent use of resource pools. As virtualization software products mature, these advanced features are becoming the key differentiators between virtual environments.

Clustering

Resource pools and *clustering* are often used interchangeably but, in fact, are quite different. Resource pools are created so the resources from within the pool can be allocated to virtual machines or applications by policy-driven software rather than by hand. Clustering, on the other hand, is when multiple physical or virtual entities are used to address a *single* task. Specific tasks include clustering for high availability or to solve a computational complex problem, as with high performance computing. Often, clustering implementations will draw their resources from resource pools.

High Availability Clustering

Most blade products have a great deal of redundancy built in (dual ports, etc.). However, even with redundancy on the blade and within the chassis, parts fail.

Fortunately, the high density of blade environments makes them ideal for creating failover capabilities within a single blade chassis or over a distance. Planning for failover from the very beginning is an essential part of any best-practices list. Adding virtualization to the blade increases the business impact associated with blade failing. Instead of just one application failing, there are now multiple virtual machines and their applications failing, affecting potentially hundreds of users.

Q   Does your management or virtualization software include high availability (HA) clustering?

> **Most vendors who provide management software also provide high availability clustering solutions. These solutions are often separate from other clustering solutions a vendor may provide.**

Q   Will you have local disks on your blades or will you use anonymous (diskless) blades?

> **The component on a blade most likely to fail is the disk(s). It has the most moving parts. If you plan to have local disks, dual mirrored disks should be implemented for HA.**

Q   Does the HA solution support auto-failover at a blade level? At a VM level?

> **Not all HA solutions support an auto-failover capability. Even fewer support auto-failover for a virtual environment, but most vendors are heading that way.**

Q   Does failover have to be an identical hardware configuration?

> **Some HA solutions require failover to an identical hardware configuration — identical chipsets, memory configuration, and so on. Other solutions will fail over to an equal or greater hardware configuration, especially in an active-active (both servers running their own set of applications) HA environment.**

TIPS

- Plan for and implement at least a blade-level high availability scenario, especially for mission critical applications. You may have to purchase an HA solution in addition to your OS or virtualization software as an add-on.

- Seamless HA failover for any software environment and especially for VM environments is dependent upon shared storage/data environments between both hosts and the storage. The easiest way to do this is with a SAN, NAS, or a clustered file system.

- Verify whether movement of the virtual environment from one blade to another requires an identical hardware environment.

- Software that migrates an environment from one blade to another is usually sold separately from the base blade or virtualization management solution.

High Performance Computing Clusters

Creating a cluster, whether for HA or for HPC (high performance computing), within a bladed or virtual environment works well. The high density and interchangeability of the blades (or virtual environments) makes an ideal environment to pull resources together to address a single task.

Q   Do you or will you implement clustering? At a blade level? At a VM level? At a data level?

 Clusters can be created between multiple blades or even multiple VMs. However, specific clustering software will be required.

Data clustering is often called *clustered file systems* or *global file systems*. This allows for multiple, clustered servers (either physical or virtual) to gain access to the same file system space and its data.

Q   Does your blade/management environment support SMP? If so, with how many blades/processors? Is it hardware-based or software-based?

 Both hardware-based and virtual SMP can be configured. Hardware-based SMP can often be provisioned dynamically, allowing for high performance and dynamic resource-sharing. Virtual SMP can be performed dynamically between VMs, making it easy to configure but at lower performance.

Q   Do you run clustered applications?

> **Relatively few commercial applications can take advantage of a clustered environment. If you use such an application, (such as Oracle 10g) you may want to take advantage of this on your blade system.**

Q   Do you or will you develop your own parallel applications?

> **If you have your own clustered applications or plan to develop your own parallel applications, you will have to purchase additional parallel compilers and debuggers as well as implement a global/clustered file system.**

TIPS

- **Check to see whether your vendor supports clustering across VMs.**
- **Blade vendors that support hardware SMP implement the SMP in different ways. Discuss SMP capabilities with your blade vendors to understand the value and limitations of the implementation.**

Resource Pools

Resource pooling is often implemented as a methodology for viewing IT resources. It is recommended, especially as the number of resources increases, that software be used to monitor and manage the resources, including automated policy-based resource managers.

Q   Do you or will you implement resource pooling? At a blade level? At a VM level? At a storage level? At a data level?

> **All resources within a blade chassis can be considered simply pools from which resources will be allocated as applications require. This can be done for hardware resources such as processors, memory, and disk, or at a higher level as virtual machines.**

TIPS

- For ease of management, all blades within a pool should be identical configurations and diskless. This approach removes most of the state from the blade, making the blades interchangeable.

- Resource pooling can also be done at a storage level, where the storage containers are accessed by many different blades via a SAN. However, if you need to pool data — that is, give data-level access to many different blades — either a NAS device or a clustered (aka global) file system is necessary.

Licensing

It is important to verify software licensing for both your blade systems and your virtual machines (if using virtualization). Some software vendors have changed their licensing to account for virtual machines and some still base their licensing on CPUs. Microsoft is accommodating virtual machines with concurrent licensing — that is, concurrently running virtual machines. If you have created virtual machines but they are not running (or active), they do not require a license. For example, Microsoft's licensing as of October 1, 2006 accommodates the use of VMs as follows:

Windows Server — Standard Edition: One license per running instance (either VMs or physical server)

Windows Server — Enterprise Edition: Up to four running instances (either VMs or physical server)

Windows Server — Datacenter Edition: Unlimited running instances (either VMs or physical server)

NOTE This information is highly subject to change, and may not reflect Microsoft's current licensing. Please check with Microsoft http://www .microsoft.com/licensing/mplahome.mspx **to verify current licensing.**

Q   How do your OS and application licenses apply in a virtual environment? In an environment using stateless, anonymous blades?

Not all software vendors have decided how they want to license their software within a virtual environment. Licenses can be based on the number of physical servers, the number of sockets, the number of cores, or even the number of concurrent environments being run. Vendors are in the midst of changing their licensing schemes, so it is important to understand how the virtual environment will affect your current licenses.

Q   Are you using management software that tracks software licenses?

Just as not all software vendors have updated their licenses, not all management applications that track software licenses have been updated to support new schemes or virtualization.

TIPS

- Ask your OS and application vendors what their licensing policy is for virtual environments. Is the licensing based on physical CPUs? Concurrent environments or total environments?

- Talk to your vendor about how (or if) your management software tracks licenses in a virtual environment.

Conclusion

Blade systems together with virtualization provide many operating options. With those options come many choices to make in implementing solutions. This chapter offers questions to ask yourself and your potential vendors. It also provides implementation tips for blades and virtualization to help avoid pitfalls and blind alleys.

This chapter completes Part III of this book. Part IV "Solutions," starts with suggestions for how to differentiate between the various vendors and solutions and moves into a more in-depth analysis of the major blade system and virtualization offerings in the market.

Differentiating and Selecting Products

With the knowledge of the basic architectures of blade systems and virtualization solutions, along with an understanding of your individual requirements and the considerations necessary for your environment, the next step is product evaluation and selection. This chapter provides a methodology for this process, including matrices to use as a starting point for an analysis of architectural approaches and features and how they map to your requirements. The features listed in these matrices can be used as core items in a checklist or a request for proposal (RFP). The matrices here cover features available by product as of late 2006, and, of course, they will need to be updated before any product selection should be made. (Check www.focusonsystems.com.)

In addition to the matrices presented in this chapter, several other sections of this book will be helpful in making product selections. Chapter 16, "Key Vendor and Product Analysis," offers overviews and analysis of the major product offerings. Chapter 17, "Case Studies," presents a variety of case studies based on user implementations of blade systems and virtualization software, ranging from smaller environments with tens of blades to very large implementations with thousands of blades and multiple blade vendors. Additional product information from the vendors is also included in Appendix A, "Vendor and Product Information."

Blade System Selection

As the blade server market continues to evolve, the range of product options is expanding significantly. Although early blade products used only low-power chips (due largely to power and cooling issues) and blades did not offer equivalent capabilities to traditional servers, this is no longer the case. Blades now offer similar functions to rack-mounted servers in terms of processor speeds, memory, and so on, while also offering the benefits of reduced space, shared components, improvements in power and cooling, and more.

Blade System Vendors

Blade offerings are now available from all the major server vendors, including IBM, HP, Dell, Sun, and Hitachi, as well as a number of interesting emerging-technology vendors, such as Egenera, Verari, PANTA Systems, and Rackable. A number of differences exist in architectural design, particularly in the approaches to storage (on-blade and/or SAN-based), networking, I/O (use of switch modules, pass-thru, pooled HBAs and NICs, and use of standardized PCI Express cards), and power and cooling (varying hardware designs and software tools).

Blade Features Matrix

The matrix in Figure 15.1 lists the major blade vendors, their chassis and blade server products, and their respective features. It identifies relationships between the chassis and blades, and the suggested application environments for the various blades. Hardware features and options are also described, along with environmental aspects such as power and cooling.

This section describes the features outlined in the matrix and how to interpret them. The matrix format can be reproduced and used for RFPs or other types of selection processes.

Vendor: Lists the vendors that offer blade solutions.

Product (Blade Chassis): Lists the available blade chassis for each vendor. Entries in this row describe the chassis-level features, such as switch modules, power and cooling capabilities, and the range of CPU speeds for blades in that chassis.

Blade(s): Describes the blades available for each chassis, and the features and options for each blade. For some vendors, there is only one blade choice, with varying configurations of processor, memory, and so on. Other vendors define various configurations as separate blade models. In the case of Egenera, they have special-function blades including their cBlade (control blade), sBlade (switch blade) and their pBlade (processor blade). More information about these blades is described in Chapter 16, "Key Vendor and Product Analysis."

Operating Systems Supported: Lists the supported operating systems for each offering — Windows, Red Hat Linux, SUSE Linux, Solaris, and so on.

Server Scale-out Applications: Not all blade systems are ideal for scale-out applications. Many that are have integrated load-balancing Ethernet switches. Web hosting is an example of server scale-out applications.

High Performance Computing (HPC): Applications that require very high performing cores and floating-point processors, scalable memory, and fast I/O can expect a blade marked "Yes" to work well in the environment, either as a single blade or as part of an HPCC.

High Performance Computing Clusters (HPCC): High performance computing clusters are used with applications that are *cluster-aware* — that is, they can distribute the application workload across a number of systems or processors to get the work done faster and more efficiently than on a single system/processor. In addition to the attributes of HPC blades, blade solutions for HPCC support an inter process communications (IPC) capability across high-speed interconnect, such as 10GigE, InfiniBand, or Myrinet. Blades with a "Yes" in this column work well in an HPCC environment and have high-speed interconnect support.

High Availability (HA): This column presents the HA features of the chassis and blades, such as N+1 redundancy, which components are hot-swappable, which components are redundant, and so on.

SMP Support (Max. #): Symmetric multiprocessing is often supported between cores on a single blade and, in some cases, by combining two or more blades within a chassis. The max. number is the maximum number of processors (cores) that can be grouped for SMP and if multiple blades can be combined into an SMP group.

Virtualization HW Assist: Lists support on the blade for chipsets that provide hardware-assisted virtualization, such as the Intel VT or AMD-V.

Virtualization SW Supported: Lists the server virtualization solutions supported, including hypervisors, (VMware ESX, Xen 3.0, MS Windows Server Virtualization), hosted approaches (VMware GSX, Microsoft Virtual Server), and OS partitioning (SWsoft, Solaris).

Virtualized or Pooled I/O (Networking and Storage) Capabilities: Lists the type of support available in the product for the use of virtualized I/O and/or pooled World Wide Names or MAC addresses. Some of these approaches allow multiple blades to share the use of a smaller group of HBAs or NICs, reducing the number of physical HBAs or NICs. Some approaches still use HBAs and/or NICs on each blade but create a pool of virtual World Wide Names or MAC addresses to be used by the blades, simplifying configuration issues. Includes support for N-Port ID Virtualization (NPIV).

Supported Interconnect — GigE, 10GigE, IB (2X, 4X...), FC (2,4,8), etc.: Lists the types of interconnects supported within the chassis and/or on each blade.

Interconnect Method — On-blade chip, Mezzanine Card, PCI Card: Describes the interconnect method used on the blade — either an onboard (on-blade) GbE NIC, a mezzanine card Fibre Channel HBA, a mezzanine card InfiniBand HCA, or use of some number of allocated slots in the chassis with standard PCI Express cards, which might be FC HBAs, high-speed NICs, or other PCI Express cards.

Switch-Module Types GbE, 10GbgE, IB (2X, 4X...), FC (2, 4, 8): Lists the types of switch modules available (standard or as options) within the chassis. "External switch" here indicates a chassis that does not support the use of switch modules, but rather the blades pass through to an external switch.

Switch Module Vendors: Lists the manufacturers of the switch modules available for this chassis.

CPU Chipsets: This column lists CPU chipsets and how many are supported on the blade (such as Intel Xeon, Intel Xeon Low Power [Sossaman], Intel Xeon Dual Core [Woodcrest], Intel E7230, Intel 5000X, Itanium, AMD Opteron DDR1, AMD Opteron DDR2, AMD Opteron DDR2, POWER PC 270, POWER 970MP, Sun SPARC).

Processor Speed: Lists the processor speed or range of speeds supported on the blade in GHz.

Max. Memory: Lists the maximum amount of memory supported on each type of blade.

Graphics Capabilities: Lists whether the blades support advanced graphics capabilities and if so, at what level.

Onboard Storage (Max. Size): Indicates whether the blade supports onboard storage, and if so, what the maximum size (in GBs).

Storage Interfaces: Lists onboard storage and storage networking interfaces supported on the blade (for example, SCSI, SAS, SATA, FC SAN, iSCSI hardware initiators, iSCSI software initiators).

Power Requirements: Shows the range of power requirements, in watts.

Cooling Potential: Indicates the cooling potential in BTUs.

Mgmt. Software: Lists the management software available from the blade-system vendor for managing software, firmware, and hardware components (including power and thermal management).

Figure 15.1-1a: Blade-features matrix

Vendor	Product (Chassis)	Blade(s)	Operating Systems Supported	Server Scale-out applications	High Performance Computing (HPC)	High Performance Cluster Computing (HPCC)
Dell	PowerEdge Modular Blade Chassis					
		PowerEdge 1955	Microsoft Windows , Red Hat Linux, Novell SUSE Linux	Yes	Yes	Yes
Egenera	BladeFrame ES	2 x c/sBlades		Yes		
		Up to 6 pBlades	Microsoft Windows, Red Hat Linux, Novell SUSE Linux, Sun Solaris	Yes	Not really a fit but could be done	Support for Microsoft and Linux Clusters across pBlades
	BladeFrame EX	2 cBlades, 2 sBlades		Yes	Not really a fit but could be done	
		Holds up to 24 pBlades	Microsoft Windows, Red Hat Linux, Novell SUSE Linux, Sun Solaris	Yes	Not really a fit but could be done	Support for Microsoft and Linux Clusters across pBlades and BladeFrame Farm
Hitachi	BS1000 Chassis			Yes	Yes	Yes
		Hitachi Blade Symphony Dual Core Intel® Xeon® Processor 2 Socket Blade	Microsoft Windows, Red Hat Linux	Yes, - Blade Architecture - Scale OUT Intel® Xeon® Processor Blades	Yes - 2Way SMP Intel® Xeon® Processor - 16GB Memory per blade - PCI Express Slots	Yes - 2Way SMP Intel® Xeon® Processor - 16GB Memory per blade - PCI Express Slots for Infiniband cards
		Hitachi Blade Symphony Dual Core Intel® Itanium® 2 Processor 2 Socket Blade	Microsoft Windows Red Hat Linux SUSE Linux	Yes, - Blade Architecture - Scale UP and OUT Intel® Itanium® 2 Processor blades	Yes - 2 to 16Way SMP Intel® Itanium® 2 Processor blades - 32GB Memory per blade (128GB @ 16ways) - PCI Express Slots	Yes - 2 to 16Way SMP Intel® Itanium® 2 Processor blades - 32GB Memory per blade (128GB @ 16ways) - PCI Express Slots for Infiniband cards

Source: Focus Consulting

Figure 15.1-1b: Blade-features matrix

High Availability (HA)	SMP Support (max #)	Virtualization HW Assist	Virtualization SW Supported	Virtualized I/O (networking and storage) capabilities	Supported Interconnect - GbE, 10GbE, IB(2X, 4X, etc) FC (2,4,8), etc	Interconnect method - on-blade chip, mezzanine card, PCI (ex) card
					GbE, 4X IB, FC4	
Yes	None	Uses Intel VT Technology	VMware (ESX, GSX, etc.), MS Virtual Server, Xen	On-Board management controller can share an IP address with the dual GB NICs	GbE, 4X IB, FC4	mezzanine HBAs, on blade GbE NICs
N + 1 hardware HA across BladeFrame, Warm pBlade Technology, Full Disaster Recovery Capability				pBlades use virtual connections to HBAs and NICs on cBlades, allowing reduced # of HBAs and NICs	2 pairs of redundant GbE, 2 pair redundant FC	cBlades use mezzainine HBA and NICs
Yes	pBlades with up to 4 CPUs, dual core both AMD and Intel	Support for Intel VT and AMD Pacifica	VMware (GSX, with ESX available by 2007), SWSoft, MS Virtual Server, Xen(2007)	Yes		no HBAs or NICs on pBlades
N + 1 hardware HA across BladeFrame and Blade Farm, Warm pBlade Technology, Full Disaster Recovery Capability				pBlades use virtual connections to HBAs and NICs on cBlades, allowing reduced # of HBAs and NICs	8 pairs of redundant GbE, 2 pair redundant FC	cblades use mezzainine HBA and NICs
Yes	pBlades with up to 4 CPUs, dual core both AMD and Intel	Support for Intel VT and AMD Pacifica	VMware (GSX, with ESX available by 2007), SWSoft, MS Virtual Server, Xen(2007)	Yes		no HBAs or NICs on pBlades
Yes - Redundant FAN, Switch, Power Supply and Management Modules	SMP Blade Interconnect Midplane with 2 blades	Yes (Hitachi Embedded [Only for VT-i])	NA		GbE Ethernet PCI-X / PCI-express (4 Lane) Slots FC 4Gbps Switch	GbE NIC PCI-Express (4 Lane)
Yes - N+M Cold Standby Fail-Over	2 Sockets (4way)	Yes (Intel® VT-x)	Yes Vmware	No	GbE Ethernet PCI-X / PCI-express (4 Lane) Slots FC 4Gbps Switch	GbE NIC PCI-Express (4 Lane)
Yes - N+M Cold Standby Fail-Over	8 Sockets (16way)	Yes (Intel® VT-I / Hitachi Embedded)	No	Virtualized HBA and NIC	GbE Ethernet PCI-X / PCI-express (4 Lane) Slots FC 4Gbps Switch	GbE NIC PCI-Express (4 Lane)

Figure 15.1-1c: Blade-features matrix

Vendor	Product (Chassis)	Blade(s)	Switch Module Types GbE, 10GbE, IB(2X, 4X...) FC (2,4,8)	Switch Module Vendors	CPU Chipsets
Dell	PowerEdge Modular Blade Chassis		4X Infiniband, FC4, Ethernet Passthru, Ethernet Switch	Brocade, McData, Dell, PowerConnect, Cisco, TopSpin InfiniBand	
		PowerEdge 1955			Intel Xeon Dual Core; Xeon Quad Core; Xeon Low Volt; Intel 5000p Chipset
Egenera	BladeFrame ES	2 x c/sBlades	c-blades connect to external switch	External Switch	
		Up to 6 pBlades			Intel and AMD
	BladeFrame EX	2 cBlades, 2 sBlades	c-blades connect to external switch	External Switch	
		Holds up to 24 pBlades			Intel and AMD
Hitachi	BS1000 Chassis		2 - L2 Gigabit Ethernet Switches and 2 - 4Gbps Brocade Switch or 2 - 8 Slot PCI-X Modules or 2 - 8 Slot PCI-Express Modules	Hitachi. Other switch applications under development	
		Hitachi Blade Symphony Dual Core Intel® Xeon® Processor 2 Socket Blade	2 - 10/100/1GbE Onboard NIC Max 4 PCI-x slots or 2 PCI-Express	Hitachi. Other switch applications under development	Intel®
		Hitachi Blade Symphony Dual Core Intel® Itanium® 2 Processor 2 Socket Blade	8 - 10/100/1GbE Onboard NIC Max 16 PCI-x slots or 8 PCI-Express	Hitachi. Other switch applications under development	Intel®

Source: Focus Consulting

Figure 15.1-1d: Blade-features matrix

Processor Speed	Max Memory	Graphics Capabilities	Onboard Storage (max size)	Storage Interfaces	Power Requirements	Cooling Potential	Mgmt SW
					All Power and cooling requirements are different per customized configuration. See dell.com for more info.	All Power and cooling requirements are different per customized configuration. See dell.com for more info.	Dell OpenManage plus complete integration into third party management tools such as Microsoft, Altiris and Novell
Latest Intel Processors	32GB FBD DIMMS	ATI 16MB Video Card	292GB - SAS	SATA or SAS	All Power and cooling requirements are different per customized configuration. See dell.com for more info.	All Power and cooling requirements are different per customized configuration. See dell.com for more info.	Dell OpenManage plus complete integration into third party management tools such as Microsoft, Altiris and Novell
		Not Supported	SAN	Fibre Channel, iSCSI ('07)	Configuration Dependant	Configuration Dependant	PAN Manager
Intel 2.2GHz - 3.6GHz AMD 2.4GHz - 2.8GHz	64GB per pBlade						
		Not Supported	SAN	Fibre Channel, iSCSI ('07)	Configuration Dependant	Configuration Dependant	PAN Manager
Intel 2.2GHz - 3.6GHz AMD 2.4GHz - 2.8GHz	64GB per pBlade						
					343 - 730W	Cooling information unavailable at print time.	Hitachi Blade Symphony Server Conductor
1.60GHz/4MB 2.33GHz/4MB 3.0GHz/4MB	16GB (8 Slots)	PCI card graphics can be supported if required	219GB	SAS	247 - 337W	Cooling information unavailable at print time.	Hitachi Blade Symphony Server Conductor
1.40GHz/12MB 1.60GHz/18MB 1.60GHz/24MB	128GB (64 Slots)	PCI card graphics can be supported if required	None (876GB Storage Expansion Blade option available)	SCSI (for storage expansion blade)	375W	Cooling information unavailable at print time.	Hitachi Blade Symphony Server Conductor

Figure 15.1-2a: Blade-features matrix

Vendor	Product (Chassis)	Blade(s)	Operating Systems Supported	Server Scale-out applications	High Performance Computing (HPC)	High Performance Cluster Computing (HPCC)
HP	HP BladeSystem p-Class Chassis					
		BL20p	Microsoft Windows , Red Hat Linux, Novell SUSE Linux, XEN, Novell Open Enterprise Server, Novell NetWare, VMWare ESX Server	Yes	N/A	Yes
		BL25p	Microsoft Windows, Red Hat Linux, Novell SUSE Linux, Novell Open Enterprise Server, Sun Solaris, VMWare ESX Server	Yes	N/A	Yes
		BL35p	Microsoft Windows, Red Hat Linux, Novell SUSE Linix, Novell Open Enterprise Server, Sun Solaris, VMWare ESX Server	Yes	N/A	Yes
		BL45p	Microsoft Windows, Red Hat Linux, Novell SUSE Linux, Novell Open Enterprise Server, Sun Solaris, VMWare ESX Server	Yes	Yes	Yes
		BL60p	Microsoft Windows, Red Hat Linux	Yes	Yes	Yes
	HP BladeSystem c-Class Chassis					
		BL460c	Microsoft Windows, Red Hat Linux, Novell SUSE Linux, Novell Open Enterprise Server, Novell NetWare, VMWare ESX Server	Yes	Yes	Yes
	c-Class	BL480c	Microsoft Windows, Red Hat Linux, Novell SUSE Linux, XEN, Novell Open Enterprise Server	Yes	Yes	Yes

Source: Focus Consulting

Figure 15.1-2b: Blade-features matrix

High Performance Cluster Computing (HPCC)	High Availability (HA)	SMP Support (max #)	Virtualization HW Assist	Virtualization SW Supported	Virtualized I/0 (networking and storage) capabilities	Supported Interconnect - GbE, 10GbE, IB(2X, 4X, etc) FC (2,4,8), etc
Yes	Yes	No	Yes	VMware, Xen, MS Virtual Server	No	2 Integrated HP NC373i PCI-X Gigabit Multifunction NICs 2 Option Dual HP NC374m Gigabit Multifunction NICs or Dual HP NC320m Gigabit NICs 1 - 10/100T iLO NIC dedicated to management
Yes	Yes	No	Yes	VMware, Xen, Micro-soft Virtual Server	No	4 PCI-X Gigabit ports (embedded) with WOL and PXE 1 - 10/100 iLO port dedicated to management
Yes	Yes	No	No	VMware, Xen, MS Virtual Server	No	2 - 10/100/1000T NICs 1 Dedicated iLO Port
Yes	Yes	No	Yes	VMware, Xen, Micro-soft Virtual Server	No	4 - 10/100/1000T ports, 1 Dedicated iLO port
Yes	Yes	No	No		No	4 Broadcom Gigabit Ethernet ports 1 - 10/100T iLO NIC dedicated to management
Yes	Yes	No	Yes	VMware, Xen, MS Virtual Server	Virtual Connect - allows sharing of pool of virtual WWN and MAC addresses	2 NICs, plus can support: 2 mezzanine cards, 2 infiniband ports, 6 NIC ports, 4 fibre channel ports, or a combination the above
Yes	Yes	No	Yes	VMware, Xen, Micro-soft Virtual Server	Virtual Connect - allows sharing of pool of virtual WWN and MAC addresses	4 NICs, plus can support 3 mezzaninie cards, 3 infiniband ports, 12 NICs, 6 fibre channel ports, or a combination of the above.

Figure 15.1-2c: Blade-features matrix

Vendor	Product (Chassis)	Blade(s)	Switch Module Types GbE, 10GbE, IB(2X, 4X...) FC (2,4,8)	Switch Module Vendors	CPU Chipsets
HP	HP BladeSystem p-Class Chassis		HP GbE2 Interconnect Switch	Cisco, Brocade	
		BL20p			Intel Xeon processor 5160 - Dual-Core/ 3.0 GHz / 1333 MHz FSB Intel Xeon processor 5150 - Dual-Core/ 2.66 GHz / 1333 MHz FSB Intel Xeon processor 5140 - Dual-Core/ 2.33 GHz / 1333 MHz FSB Intel Xeon processor 5130 - Dual-Core/ 2.0 GHz / 1333 MHz FSB Intel Xeon processor 5120 - Dual-Core/ 1.86 GHz / 1333 MHz FSB Intel Xeon processor 5110 - Dual-Core/ 1.6 GHz / 1333 MHz FSB Intel Xeon processor 5080 - Dual-Core/ 3.73 GHz / 1066 MHz FSB Intel Xeon processor 5060 - Dual-Core/ 3.2 GHz / 1066 MHz FSB Intel Xeon processor 5050 - Dual-Core/ 3.0 GHz / 667 MHz FSB
		BL25p			Single-Core AMD OpteronTM Model 254 (2.8 GHz) Single-Core AMD OpteronTM Model 252 (2.6 GHz) Single-Core AMD OpteronTM Model 250 (2.4 GHz) Dual-Core AMD OpteronTM Model 285 (2.6 GHz) Dual-Core AMD OpteronTM Model 280 (2.4 GHz) Dual-Core AMD OpteronTM Model 275 (2.2 GHz) Dual-Core AMD OpteronTM Model 270 (2.0 GHz) Dual-Core AMD OpteronTM Model 265 (1.8 GHz)
		BL35p			Dual-Core AMD Opteron™ Model 280 (2.4 GHz - 68W) Dual-Core AMD Opteron™ Model 275 (2.2 GHz - 68W) Dual-Core AMD Opteron™ Model 270 (2.0 GHz - 68W) Dual-Core AMD Opteron™ Model 265 (1.8 GHz - 68W)
		BL45p			Single-Core AMD Opteron™ Model 852 (2.6GHz) Single-Core AMD Opteron™ Model 854 (2.8GHz) Dual-Core AMD Opteron™ Model 865 (1.8GHz) Dual-Core AMD Opteron™ Model 870 (2.0GHz) Dual-Core AMD Opteron™ Model 875 (2.2GHz) Dual-Core AMD Opteron™ Model 880 (2.4GHz) Dual-Core AMD Opteron™ Model 885 (2.6GHz)
		BL60p			Intel Itanium® 2 1.6GHz 3MB cache (Madison 9M)
	HP BladeSystem c-Class Chassis		Cisco Catalyst Blade Switch 3020, HP GbE2c Ethernet blade Switch, Brocade 4Gb SAN Switch	Cisco, Brocade	
		BL460c			Intel® Xeon® Processor 5160 - Dual core / 3.00 GHz / 1333MHz FSB Intel® Xeon® Processor 5150 - Dual core / 2.66 GHz / 1333MHz FSB Intel® Xeon® Processor 5140 - Dual core / 2.33 GHz / 1333MHz FSB Intel® Xeon® Processor 5130 - Dual core / 2.03 GHz / 1333MHz FSB (1) Intel® Xeon® Processor 5120 - Dual core / 1.86 GHz / 1066MHz FSB (1) Intel® Xeon® Processor 5110 - Dual core / 1.6 GHz /1066MHz FSB Intel® Xeon® Processor 5063 - Dual core / 3.20MV GHz / 1066MHz FSB Intel® Xeon® Processor 5050 - Dual core / 3.00 GHz / 667MHz FSB (1) [Note: (1) Available through CTO or specials only]
	c-Class	BL480c			Intel Xeon Processor 5160 - Dual-core/ 3.00 GHz/ 1333MHz FSB Intel Xeon Processor 5150 - Dual-core/ 2.66 GHz/ 1333MHz FSB Intel Xeon Processor 5140 - Dual-core/ 2.33 GHz/ 1333MHz FSB Intel Xeon Processor 5130 - Dual-core/ 2.00 GHz/ 1333MHz FSB (1) Intel Xeon Processor 5120 - Dual-core/ 1.86 GHz/ 1066MHz FSB (1) Intel Xeon Processor 5110 - Dual-core/ 1.60 GHz/ 1066MHz FSB Intel Xeon Processor 5080 - Dual-core /3.73 GHz/ 1066MHz FSB (1) Intel Xeon Processor 5063 - Dual-core /3.20MV GHz/ 1066MHz FSB (1) Intel Xeon Processor 5060 - Dual-core /3.20 GHz/ 1066MHz FSB Intel Xeon Processor 5050 - Dual-core /3.00 GHz/ 667MHz FSB (1) [Note: (1) Available through CTO or specials only]

Source: Focus Consulting

Figure 15.1-2d: Blade-features matrix

Processor Speed	Max Memory	Graphics Capabilities	Onboard Storage (max size)	Storage Interfaces	Power Requirements	Cooling Potential	Mgmt SW
					Rack-centralized External shared redundant hot-plug power	internal fans	
3.0GHz	32GB	ATI RN-50	2 drive bays - 2.5" - size configurable	Hot plug 2.5" SAS Hot plug Serial ATA			ProLiant/Blade Essentials
2.8GHz	32GB max	ATI RN-50	2 drive bays - size configurable	Hot Plug SCSI			ProLiant/Blades essentials
2.4GHz	16GB max	ATI Rage XL	2 drive bays - size configurable	Non-hot plug ATA Non-hot plug SAS			ProLiant/Blade Essentials
2.8GHz	64GB max	ATI RN-50	2 drive bays - size configurable	Hot plug SCSI			ProLiant/Blades essentials
1.6GHz	8GB max	ATI RN-50	2 drive bays - 3.5" ea	SCSI Hot Plug			ProLiant/Blades essentials
		ATI RN-50			Enclosure Based Power	Enclosure fan: HP Active Cool Fan	
3.0GHz	32 GB	ATI RN-50	2 drive bays - size configurable	Small Form Factor Hot Plug Serial Attached SAS or SATA			ProLiant/Blade Essentials
3.73GHz	48GB	ATI RN-50	4 drive bays - size configurable	Small Form Factor Hot Plug Serial Attached SAS or SATA			ProLiant/Blades essentials

Figure 15.1-3a: Blade-features matrix

Vendor	Product (Chassis)	Blade(s)	Operating Systems Supported	Server Scale-out applications	High Performance Computing (HPC)	High Performance Cluster Computing (HPCC)
IBM	BladeCenter (general purpose)	All blades fit into all chassis, except higher power (95W) processor is BladeCenter H only				
	BladeCenter H (high performance)				Yes	Yes
	BladeCenter T (Telco - ruggedized)					
		HS20 - Intel Xeon	Microsoft Windows, Red Hat Linux, Novell, Novell NetWare, Turbolinux	Yes	Yes	Yes
		HS20 ULP	Microsoft Windows, Red Hat Linux, Novell SUSE	Yes	Yes	Yes
		HS21 - Intel Dual Core Xeon	Microsoft Windows, Red Hat Linux, Novell, Novell NetWare	Yes	Yes	Yes
		LS20 - AMD Opteron	Microsoft Windows, Microsoft Windows3, WinXP, Red Hat Linux, Novell, Novell NetWare	Yes	Yes	Yes
		LS21 - AMD Opteron DDR2	Microsoft Windows, Red Hat Linux, Novell, Novell NetWare, Sun Solaris	Yes	Yes	Yes
		LS41 - 4 socket AMD Opteron DDR2	Microsoft Windows, Red Hat Linux, Novell, Novell NetWare, Sun Solaris	Yes	Yes	Yes
		JS20 - IBM PowerPC 970FX Single-core	IBM AIX, Novell SUSE Linux, Red Hat Linux	Yes	Yes	Yes
		JS21 - IBM PowerPC 970MP Single-core	IBM AIX, Novell SUSE Linux, Red Hat Linux	Yes	Yes	Yes (CSM)
		JS21 - IBM PowerPC 970MP Dual-core	IBM AIX, Novell SUSE Linux, Red Hat Linux	Yes	Yes	Yes (CSM)
PANTA Systems	PANTAmatrix shelf (8U - 14 inches tall)	Up to 8 blades; servers dynamically configurable independent of blades	Red Hat Linux, Novell SUSE Linux, Microsoft Windows	Yes	Yes	Yes
	PANTAmatrix	4-socket compute blades	Red Hat Linux, Novell SUSE Linux, Microsoft Windows	Yes	Yes	Yes

Source: Focus Consulting

Figure 15.1-3b: Blade-features matrix

High Performance Cluster Computing (HPCC)	High Availability (HA)	SMP Support (max #)	Virtualization HW Assist	Virtualization SW Supported	Virtualized I/O (networking and storage) capabilities	Supported Interconnect - GbE, 10GbE, IB(2X, 4X, etc) FC (2,4,8), etc
	All blades have 2 connections to the chassis midplane. They also benefit from the highly redundant features of the chassis: redundant power, cooling, switching and management					
Yes					Yes	
Yes	Yes	2	No	Vmware, MS Virtual Server, Xen	N/A	GbE,IB2X,FC2
Yes	Yes	2	No	MS Virtual Server	N/A	GbE,IB2X,FC2
Yes	Yes	2	Intel VT	Vmware, MS Virtual Server, Xen	N/A	10GbE, IB4X, FC8
Yes	Yes	2	No	Vmware, MS Virtual Server, Xen	N/A	GbE,IB2X,FC2
Yes	Yes	2	AMD-V	Vmware, MS Virtual Server, Xen	N/A	10GbE, IB4X, FC4
Yes	Yes	4	AMD-V	Vmware, MS Virtual Server, Xen	N/A	10GbE, IB4X, FC4
Yes	Yes	2	No	N/A	N/A	GbE,IB1X,FC(QLogic 4Gb)
Yes (CSM)	Yes (HACMP)	2	Micro-partitioning	Advanced POWER Virtualization	Virtual I/O Server	10GbE, IB4X, FC4
Yes (CSM)	Yes (HACMP)	2	Micro-partitioning	Advanced POWER Virtualization	Virtual I/O Server	10GbE, IB4X, FC4
Yes	Hot swappable	Up to 16-way and 128GB memory with 2 blades	Yes	Xen, MS Virtual Server	Unlimited virtualized I/O with integrated management; sharing of storage, HBAs and NICs; pooled MAC addresses	IB 4X (2-12 links per server), and HyperTransport (2-4 per server)
Yes	Hot swappable	Up to 16-way and 128GB memory with 2 blades	No	Xen, MS Virtual Server	Unlimited virtualized I/O with integrated management; sharing of storage, HBAs and NICs; pooled MAC addresses	IB 4X (2-12 links per server), and HyperTransport (2-4 per server)

Figure 15.1-3c: Blade-features matrix

Vendor	Product (Chassis)	Blade(s)	Switch Module Types GbE, 10GbE, IB (2X, 4X…) FC (2,4,8)	Switch Module Vendors	CPU Chipsets
IBM	BladeCenter (general purpose)	All blades fit into all chassis, except higher power (95W) processor is BladeCenter H only	Layer 2/3 Cisco Copper Uplink, Layer 2/3 Nortel Fibre Uplink, Layer 2-7 Nortel, Nortel 10Gb Uplink Ethernet, Server Connectivity Module, Copper Pass Through Module, Cisco 1X & 4X InfiniBand, Myrinet, Brocade 10 & 20 port 4Gb Fibre Channel, McDATA 10 & 20 port 4Gb Fibre Channel, QLogic 10 &20 port 4Gb Fibre Channel, Optical Pass Through	Cisco, Nortel, IBM, Brocade, McData, Qlogic	
	BladeCenter H (high performance)				
	BladeCenter T (Telco - ruggedized)				
		HS20 - Intel Xeon			Intel Xeon
		HS20 ULP			Intel Xeon Low power (Sossaman)
		HS21 - Intel Dual Core Xeon			Intel Xeon Dual Core (Woodcrest)
		LS20 - AMD Opteron			AMD Opteron DDR1
		LS21 - AMD Opteron DDR2			AMD Opteron DDR2
		LS41 - 4 socket AMD Opteron DDR2			AMD Opteron DDR2
		JS20 - IBM PowerPC 970FX Single-core	GbE, IB 1X, FC(all vendors)	Cisco, Nortel, IBM, Brocade, McData, Qlogic	PowerPC 970FX
		JS21 - IBM PowerPC 970MP Single-core	GbE, IB 1X, FC(all vendors)	Cisco, Nortel, IBM, Brocade, McData, Qlogic	PowerPC 970MP
		JS21 - IBM PowerPC 970MP Dual-core	GbE, IB 1X, FC(all vendors)	Cisco, Nortel, IBM, Brocade, McData, Qlogic	PowerPC 970MP
PANTA Systems	PANTAmatrix shelf (8U - 14 inches tall)	Up to 8 blades; servers dynamically configurable independent of blades	Internal IB 4X; external GbE, 10GbE, FC (2, 4)	Cisco, SilverStorm, Voltaire	Opteron DDR1 and DDR2
	PANTAmatrix	4-socket compute blades	Internal IB 4X; external GbE, 10GbE, FC (2, 4)	Cisco, SilverStorm, Voltaire	Opteron DDR1

Source: Focus Consulting

Figure 15.1-3d: Blade-features matrix

Processor Speed	Max Memory	Graphics Capabilities	Onboard Storage (max size)	Storage Interfaces	Power Requirements	Cooling Potential	Mgmt SW
			* the Storage/IO expansion unit attaches to a blade and adds an additional 3 hot-swap drives to the blade				Management Module interface and IBM Director with Power Executive
2.8-3.8 GHz	16GB	XGA	146/373GB	SCSI	350W/Blade	1190BTU	
1.67-2.0 GHz	16GB	XGA	146GB	SAS	180W/Blade	615BTU	
1.66-3.0 GHz	32GB	XGA	146/367GB	SCSI	260W/Blade	890BTU	
2.0-2.8 GHz	16GB	XGA	146/367GB	SCSI	240W/Blade	820BTU	
2.0-2.6 GHz	32GB	XGA	146/293GB	SAS	240W/Blade	820BTU	
2.0-2.6 GHz	64GB	XGA	146/367GB	SAS	400W/Blade	1365BTU	
2.2 GHz	8GB	N/A	120GB	IDE	250W	850BTU	
2.7 GHz	16GB	XGA	146GB	SAS	300W	1020BTU	
2.3-2.5 GHz	16GB	XGA	146GB	SAS	308W	1050BTU	
Varies by processor	Up to 512GB	Vizualization blades optional	None; simplified provisioning through diskless blades	All storage interfaces supported via InfiniBand	Up to 3200W per chassis, including blades	Up to 10000 BTUs/ hour per chassis, including blades	PANTA System Manager, with GUI and API; instant server provisioning; restart of servers will automatically use spare blades, retaining the same I/O configuration
Varies by processor	Up to 128GB (64GB/ blade)	Attachment to vizualization blades optional	None; simplified provisioning through diskless blades	All storage interfaces supported via InfiniBand	Up to 375W	Up to 1200 BTUs/hour	PANTA System Manager, with GUI and API; instant server provisioning; restart of servers will automatically use spare blades, retaining the same I/O configuration

Figure 15.1-4a: Blade-features matrix

Vendor	Product (Chassis)	Blade(s)	Operating Systems Supported	Server Scale-out applications	High Performance Computing (HPC)	High Performance Cluster Computing (HPCC)
	PANTAmatrix	2-socket compute blades	Red Hat Linux, Novell SUSE Linux, Microsoft Windows	Yes	Yes	Yes
Rackable Systems	Scale Out Blade Server Series	ScaleOut 1.5	Red Hat Enterprise Linux, Novell SUSE Linux, Microsoft Windows	Yes (Optimal application)	Yes	Yes
Sun	Sun Blade 8000 Chassis					
		Sun Blade 8400	Sun Solaris	Database, applications, consolidation, virtualisation	Analytics	No
Verari Systems	BladeRack 2					
		VB1205	Red Hat Linux, Novell SUSE Linux, Fedora Core, CentOS, Microsoft Windows	Yes	Yes	Yes
		VB1220	Red Hat Linux, Novell SUSE Linux, Fedora Core, CentOS, Microsoft Windows	Yes	Yes	Yes
		VB1505	Red Hat Linux, Novell SUSE Linux, Fedora Core, CentOS, Microsoft Windows	Yes	Yes	Yes
		VB1506	Red Hat Linux, Novell SUSE Linux, Fedora Core, Novell, CentOS, Microsoft Windows	Yes	Yes	Yes
		VB1507	Red Hat Linux, Novell SUSE Linux, Fedora Core, Novell, CentOS, Microsoft Windows	Yes	Yes	Yes
		VB1510	Red Hat Linux, Novell SUSE Linux, Fedora Core, Novell, CentOS, Microsoft Windows	Yes	Yes	Yes
	BladeRack 2 Extended					
		VB1150/1055	Red Hat Linux, Novell SUSE Linux, Fedora Core, Novell, CentOS, Microsoft Windows	Yes	Yes	Yes
		VB1250	Red Hat Linux, Novell SUSE Linux, Fedora Core, Novell, CentOS, Microsoft Windows	Yes	Yes	Yes
		VB1260	Red Hat Linux, Novell SUSE Linux, Fedora Core, Novell, CentOS, Microsoft Windows	Yes	Yes	Yes
		VB1155M	Red Hat Linux, Novell SUSE Linux, Fedora Core, Novell, CentOS, Microsoft Windows	Yes	Yes	Yes
		VB1550	Red Hat Linux, Novell SUSE Linux, Fedora Core, Novell, CentOS, Microsoft Windows	Yes	Yes	Yes

Source: Focus Consulting

Figure 15.1-4b: Blade-features matrix

High Performance Cluster Computing (HPCC)	High Availability (HA)	SMP Support (max #)	Virtualization HW Assist	Virtualization SW Supported	Virtualized I/O (networking and storage) capabilities	Supported Interconnect - GbE, 10GbE, IB(2X, 4X, etc) FC (2,4,8), etc
Yes	Hot swappable	Up to 8-way and 64GB memory	Yes	Xen, MS Virtual Server	Unlimited virtualized I/O with integrated management; sharing of storage, HBAs and NICs; pooled MAC addresses	IB 4X (2-12 links per server), and HyperTransport (2-4 per server)
Yes	Optional high-MTBF DC Power with support for redundant power feeds	No	Yes. Intel VT or AMD V	Yes (Open architecture). E.g. VMware ESX, Xen, SWsoft Virtuozzo	Yes via optional Infiniband interconnect	Dual GbE and out-of-band serial management standard. 10 GbE, Infiniband, FC optional.
			Exploit AMD Opteron			
No	Infiniband	4 dual core processors in 2006, 6+ quad core processors in 2007	Exploit AMD Opteron	VMware	None	GbE, 4X Infiniband, 4Gbps FC
Yes	No	2	No	No	No	GbE, 10GbE, IB (4x/8X), FC (2/4), SolarFlare
Yes	No	8	Yes	Yes	Yes	GbE, 10GbE, IB (4x/8X), FC (2/4), SolarFlare
Yes	No	4	Yes	No	No	GbE, 10GbE, IB (4x/8X), FC (2/4), SolarFlare
Yes	No	4	Yes	No	No	GbE, 10GbE, IB (4x/8X), FC (2/4), SolarFlare
Yes	No	4	Yes	No	No	GbE, 10GbE, IB (4x/8X), FC (2/4), SolarFlare
Yes	No	8	Yes	Yes	Yes	GbE, 10GbE, IB (4x/8X), FC (2/4), SolarFlare
Yes	Yes	2	Yes	Yes	Yes	GbE, 10GbE, IB (4x/8X), FC (2/4), SolarFlare
Yes	Yes	8	Yes	Yes	Yes	GbE, 10GbE, IB (4x/8X), FC (2/4), SolarFlare
Yes	Yes	8	Yes	Yes	Yes	GbE, 10GbE, IB (4x/8X), FC (2/4), SolarFlare
Yes	Yes	2	Yes	Yes	Yes	GbE, 10GbE, IB (4x/8X), FC (2/4), SolarFlare
Yes	Yes	8	Yes	Yes	Yes	GbE, 10GbE, IB (4x/8X), FC (2/4), SolarFlare

Figure 15.1-4c: Blade-features matrix

Vendor	Product (Chassis)	Blade(s)	Switch Module Types GbE, 10GbE, IB(2X, 4X...) FC (2,4,8)	Switch Module Vendors	CPU Chipsets
	PANTAmatrix	2-socket compute blades	Internal IB 4X; external GbE, 10GbE, FC (2, 4)	Cisco, SilverStorm, Voltaire	Opteron DDR2
Rackable Systems	Scale Out Blade Server Series	ScaleOut 1.5	4U per cabinet side available for standard 19" rack compatible external switches	Flexible	All 2-socket x86 architecture cpus (Intel and AMD)
Sun	Sun Blade 8000 Chassis		None - system has passthru	N/A	
		Sun Blade 8400			AMD Opteron in 2006, SPARC in 2007
Verari Systems	BladeRack 2				
		VB1205	GbE,10GbE,IB, FC	HP, Cisco, Force 10, Silverstorm, Qlogic, Foundry	Intel E7230
		VB1220	GbE,10GbE,IB, FC	HP, Cisco, Force 10, Silverstorm, Qlogic, Foundry	Intel 5000X
		VB1505	GbE,10GbE,IB, FC	HP, Cisco, Force 10, Silverstorm, Qlogic, Foundry	AMD 8111
		VB1506	GbE,10GbE,IB, FC	HP, Cisco, Force 10, Silverstorm, Qlogic, Foundry	Nvidia 2200 Pro Chipset
		VB1507	GbE,10GbE,IB, FC	HP, Cisco, Force 10, Silverstorm, Qlogic, Foundry	AMD 8111
		VB1510	GbE,10GbE,IB, FC	HP, Cisco, Force 10, Silverstorm, Qlogic, Foundry	Nvidia 2200 Pro Chipset
	BladeRack 2 Extended				
		VB1150/1055	GbE	HP, Cisco, Force 10, Silverstorm, Qlogic, Foundry	Intel 3000
		VB1250	GbE,10GbE,IB, FC	HP, Cisco, Force 10, Silverstorm, Qlogic, Foundry	Intel 5000X
		VB1260	GbE,10GbE,IB, FC	HP, Cisco, Force 10, Silverstorm, Qlogic, Foundry	Intel 5000X
		VB1155M	GbE,10GbE,IB, FC	HP, Cisco, Force 10, Silverstorm, Qlogic, Foundry	Intel 3000
		VB1550	GbE,10GbE,IB, FC	HP, Cisco, Force 10, Silverstorm, Qlogic, Foundry	Nvidia 2200 Pro Chipset

Source: Focus Consulting

Figure 15.1-4d: Blade-features matrix

Processor Speed	Max Memory	Graphics Capabilities	Onboard Storage (max size)	Storage Interfaces	Power Requirements	Cooling Potential	Mgmt SW
Varies by processor	Up to 64GB (32GB/blade)	Attachment to vizualization blades optional	None; simplified provisioning through diskless blades	All storage interfaces supported via InfiniBand	Up to 325W	Up to 1100 BTUs/hour	PANTA System Manager, with GUI and API; instant server provisioning; restart of servers will automatically use spare blades, retaining the same I/O configuration
Fastest available	Up to 64 GB	Onboard graphics standard. Advanced options via PCI-X/PCI-E card.	2 - 3.5" drives (1.5 TB)	Internal (SATA/SAS/SCSI) or FC card	Configuration dependent	Configuration dependent	Data center-level management: Cittio Watchtower, Industry-standard SNMP-compatible software. Server-level management: Rackable Systems Roamer™ and IPMI.
					7175 Watts for 10 blades plus chassis and all optional components	30,000 BTU	N1
2.8 GHz	64GB 2006, 128GB 2007		2 - SAS disks - size configurable				
3.6GHz	12GB	Onboard VGA	1TB	IDE/SATA/FC SAN	26Kw	40,000+ BTU per Hour	Verari Command Center
3GHz	32GB	Onboard VGA	1TB	SATA/FC SAN	26Kw	40,000+ BTU per Hour	Verari Command Center
3GHz	16GB	Onboard VGA	1.5TB	IDE/SATA/FC SAN	23Kw	40,000+ BTU per Hour	Verari Command Center
3GHz	32GB	Onboard VGA	750GB	IDE/FC SAN	26Kw	40,000+ BTU per Hour	Verari Command Center
3GHz	16GB	Onboard VGA	1.5TB	IDE/FC SAN	23Kw	40,000+ BTU per Hour	Verari Command Center
2.8GHz	64GB	Onboard VGA	750GB	SATA/SAS/FC SAN	26Kw	unavailable at print time.	Verari Command Center
2.6GHz	8GB	Onboard VGA	1.5TB Internal / 36TB Ext.	SATA/SAS	12Kw	unavailable at print time.	Verari Command Center
3GHz	32GB	Onboard VGA or PCI-E Card	1.5TB	SATA/SAS/FC SAN	26Kw	unavailable at print time.	Verari Command Center
3GHz	64GB	Onboard VGA or PCI-E Card	750GB	SATA/SAS/FC SAN	26Kw	unavailable at print time.	Verari Command Center
2.6GHz	8GB	Onboard VGA	1.5TB	SATA	20Kw	unavailable at print time.	Verari Command Center
3GHz	64GB	Onboard VGA or PCI-E Card	750GB	SATA/SAS/FC SAN	26Kw	unavailable at print time.	Verari Command Center

Virtualization Software Selection

As previously discussed, the server virtualization space has changed dramatically over the past few years. The market has gone from the experimental phase, with only one viable product, to a more mature market, with multiple competitive solutions and tools. Most recently, pricing changes (including some free options) and open source offerings have changed the market again.

Server Virtualization Software Vendors

In the beginning, the market was almost completely dominated by VMware, due to the complexity of virtualizing the x86 environment. In the Sun space, Solaris containers allowed partitioning of the Solaris environment. Microsoft entered the space slowly and continues to roll out products to catch up with others. Emerging companies such as SWsoft and Virtual Iron joined in with variations of OS and server virtualization offerings. Virtualization migration and management solution vendors such as PlateSpin also appeared.

The advent of virtualization hardware assists and the release of Xen 3.0 (based on the Xen open source project) in 2006 changed the landscape substantially, making Xen the basis of most other virtualization software and leveling the playing field to a large extent. As this process continues, the differentiation will move from the virtualization approach into the management and services of the virtual environment.

Virtualization-Features Matrix

Figure 15.2 lists the major vendors of server virtualization software (including hypervisors, host approaches, and partitioning products) as well as the primary virtualization management software and utilities. Because this matrix is focused on features analysis for differentiating virtualization software, management products from the blade vendors that assist with virtualization management have not been included. In addition, management products for managing physical environments as well as virtual environments are not included.

This section describes the features outlined in the virtualization matrix and how to interpret them. The matrix format can be reproduced and used for RFPs or other types of selection processes.

Vendor: Lists the vendors that offer server-virtualization solutions and VM management solutions.

Product: Lists the server-virtualization and VM management products from each vendor.

Type of Virtualization: Describes the type of server-virtualization approach — hypervisor, hosted (Windows and/or Linux), or OS partitioning, (or the server virtualization products that are supported).

Supported Processors: Lists the category of processors supported by the product (Intel x86, AMD x86, Intel VT, AMD-V, Sun SPARC, etc.).

Virtualization HW Assist: Describes the relationship to virtualization hardware assists, such as Intel VT and AMD-V — whether such virtualization hardware is required for the product, not required in order to run but utilized for improved performance, or not utilized in any case.

# of CPUs Supported: Lists the maximum number of processors (cores) supported by the server virtualization software. (For this listing, dual-core counts as two CPUs, and two sockets count as two CPUs. Dual-core, two-socket counts as four CPUs.)

RAM Supported: Maximum amount of physical memory supported by the server virtualization software.

Virtual SMP Support (in #of Cores): Maximum number of virtual CPUs supported in an SMP environment (in number of cores).

Supported Guests: Lists the operating systems that are supported as guest operating systems running in the virtual environment.

Paravirtualization/Enlightened Guest OS: Does the VMM support operating systems modifications to make them aware of running in a virtual environment? Paravirtualization typically provides performance improvements for guest operating systems.

Number of VMs per Physical Server: Lists the maximum number of VMs per server — either as a hard-coded limit or as a practical recommended number.

VM Clustering: Describes the clustering capabilities and restrictions within the virtual environment, for both the virtualization software and guest OSs. Also indicates whether clustering is available only within a single physical host, or across multiple hosts.

Migration Utilities: Lists the migration utilities offered for moving from one environment to another, including P2V, V2V, V2P, and Image to Virtual (I2V).

Move Running VMs: Describes the ability or inability to move virtual machines while they are running. Some products allow a full move without stopping operation; some support a move, but require a stop/ quiesce followed by a move and restart; and some do not support move in any way.

Hot Add of Virtual Resources: Lists the types of virtual resources that can be modified during virtual machine operation, such as CPU, amount of memory, virtual networking, and so on.

VM Usage Accounting: Describes any features related to usage statistics for accounting and billing purposes.

Offline VM Disk-Format Manipulation: Indicates whether the virtual environment allows changes to the VM disk (configuration and environment) while the VM is not running.

Granularity of Resource Management (Examples and # of Parameters): Describes the level of granularity available for managing the virtual environment, including changing virtual resources, setting thresholds, and so on. Provides examples of the types of parameters and gives the total number of parameters available.

Workload Performance Monitoring/Mgmt. of VMs: Describes the ability or inability to monitor the performance and manage workloads across virtual machines. The more sophisticated of these products provide policy-based management functions, such as moving virtual machines within or across resource pools based on certain performance thresholds.

Policy-Based Mgmt.: Indicates whether the software allows policies to be set based on specific criteria, with automated actions taken when those criteria (thresholds) are met or exceeded.

Conclusion

Differentiating between available product offerings, narrowing down to a short list and eventually down to a final choice, is a complex process. Understanding your requirements and priorities and incorporating your own experiences with various vendors must come first. With those considerations as a backdrop, the matrices in this chapter present a framework for evaluating various approaches and products. This framework, of course, is no substitute for hands-on evaluation of the products. Rather, it can start the process, providing the basis for an RFP (or less formal selection process), and can help narrow down the choices before any onsite testing and evaluation are performed.

The next chapter discusses the major blade and server virtualization products (available as of late 2006) in more detail and offers assessments of these products, including technical differentiators, technology firsts, unique value propositions, and an overall analysis.

Figure 15.2-1a: Virtualization features matrix

Vendor	Product	Type of Virtualization	Supported Processors	Virtualization HW Assist	# of CPUs supported
VMware	ESX Server	Hypervisor or "bare metal" architecture	Intel x86, AMD x86, Intel -VT, AMD-V.	not required in order to run, but utilized for improved performance with 64-bit guests if it is there	32
	Server (GSX)	Hosted - Windows, Linux	Intel x86, AMD x86, x86-64, Intel -VT, AMD-V.	Experimental support for Intel VT. Not required in order to run, but utilized for improved performance if it is there	16
	Workstation	Hosted - Windows, Linux	Intel®: Celeron®, Pentium® II, Pentium III, Pentium 4, Pentium M (including computers with Centrino™ mobile technology), Xeon™ (including "Prestonia") AMD™: Athlon™, Athlon MP, Athlon XP, Duron™, Opteron™, 64-bit processor support for AMD64 Opteron, Athlon 64 and Intel IA-32e CPU (including "Nocona")	NA	Multiprocessor systems supported
	Virtual Center	works with ESX Server, VMware Server	same as ESX Server	NA	NA
	DRS (Distributed Resource Scheduler)	works with ESX Server	same as ESX Server	same as ESX Server	same as ESX Server
	HA (High Availability)	works with ESX Server	same as ESX Server	same as ESX Server	same as ESX Server
	VMotion	works with ESX Server	same as ESX Server	same as ESX Server	same as ESX Server
	Virtual Consolidated Backup (VCB)	works with ESX Server	same as ESX Server	same as ESX Server	same as ESX Server

Source: Focus Consulting

Figure 15.2-1b: Virtualization features matrix

RAM supported	Virtual SMP Support (in #of cores)	Supported Guests	Para- virtualization/ Enlightened Guest OS	# of VMs per physical server	VM Clustering
64GB	Up to 4 CPUs, which can be dual core	32-bit and 64-bit guest OS, Microsoft Windows, Red Hat Linux, Novell SUSE Linux, Novell NetWare, Sun Solaris.	No	up to 128 powered-on VMs per server	same physical host &across physical hosts. Supports Microsoft® Clustering Services.
64GB	Up to 4 CPUs, which can be dual core	DOS, Microsoft Windows, Red Hat Linux, Novell SUSE Linux, FreeBSD, Mandrake Linux, Turbolinux Linux, Ubuntu Linux, Novell NetWare, Sun Solaris	No	up to 64 powered-on VMs per server	Across physical hosts. Supports MS Clustering Services, MS Network Load Balancing, Veritas Clustering Service, Novell Clustering Services
128 MB minimum (256 MB recommended)	No	DOS, Microsoft Windows, Red Hat Linux, Novell SUSE Linux, Mandrake Linux, Ubuntu Linux, FreeBSD, Sun Java Desktop System, Sun Solaris, Novell NetWare	No		No
NA	NA	NA	NA	No limit	NA
same as ESX Server	same as ESX Server	same as ESX Server	same as ESX Server	same as ESX Server	HA restarts virtual machines affected by hardware failure
same as ESX Server	same as ESX Server	same as ESX Server	same as ESX Server	same as ESX Server	same as ESX Server
same as ESX Server	same as ESX Server	same as ESX Server	same as ESX Server	same as ESX Server	same as ESX Server
same as ESX Server	same as ESX Server	same as ESX Server	same as ESX Server	same as ESX Server	same as ESX Server

Figure 15.2-1c: Virtualization features matrix

Vendor	Product	Migration Utilities	Move running VMs	Hot Add of virtual resources	VM Usage Accounting
VMware	ESX Server	VMware Converter - convert physical environments to VMs, and non-VMware VM formats into VMware VM formats	with VMotion	Yes - Hot add of virtual disks to a running virtual machine to increase available resources or for backup. CPU, memory, network and storage require power off to be added.	All VM monitoring data generated by VirtualCenter can be exoprted to HTML and Excel formats for integration with other reporting tools and offline analysis.
	Server (GSX)	VMware Converter - convert physical environments to VMs, and non-VMware VM formats into VMware VM formats	No	No	All VM monitoring data generated by VirtualCenter can be exoprted to HTML and Excel formats for integration with other reporting tools and offline analysis.
	Workstation	VMware Converter - convert physical environments to VMs, and non-VMware VM formats into VMware VM formats	No	No	No
	Virtual Center	VMware Converter	with VMotion	Hot add of physical resources to resouce pools.	All VM monitoring data generated by VirtualCenter can be exoprted to HTML and Excel formats for integration with other reporting tools and offline analysis.
	DRS (Distributed Resource Scheduler)	VMware Converter	continuously monitors utilization across resource pools and allocates available resources among VMs based on pre-defined rules and policies. Generates recommendation to migrate a specified workload, which is then executed by VMotion.	DRS will automatically balance hod-added physical resources.	NA
	HA (High Availability)	VMware Converter	NA	NA	NA
	VMotion	VMware Converter	Yes	NA	NA
	Virtual Consolidated Backup (VCB)	NA	NA	NA	NA

Source: Focus Consulting

Figure 15.2-1d: Virtualization features matrix

Offline VM Disk Format Manipulation	Granularity of Resource Management (examples & # of parameters)	Workload Performance Monitoring/ Mgmt of VMs	Policy based Mgmt
ESX Server uses VMFS cluster file system which stores and manipulates virtual disk files. Offline VM disk manipulation is not encouraged.	min,max and proportional resource shares-CPU, memory, disk, network bandwidth. Modify running VMs. Dynamically acquire more resources for peaks. CPU capacity prioritization. Allow absolute min level of CPU. Storage I/O traffic prioritization. priority access to storage. I/O traffic prioritized on "fair share" basis. Network Traffic Shaper.priority access to network bandwidth. Network traffic prioritized on a "fair share" basis. Network Traffic Shaper manages VM network traffic to meet peak bandwidth, average bandwidth and burst size constraints.	Command-line and SDKK granular resource tool under ESX service console. VirtualCenter - comprehensive perf monitoring of servers, storage devices, resource pools and virtual machines. detailed performance graphs. Performance metrics defined with several levels of granularity. viewed real time, or across specified time interval. Export to HTML and Excel	VMware DRS continuously monitors utilization across resource pools and intelligently allocates available resources among virtual machines based on predefined rules and policies.
VMware Virtual Disk Manager utility creates,manages, and modifies virtual disk files from command line or scripts.	Allows allocation of portion of VMware Server host memory to each VM. Set size of individual VM's memory in VM settings editor or VMware Management Interface.	Set of counters that work with MS Performance console for collection of performance data from running VMs. (available only on Windows hosts).cannot monitor performance for VMs on Linux hosts. can monitor performance of any guest OS on the Windows host, including Linux guests.	No
VMware Virtual Disk Manager is a utility in VMware Workstation that allows you to create, manage and modify virtual disk files from the command line or within scripts.	No	Set of counters that work with MS Performance console for collection of performance data from running VMs. (available only on Windows hosts).cannot monitor performance for VMs on Linux hosts. can monitor performance of any guest OS on the Windows host, including Linux guests. Monitors reading and writing to virtual disks, memory used by VM, virtual network traffic	No
NA	min,max and proportional resource shares-CPU, memory, disk, network bandwidth. Modify running VMs. Dynamically acquire more resources for peaks. CPU capacity prioritization. Allow absolute min level of CPU. . Storage I/O traffic prioritization. priority access to storage. I/O traffic prioritized on "fair share" basis. Network Traffic Shaper.priority access to network bandwidth. Network traffic prioritized on a "fair share" basis. Network Traffic Shaper manages VM network traffic to meet peak bandwidth, average bandwidth and burst size constraints.	Comprehensive perf monitoring of servers, storage devices, resource pools and virtual machines. detailed performance graphs. Performance metrics defined with several levels of granularity.viewed real time, or across specified time interval. Export to HTML and Excel	VMware DRS continuously monitors utilization across resource pools and intelligently allocates available resources among virtual machines based on predefined rules and policies.
same as ESX Server	Same as ESX Server and VirtualCenter	Same as ESX Server and VirtualCenter	continuously monitors utilization across resource pools and allocates available resources among VMs based on predefined rules and policies. Generates recommendation to migrate a specified workload, which is then executed by VMotion.
same as ESX Server	Same as ESX Server and VirtualCenter	Same as ESX Server and VirtualCenter	NA
same as ESX Server	Same as ESX Server and VirtualCenter	Same as ESX Server and VirtualCenter	NA
VCB provides agentless backup of virtual machines	NA	NA	NA

Figure 15.2-2a: Virtualization features matrix

Vendor	Product	Type of Virtualization	Supported Processors	Virtualization HW Assist	# of CPUs supported
Microsoft	Virtual Server 2005 R2	Hosted - Windows 2003, XP	Intel x86, AMD x86, Intel -VT, AMD-V	R2 - Utilzed, not required	based on host OS. up to 8 (for Standard Edition), up to 64 (for Datacenter Edition)
	Windows Server Virtualization (Windows Server "Longhorn Viridan")	Hypervisor	Intel x86, AMD x86, Intel -VT, AMD-V	Required	Unavailable at time of print
Sun	Solaris	OS Virtualization - Solaris Containers	x86, SPARC	Not required	up to 144
SWSoft	Virtuozzo	OS Virtualization - Windows, Linux	Intel x86, AMD x86, x86-64, Intel -VT, AMD-V	Utlized, not required	16
Virtual Iron	Virtual Iron 3.0/3.1	Hypervisor (Based on Xen 3.0)	Intel -VT, AMD-V	Required	32 Physical
XenSource	Xen™ 3.0	Hypervisor: Xen 3.0	Intel -VT, AMD-V; Pre VT and AMDV for Linux, Sun Solaris, BSD	Required for Windows, not for Linux, BSD, Sun Solaris	64 in Xen 3.0.3
XenSource	XenEnterprise™	Works with any Xen Server	Any Xen Server	Required for Windows, not for Linux or other Xen guests	32
PlateSpin	PowerConvert	works with any VM	x86, any VM	not required	Can migrate VMs on any number of CPUs
PlateSpin	PowerRecon	works with any VM	x86, any VM	not required	Can monitor any number of CPUs

Source: Focus Consulting

Figure 15.2-2b: Virtualization features matrix

RAM supported	Virtual SMP Support (in #of cores)	Supported Guests	Para- virtualization/ Enlightened Guest OS	# of VMs per physical server	VM Clustering
64GB, extensible with Physical Addressing Extensions (PAE)	No	Microsoft Windows, Red Hat Linux, Novell SUSE Linux	No	R2 - up to 64	Up to 8 host systems by leveraging Virtual Server Host Clustering
Unavailable at time of print	yes up to 8 virtual processors per VM	Microsoft Windows, Linux, 64-bit and 32-bit guests	supported	> 64 (exact # unavailable at time of print)	Yes - Details unavailable at print time
up to 1 TB	up to 144	Solaris, Linux (2007)	supported with Linux guest	~500 on a 4-way (limit is 8192)	across physical hosts- Sun Cluster and Veritas Cluster Server
64 GB	16 processors + multi-core	Microsoft Windows, Linux - most distributions including Red Hat Linux, Novell SUSE Linux	NA	100s	Yes - across physical hosts
96GB	Up to 8 CPU's	Virtual Iron, Red Hat Linux, Novell SUSE Linux, Microsoft Windows	No	Max 5 per CPU	Clustering software works with the guests
16 GB	Up to 64	Linux, NetBSD, FreeBSD, OpenBSD, OpenSolaris, Microsoft Windows	supported	Highly Server Dependent; For 2-way typical would be up to 32	virtual block devices; no clustering abstraction
16 GB	32	Red Hat Linux, Novell SUSE Linux, Microsoft Windows	supported	Highly Server Dependent; For 2-way typical would be up to 32	no cluster File System
Can migrate VMs and adjust RAM to any amount post-conversion	As much as VM can support	Any VMs (Microsoft Windows or Linux)	NA	Same as what Virtual Host can support	Supports migrations of clustered environments one node at a time
Can monitor servers with any amount of RAM	As much as VM can support	Any VMs (Microsoft Windows or Linux)	NA	Same as what Virtual Host can support	Can monitor clustered environments but is not currently cluster-aware

Figure 15.2-2c: Virtualization features matrix

Vendor	Product	Migration Utilities	Move running VMs	Hot Add of virtual resources	VM Usage Accounting
Microsoft	Virtual Server 2005 R2	Virtual Server Migration Toolkit (P2V, V2V)	No	No	Microsoft Operations Manager (MOM) 2005 and Systems Management Server (SMS) 2003
	Windows Server Virtualization (Windows Server "Longhorn Viridan")	System Center Virtual Machine Manager	Yes	CPU, Memory, Networking	Unavailable at time of print
Sun	Solaris	Cold migration. No live migration. Third party for P2V.	No	CPU, Memory, Networking, Storage	Yes, if enabled
SWSoft	Virtuozzo	P2V as well as Live Migration (moving between phyiscal servers without downtime)	Yes	Yes in real-time, and also real hardware resources	Yes for CPU, memory, bandwidth and other parameters
Virtual Iron	Virtual Iron 3.0/3.1	Yes	Yes	No	Yes
XenSource	Xen™ 3.0	No P2V	Linux, BSD, OpenSolaris	VCPUs, Memory, VNICs, Vblock	Yes
XenSource	XenEnterprise™	Yes	Not exposed in first version	VCPUs, Memory, VNICs, Vblock	Graphical display of all resources
PlateSpin	PowerConvert	P2V,P2I, V2P, V2V,V2I, I2V,I2P,P2P	yes and w/o shared storage	Reconfiguration occurs during migration	Not applicable
PlateSpin	PowerRecon	P2V,P2I, V2P, V2V,V2I, I2V,I2P,P2P	yes and w/o shared storage	Not applicable	CPU, Network, Disk, Memory historical data / metering

Source: Focus Consulting

Figure 15.2-2d: Virtualization features matrix

Offline VM Disk Format Manipulation	Granularity of Resource Management (examples & # of parameters)	Workload Performance Monitoring/ Mgmt of VMs	Policy based Mgmt
In Virtual Server 2005 R2 SP1	Virtual Machine memory, Virtual hard disk configuration,Virtual hard disk size, Virtual hard disk bus type, Virtual hard disk location, Virtual network adapters, SCSI adapaters,CD / DVD drives connected to the Virtual machines,Scripts associated with the virtual machine, CPU resource allocation,and more	Integrated with MOM and SMS. SMS 2003 SP2 adds- Virtual Server 2005 called out in hardware inventory information, new node called Virtual Machine in SMS admin console,discovery of virtual host/guest relationships	Integrated with MOM
Yes	Unavailable at time of print	Integrated with MOM	Integrated with MOM
Yes	CPU, memory,network I/O, file system size, environment variables (20+ parms)	Third party products which are container aware	Yes, policy engine - Dynamic Resource Pools
Yes	CPU (1/1000th), memory (1/1000th), disk (1 kb), I/O allocation (30+parms), bandwidth (1 kbps)	Yes, alerts at performance levels	Performance management
Yes	Yes	Yes	Yes
No	CPU: share & vcpu; Memory: MB; Block I/O Blk/s; Net: KB/s	Basic, yes	No
Not in first release	Auto-configured from wizards; no user direct manipulaton	Comprehensive	No (open interfaces to higher level mgt)
Planned	NA	Takes configuration information from current environment and uses it to migrate to new environment	Planned
Not applicable	Planned	Matches workloads and resources and creates consolidation / optimization plan	Planned

Key Vendor and Product Analysis

Blade and virtualization products and solutions are continuing to advance and evolve at a rapid pace. It would be impossible to describe all the features and functions of all these products in this book, since it would be out-of-date by the time it went to press. It would also be impossible not to discuss the vendors and products at all. Therefore, this chapter will provide our analysis of the major vendors and their solutions at a high level, from a snapshot in time. This analysis will be aimed at helping to differentiate the unique aspects of the various vendors and solutions, key differentiators and technology firsts, value propositions, major areas where vendors are focused in the market, strategic business relationships, and high-level strengths and limitations.

In addition to our analysis presented in this chapter, Chapter 17, "Case Studies," presents a variety of case studies of users who have implemented many of these solutions. In addition, Appendix A, "Vendor and Product Information," includes information provided by the vendors themselves as of September 2006. Our product analyses in this chapter, the user commentary in Chapter 17, and the vendor information in the appendix should provide a solid foundation for your next steps. However, it will be important to check vendor websites (listed in Appendix A) and to speak with both vendors and users to obtain updated information before making final purchase decisions.

Blade Server Systems

The early days of blades in 2001 were defined by a number of start-up vendors, and shortly thereafter, by the entry of several major vendors. As of 2006 the market is defined by the major server vendors (IBM, HP, Dell, Sun, and Hitachi) along with several smaller innovative technology vendors. The innovators include Egenera (who was one of the first), Rackable Systems, Verari, and PANTA Systems, each of whom has a uniquely different perspective on blade systems. Analysis of all of these vendors follows here, listed in order of market share, according to IDC, as of late 2006.

IBM

With roughly a 40% market share throughout 2006, IBM continues to be the leader in the blade market. IBM entered the blade space early on, in 2002, and has continued to advance their product line in terms of both blade and chassis options. IBM's focus with BladeCenter is to offer better computing performance for less power, cooling, air, and space. With three chassis options, numerous blade options, complete backward-compatibility for all blades across all IBM chassis, and hundreds of third-party options available, IBM offers advantages in several areas.

Creating a Blade Ecosystem

As has been previously discussed, none of the major vendors are willing to create an industry-wide blade standard specification, since they each have their unique differentiation based on their own architecture. That said, IBM has published the specification for their BladeCenter and licenses it to vendors wanting to develop products for BladeCenter. In 2006, IBM and Intel created the Blade.org organization to advance the development of IBM-centric blade solutions and encourage the BladeCenter development effort. These efforts have been very successful in creating an ecosystem of vendors and products for BladeCenter. As of 2006, Blade.org has 75-plus members, with more than 350 vendors licensing the BladeCenter specification. The BladeCenter ecosystem continues to grow and includes a broad selection of hardware and software products such as IP, Fibre Channel, and InfiniBand switches, firewalls, load balancers, and so on, as well as solutions for retail, banking, SMB, and others. IBM also has had significant success delivering on the concept of a "Solution in a Box," with preconfigured, pretested solutions designed for specific industries, such as the Business in a Box for SMBs, Systems Solutions for Branch Banking, and Systems Solutions for Retail Stores.

Long-Term Compatibility with Broad Options

IBM views the BladeCenter chassis as their foundation for the future. The original BladeCenter, BladeCenter T (for Telco), and BladeCenter H (for high performance) chassis are all still offered, with both the original and newer server blades fitting into any chassis (the only exception being that very high-end blades can go only into the high-performance chassis).

IBM offers many configuration choices; processors from low-end processing speeds to high-end processing multicore CPUs, memory up to 32 GB, 32- and 64-bit support, and various I/O interconnects. Options continue to expand, including support for newer chips with virtualization assists (Intel VT and AMD-V) and improved power and cooling techniques, along with advances in software supporting the chip advances. Blade offerings are available based on Intel, AMD, and PowerPC chips. Blades with a snap-in function were introduced in mid 2006, allowing a blade to be upgraded from a one-socket to a two-socket system (for example to go from a two-way to a four-way), targeting database and HPC clustered applications, and benefiting virtualization as well. (The snap-in architecture requires a second blade slot.)

The high-performance chassis, BladeCenter H (see Figure 16.1), introduced in 2006, was the first blade chassis in the industry to include 10GbE in the backplane, as well as 4X InfiniBand. IBM was the first to announce support for the first 10GbE switch module, an OEM product from Blade Network Technologies (BLADE), formerly part of Nortel. IBM was also one of the first major vendors to offer AMD Opteron-based blades.

Figure 16.1: IBM BladeCenter H
Source: IBM

The BladeCenter architecture supports up to 14 server blades per chassis, (chassis range from 7U to 9U for BladeCenter and BladeCenter H) and utilizes a passive midplane. Server blades and hot-swappable, redundant load-balancing power supplies are inserted into the front of the chassis. Shared hot-swap, redundant switch modules, management modules, and blowers are inserted in the back. On-blade storage is available, as is shared storage through NAS or SAN. Switch modules are available for GbE, 4 Gig Fibre Channel, 1x InfiniBand, Myrinet, and 4x InfiniBand. Bridges and gateways are available for IB to FC and Ethernet.

Blade networking options include additional GbE or 10GbE NICs, iSCSI software initiator for boot from SAN, Fibre Channel HBA daughter cards, and InfiniBand HCAs. Standard Ethernet and Fibre Channel implementations require networking adapters on each blade, which connect to the appropriate switch module in the chassis. Virtualized I/O is available through the IB implementation, with gateways and bridges to connect to non-IB devices. Future plans in this area for Fibre Channel include N-port identifier virtualization (NPIV), which will allow sharing of adapters so that the 14 blades share access to 6 HBAs.

Focus on Better Performance for Less Space, Power, and Cooling

As an early entrant into the blade market and a long-time player in the mainframe arena (where power and cooling have long been an issue), IBM is highly attuned to the power and cooling concerns related to blades. Although blade detractors point to cooling issues as the prime barrier to blade acceptance, claiming that blade chassis and racks can be only partially populated (meaning left partially empty) due to cooling problems, IBM, along with other blade vendors and many existing blade customers, disagrees. The largest customer installation of BladeCenter at a single site consists of 5,000 blades, 7,000 worldwide, with racks and chassis fully populated.

IBM's view of cooling is threefold: keep the blade cool (pack to full density), keep the rack cool, and keep the room cool. IBM takes responsibility for the first two of these and provides professional services to help the customer do the last. Feature enhancements that affect blade cooling include increasing the efficiency of the power supply from 65% in a 1U server (where 35% of the power is lost and enters the room in the form of heat) to 91% efficiency in BladeCenter H. (For more information on power efficiency, see Chapter 13, "Power and Cooling.") In addition, BladeCenter H adds chassis-level cooling through what BladeCenter terms "blowers," in addition to blade-level cooling fans. Additional fans were also added in the front to cool power supplies and switches. At the room level, IBM will help with planning and partnering. For example, if the ceiling is too low, the floor is too thin, or there is not enough air, they may suggest water chillers in the room or at the rack level through APC or Liebert. (IBM mainframes have used water cooling for decades.)

IBM also introduced software to help with power and cooling issues. Power-Executive monitors power usage and heat to assist with data-center planning and management. Thermal Dynamics helps pinpoint heat-related issues in the data center. IBM servers include hardware features that assist as well; for example, circuitry on the blade communicates with the base controller to keep blades running even if there is not enough power — the management module tells the processors to reduce power by slowing the clock speed. Additional software features are planned, such as allowing customers to cap power. The PowerExecutive suite integrates into IBM Director with a free plug-in.

Automating Virtualization Management

Although IBM is not in the business of providing a virtualization hypervisor for x86 servers, it is using the expertise gained from decades of mainframe virtualization to deliver a number of complementary virtualization products. Under the umbrella of the IBM Virtualization Engine platform, IBM offers a variety of products that support and interface with VMware, Xen, and Microsoft Virtual Server (IBM is the leading reseller of VMware). In addition to the virtualization-assist capabilities in BladeCenter, for virtual access and management, key functions are provided by IBM Director and the Enterprise Workload Manager (EWLM). IBM Director has a plug-in Virtual Machine Manager for VMware ESX and MS Virtual Server. EWLM, which runs on a server or a mainframe, allows automated discovery of servers and application topology, collection of performance against goals, and the ability to adjust resources dynamically, including load balancing across multiple physical and virtual resources. Building on that foundation, Tivoli Provisioning Manager, Tivoli Intelligent Orchestrator, and Tivoli Workload Scheduler add advanced policy management and automated workflow for provisioning.

Final Analysis

IBM has been a leader in the blade market for a variety of reasons. As a leader in the traditional server market and an early entrant in the blade market, IBM offered early adopters an easy decision to migrate from IBM rack servers to IBM blades. With a strong history of backward- and forward-compatibility (as exemplified by compatibility from the original chassis through BladeCenter H), IBM offers a way to implement a wide variety of blade choices, with the low-risk comfort factor of choosing IBM as a long-term blade foundation. Although IBM may not always be the first vendor to offer products with the latest technology, they continue to deliver reliable products which, if not first, follow closely enough thereafter. Finally, the BladeCenter ecosystem continues to grow, with contributions from hundreds of participating vendors, offering a wide array of products for both horizontal and vertical solutions based on BladeCenter.

HP

HP has consistently held the number-two spot in the blade market, with 35% market share as of 2006. With their first HP blade products in 2001, HP was part of the blade movement almost from the beginning. Like IBM, HP has offered their server customer base a low-risk way to move into blade implementations early on. As blade technology evolved, however, HP chose to redo their architecture to leverage these advances and focused on re-architecting for the future. The HP blade strategy going forward is to deliver the same choices of servers, storage, and networking options available in rack-mounted infrastructure in a blade design.

Third-Generation Architecture

HP's initial BladeSystem in 2001 was focused purely on ultradense computing. In late 2002, they launched their second-wave product, the p-Class chassis, which was designed not only for density, but also to integrate in the edge components of the data center, with switching as a key component. The p-Class includes Cisco and Brocade solutions for Ethernet and Fibre Channel switch modules. In June 2006, the c-Class (see Figure 16.2) was introduced as the third-wave, next-generation data-center solution. It was designed to run everything from low-end, scale-out solutions through high-end, scale-up applications, all managed through the same chassis. HP will continue its support for existing p-Class customers (for example, a new Intel Woodcrest blade was announced in 2006 for p-Class); however, c-Class is the recommendation for all new customers.

Figure 16.2: HP BladeSystem c-Class
Source: Hewlett-Packard

The redesign of the c-Class includes changes for cost efficiency, increased high-speed interconnects, enhancements in virtualization, and improvements in power and cooling. With the c-Class, HP is the first in the industry to offer a four-socket Opteron blade, the first support for 20Gb InfiniBand, and the first cooling provided through an active (ducted high-pressure) cooling fan. The backplane was redesigned, with all active components designed out, and was optimized for serial technology. It supports Ethernet, Fibre Channel, InfiniBand, SAS, and SATA, with a total 5 Terabits per second (Tbps) I/O throughout. Switches include Cisco (Ethernet), Blade Network Technologies (Ethernet and FC), and Mellanox (20Gb per second InfiniBand). All three types of switches can coexist in the same chassis. Multifunction NICs on the server blades offer acceleration for iSCSI through TCP Offload Engines (TOEs) and RDMA. (Check your OS vendor for corresponding software support for these functions.)

The c-Class also introduced improvements in power and cooling with HP Thermal Logic. High-pressure fans were added, and the chassis and blades have been instrumented to monitor temperature and power. According to HP, these enhancements make the c-Class 30% more power-efficient than a traditional rack server.

The strategy going forward is to deliver the same choices of servers, storage, and networking options in rack-mounted infrastructure in a blade design. The blade enclosure becomes the modular building block, with all elements virtualized and all management processes automated. The BladeSystem will support blades with multicore processors, plus storage, network, PC, and workstation blades. (HP's Consolidated Client Infrastructure [CCI] offers PC blades as an additional option, and HP supports a variety of Virtual Client PC solutions on HP BladeSystem based on VMware and Citrix.) HP describes this modular agenda as "blade everything."

Virtualization Enhancements

The new Virtual Connect architecture announced with c-Class adds an interesting level of virtualization in networking. Virtual Connect enables virtual networking for Ethernet and FC (1 Gig and 10GbE, and 4 Gig FC). The blades themselves are configured with the appropriate NICs, HBAs, and firmware, but they share a pool of Worldwide Names and MACs, with virtualized connections. This simplifies configuration management, because it avoids maintaining Worldwide Names and MAC addresses by physical blade. It also removes state from the blades, making them more interchangeable. Plans are to grow this virtualization to extend to direct-attached storage (DAS) on storage blades within the chassis.

Additionally, HP offers software tools to help with server virtualization. The ProLiant Essentials Virtual Machine Management software (PEVMS) is designed to unify management of physical and virtual resources and supports VMware, Xen, and Microsoft Virtual Server, as well as physical servers. PEVMS allows movement of virtual machine guests between physical hosts, and provides migration facilities for V2V, V2P, and P2P for rapid migration and consolidation. PEVMS ties into HP's System Insight Manager, as does the Control Tower Linux management software, acquired from RLX Technologies.

Final Analysis

HP continues to be a leading player in the blade space, offering an easy choice to loyal HP customers and a solid offering to others. With the latest c-Class products, HP has learned from the past and leveraged advances in chipsets, high-speed interconnects, virtualization, and power and cooling. Although HP has been criticized for lack of compatibility between the newer c-Class and its predecessor p-Class, the new architecture is clearly an improvement, and a strong platform moving forward. With their innovations in the HP Blade-System, virtualization, and power and cooling, they continue to help drive the industry forward.

Dell

With 15% market share, Dell comes in third in the blade space, while they are second worldwide for all x86 servers, and first in the United States. The initial Dell blade offering, the PowerEdge 1655, was delivered in 2003. It delivered density, but no other significant features. A common perception was that it was withdrawn from the market; in fact, it was still available but not heavily promoted. In late 2004, Dell introduced a new blade chassis and the PowerEdge 1855, aimed at offering the same features as Dell rack servers, but delivered in a blade form factor and with the additional benefits thereof. In 2006, the Power-Edge 1955 was introduced (see Figure 16.3), bringing additional speed.

Best at Commodity Servers

Dell's approach to blades is in line with its overall approach to servers. Dell's goal is to be best in the commodity market, using standard components and factory-tested configurations at the best price. The Dell philosophy is to leverage common components and reduce complexity. As part of this approach, blades are treated just like other servers wherever possible.

The Dell blade promise is "Blade servers without compromise," meaning PowerEdge blades offer the benefits of high-density blades but with all the latest high-performance server options. This approach addresses one of the chief complaints users had with early blade offerings — why pay more for blades

Figure 16.3: Dell PowerEdge 1955
Courtesy of Dell Inc.

that offer less power than a rack server? Although other vendors have also evolved their product lines to address this issue, Dell will undoubtedly do it as well or better than anyone else from a commodity/price perspective. It is this approach that has made Dell number one in servers in the United States, and as the blade market matures, will allow Dell to succeed in that market as well.

The PowerEdge chassis is a 7U enclosure that holds up to 10 server blades. The passive midplane supports up to 10Gb/s. InfiniBand is supported up to 10 Gig, along with 4 Gig Fibre Channel and Gigabit Ethernet (10 GbE was not available at press time). Dell offered 10 Gig InfiniBand in 2004, before IBM and HP. Switch modules are available for Ethernet (Cisco and Dell), and Fibre Channel (McData and Brocade), along with InfiniBand pass-through (Cisco Topspin).

Blades are available with up to two dual core 64-bit Intel Xeon processors, running up to 3.0 GHz with up to 32 Gig fully buffered DIMM memory. PowerEdge supports virtualization through the Intel VT chip and will support multicore when it becomes available. At press time, Dell supported only Intel chips but had just signed a partnership with AMD.

While Dell has continued to add higher-power chips to their blades, no change has been made or required thus far to their power supply. The patent-pending, low-flow fans are adaptive fans that spin down to whatever cooling level is needed at the moment. The Dell Data Center Assessment service helps users plan for power and cooling needs, providing advice on hot aisle/cold aisle design (which Dell says is not required, but is generally recommended).

Dell's management philosophy is to leverage the blade management module and integrate with all other management just as traditional servers do. Dell blades support the IPMI (Intelligent Platform Management Interface) standard, use the same Dell Remote Access Card (DRAC) as their servers and the same KVM from Avocent, and are manageable from Dell OpenManage, which integrates with Microsoft management (for example, MOM, SMS), Altiris, Novell, and so on.

Final Analysis

For blades, as with servers in general, Dell does not aim to lead in innovation. However, as number one in x86 servers in the United States, they are clearly doing something right with their low-cost commodity approach. As the blade market matures, this approach is likely to gain additional market share for Dell, especially in the midmarket. Dell's philosophy is to treat blades like traditional servers as much as possible, and over time it will pay off.

Egenera

Egenera was one of the first entrants into the blade space, shortly after RLX, in late 2001. The founder and CTO of Egenera, Vern Brownell, had been CTO at Goldman Sachs, responsible for their worldwide IT infrastructure, including their Unix-based trading floor, an infrastructure of 15,000 servers, and an IT staff of 1,500. Managing the complexities that had come from the shift of a centralized mainframe environment to this distributed environment, Brownell believed that the complexity stemmed from two key issues: the model of one server (or many servers) per application, and the amount of technology necessary per server with incomplete management solutions for those technologies. Brownell had an idea for simplifying the server environment with a new architecture, separating the processor components from other components and creating a processor area network (PAN) that could then be managed as a resource pool, much the way that LAN and SAN resources are managed.

A Different Architectural Approach

Egenera's architectural approach is focused on simplifying data-center management through virtualization and commoditized components, reducing the number of components required with traditional servers by up to 80%. According to Egenera, one customer with traditional servers counted more than 8,000 manageable components before moving to BladeFrames, and as a result of the move, reduced that number of components to 500.

The PAN architecture is based on shared pools of resources, down to the processor level. Each Processor blade (pBlade) contains only processors and memory, with no NICs or HBAs and no storage. These blades communicate across the BladeFrame high-speed interconnect to redundant Control blades (cBlades), which contain a smaller number of shared network adapters (NICs and/or HBAs), with typically two to four of each *per BladeFrame*, rather than one or two *per blade*. (The number of ports can be expanded up to 16 if needed, depending on the frame.)

Processor blades are completely stateless — not only in terms of being disk-less, but also by not being tied to MAC addresses or World Wide Names — and are managed as a shared virtual pool through the Control blade. (Egenera has filed for patents on this technology.) This allows each type of component to be managed as a pool — processor and memory components, shared net-working adapters, and shared external storage (through a SAN). In addition to simplifying the environment and improving manageability, it also helps improve the speed of provisioning for both users and service providers.

Processor blades are offered in more than 20 combinations with both Intel and AMD chips, from single-core two-sockets with 2GB of memory, through dual-core, four-sockets with 32GB of memory and either 32- or 64-bit address-ing. There is a maximum of 24 blades per BladeFrame chassis (see Figure 16.4). Since the number of connections is drastically reduced by eliminating the need for one or two adapters per blade, there is no need to aggregate connections in a switch module. The few NICs and/or HBAs on the Control blade simply connect to external switches, giving the flexibility to use whatever Ethernet or Fibre Channel switches already exist in the environment.

The backplane, originally designed before InfiniBand had gained traction, is a cell-based ATM fabric from Emulex, InfiniBand-like in terms of latency. It operates with a data transfer rate of 2.5Gbps over redundant point-to-point switched fabric interconnects. This is likely to change to 10GbE over time.

The software that manages the entire virtualized environment is called PAN Manager, and it provides a broad range of functionality. Features include the pooling and partitioning of blades within and across BladeFrames, allowing work to be assigned to appropriately sized blades, within a BladeFarm. PAN Manager also provides clustering and failover capability for HA, Disaster Recovery snapshot functions, named processor pools, warm blades (powered up and run in a low power setting, essentially on standby), and the ability to change configurations while running — adding HBAs, NICS, storage, and so on.

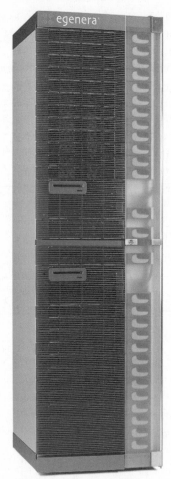

Figure 16.4: Egenera BladeFrame
Source: Egenera

BladeFrames support blades running Red Hat Linux, SUSE Linux, Windows, and Solaris 10. There are also specific solutions for Oracle Grid, 9i and 10g with RAC applications, Microsoft Exchange, and SAP. Since the virtualized I/O architecture requires customized drivers, OS environments may require some level of development from Egenera. As of late 2006, efforts were underway to add support for VMware ESX and Xen virtualization environments.

The Egenera architecture is different in its approach to power and cooling as well. The elimination of disks, NICs, and HBAs from the processor blades reduces their individual power and cooling requirements. In general, the reduction in the number of components per chassis reduces the overall power and cooling requirements per BladeFrame. In addition, each blade has power and cooling on the blade, sized to each chipset, which means that there is no need to change power supplies as newer, denser blades are introduced and added into an existing BladeFrame. The BladeFrame is cooled front-to-back and can be positioned as close as six inches from the back wall (all components are inserted from the front, with only four power cables out the back). Egenera holds four patents focused on power management, virtualized I/O, and clustering.

An Innovative, Emerging Company

Founded in 2000, Egenera started with a focus on mission-critical applications while other start-ups were focused on replacing rack servers for scale-out web services. The first BladeFrame shipped in late 2001 and went into production in early 2002 at Credit Suisse. Egenera continues to focus on large enterprise, service-provider, and government data centers. The company is small and privately held, with more than $150 million in funding as of 2006. Investors include Goldman Sachs, Credit Suisse, Austin Ventures, Lehman Brothers, Pharos Capital, Fujitsu Siemens Computers, and others.

Egenera has a large number of partners, including technology, OEM, and reseller relationships. Most significantly, in 2005 they closed a $300 million OEM agreement with Fujitsu Siemens Computers, granting Fujitsu Siemens exclusive sales rights in Europe, the Middle East, and Africa. Egenera also worked with Liebert to jointly develop an extended cooling offering called CoolFrame, which adds a set of fans/radiators over the back of the Blade-Frame Processor blades to capture heat and move it through tubing (out the top) to a Liebert XDP refrigerant-based coolant system. This option is sold and maintained by Liebert.

Final Analysis

Egenera is a great example of innovation coming from outside the ranks of the big players. The PAN architecture brings flexibility to the allocation and management of processors in much the way that SANs have for storage. Forward-thinking customers understand the value of this innovation and have been very pleased with their implementations, including some extremely large, mission-critical applications. The BladeFrame offering is a great example of the combination of blades and virtualization as building blocks for the next generation of data centers. Although other system vendors such as IBM and HP have evolved their product lines to include some similar functionality, Egenera has proven itself a strong and innovative player in this market and is well worth considering for a high-availability enterprise solution.

Rackable Systems

Rackable was founded in 1999 and has been providing rack-mount server systems for years. It was not much of a stretch for them to quickly move into the blade space and gain the rank of fifth in the blade market (according to IDC).

Known for their ultradense rack solutions, Rackable leveraged this capability in creating their Scale Out Series of blade solutions.

Blade Hybrid

Rackable has created something of a hybrid between rack-mount servers and blades. Rather than putting the blades vertically in a chassis, the Scale Out Series uses a standard rack to hold horizontal blades in a patented side-to-side and back-to-back configuration to support up to 88 blades (176 processors or 352 cores) per rack (see Figure 16.5). The rack holds two blades next to each other (side-to-side) in the front and two blades next to each other in the back (back-to-back). This design allows Rackable to use readily available processors and components, lowering their cost to build and maintain the systems (enabling them to pass those reductions on to customers).

All power and cooling for the solution is distributed through the center of the rack, which uses a wired backplane of GbE, 100baseT, or serial interconnects. Power is shared throughout the rack via a bridge rectifier that converts AC power to DC, then it is distributed on a shared bus.

Figure 16.5: Rackable Scale Out Series
Source: Rackable Systems

Customized Solutions

Rackable is focused on large-scale customers who are very technically sophisticated and know exactly what they want in a blade system: what processors, what speed I/O, how much memory, and so on. This allows Rackable to build a customized solution to fit their customers' specific application and infrastructure requirements.

Final Analysis

Rackable's high-density, side-to-side, and back-to-back design efficiently uses all possible space within a rack to provide more processing power in a smaller footprint. For customers who want many of the benefits of blades with the standardization of rack servers, Rackable's Scale Out Series provides an extremely customizable hybrid solution.

Verari Systems

Verari Systems is making its mark in the blade market using commercial off-the-shelf (COTS) components, putting their value-add into the chassis, power, and cooling design. Verari has been around since 1996 and shipped their first blade product, the BladeRack, in 2002. With only 250 employees, they have worked hard to be ranked sixth in the market by IDC and Gartner (2005). Their high-end blade solution can accommodate up to 176 processors with more than 1.4 Teraflops (Tflops) of computing power in a standard seven-foot (48U) cabinet, making them the first to offer this level of power in a standard rack configuration (see Figure 16.6). The bulk of their sales have been to three customers who have deployed more than 10,000 Verari blades.

Everything on a Blade

Verari offers "everything on a blade," from workstations (thin clients or client blades), to servers, to storage. All BladeRack solutions are built with COTS components, eliminating the cost associated with building and servicing proprietary hardware. They currently have a patent pending on their design that allows the use of standard motherboards, positioned vertically in the chassis and using standard interface cards, NICs, HBAs, and HCAs, with all cables built into the rack. The motivation for building the BladeRack architecture around COTS components was to impose no limitations on the configurations, or as Verari describes it, "blades without boundaries."

To sustain the power requirements of the BladeRack, Verari uses high-voltage DC power to the blade to mitigate power loss. The BladeRack supports up to 25kVA, 208V three-phase power with automatic balancing.

Figure 16.6: Verari BladeRack
Source: Verari Systems

Management of the BladeRacks is done on a tiered system. Each chassis has a management module built into it, with a management point every 11 blades; each management point talks to higher-level Verari Service Module (VSM) with Verari Command Center (VCC). This tiered approach allows the ability to control over 10,000 blades through one interface.

Server Blades

Verari offers two blade platforms: the BladeRack and the BladeRack 2. The BladeRack Platforms can be configured with either 66 or 88 dual-processor blade configurations, with support for up to 176 dual-core processors with their patented back-to-back vertical mount design. The BladeRack 2 Platform holds up to 66 blades, supporting as many as 132 dual-core processors. The server blades use both the Intel Xeon and AMD Opteron processors with support for virtual hardware assist.

Workstation Blades

Blades within the BladeRack Platforms can be configured to be client blades. This is accomplished using KVM/IP from Avocent. Verari plans to support dual digital video interface (DVI) per blade by the end of 2006. The addition of a graphics accelerator card on the motherboard is supported.

Storage Blades

Using up to 12 3.5-inch SAS or SATA II drives per blade, Verari can configure up to one-half petabyte of storage in a BladeRack Platform. Up to four storage blades connect into a HeadBlade via SAS to create a storage brick. The HeadBlade provides the power, monitoring, and management functions and can interface to the server, via GbE, 10 GbE, 2Gb and 4Gb Fibre Channel, or 10Gb InfiniBand.

Virtualization and Clustering

Verari is partnering with both XenSource and VMware to provide server virtualization capabilities to their customers. They see no need to reinvent this wheel. However, prior to blade systems, Verari developed a solid business around cluster management solutions that provide users and administrators the capability to optimize application performance while maximizing cluster resource utilization and uptime. The VCC software simplifies tasks such as software configuration control across the entire cluster. Verari also offers a leading message passing interface (MPI) middleware product MPI/Pro used to create and optimize parallel processing applications for customers who are developing their own parallel solutions.

Vertical Cooling Technology

Verari's patented Vertical Cooling Technology is what allows them to offer the extremely high density without heat problems. Their premise in creating this technology is that heat naturally rises, so why not take advantage of physics by cooling their BladeRack from the bottom? This technology eliminates data-center hot spots (hot and cool aisles) by drawing air from the cool floor and forcing it up through the entire rack and exhausting through the top, then into the ceiling; this provides a cooling solution that is, according to Verari, 30% more efficient than standard blade solutions. This is done with modular and hot-swappable fan trays.

Final Analysis

Verari is an excellent example of a company with strong, innovative products seeing further opportunity in the next-generation server architectures. Their unique design utilizes components that are readily available off the shelf, passing on to their customers the reduced production and lower maintenance costs that come with using standard components. They address blade system challenges, such as power and cooling, in a new and different way. Their innovative clustering capabilities and partnering with VMware and Xen to bring virtualization options add considerable value to their solutions. Verari created a variety of blade offerings that complement their previous products, thus enhancing their position in the market. Their ability and willingness to take the blade architecture to the next level, creating not only server blades but also workstation blades and storage blades, is impressive.

PANTA Systems

PANTA Systems is one of the innovative newcomers to the blade industry. Founded in 2004, PANTA's target market has been the high performance and flexibility needs of the core of the data center rather than the scale-out edge computing targeted by many of the first blade vendors. PANTA's high-speed I/O architecture is designed to ensure fast movement of data to and from the processors.

Architected for Speed

PANTA's PANTAmatrix blade solutions can hold up to 128 blades per standard rack. Within each chassis or 8U subrack, PANTA supports three types of blades (or as PANTA calls them, "modules"): compute modules, visualization modules, and switch modules (see Figure 16.7). Compute modules support two- or four-processor Opteron chips, single- or dual-core, with dual 4x Infini-Band interconnects (20Gbps expandable to 60Gbps), and GbE ports for system management. PANTA uses HyperTransport (80Gbps) to create dynamic SMP between two adjacent computing modules (blades) (up to 16 processors — 8 dual-core). Computing modules support both diskless and local disk configurations. Visualization modules support two NVIDIA graphic-processing boards per blade/module for applications that require high-performance visualization capabilities. Their switch modules, which are in effect switch blades (different form factor than other vendors' switch modules), are 24-port 4x InfiniBand switches, which create the I/O subnet(s) across all modules. The switch module can interface to external gateways for GbE, FC, or IB subsystems, in effect virtualizing the I/O into the PANTAMatrix.

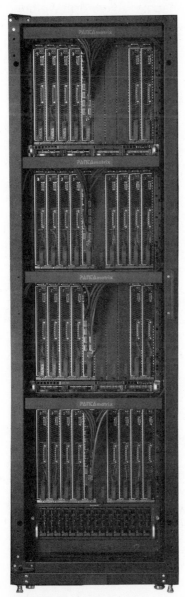

Figure 16.7: PANTAmatrix
Source: PANTA Systems

Interesting Business Model

PANTA Systems started shipping their first products in the third quarter of 2005. A year later, they had approximately 12 revenue-generating customers and a goal for profitability in the 2008 timeframe. What makes PANTA different is that they perform only the design and development functions, and depend on strategic partners to manufacture and support their offerings. Some of these partners include Tatung, AMD, Mellanox, SilverStorm, Voltaire, and Akivia.

Final Analysis

PANTA is well positioned to bring high-performance blade solutions to the data center with their PANTAmatrix solutions. Their dynamic reconfigure capability to support hardware-based SMP gives customers the ability to focus computational and I/O resources when needed. PANTA's base architecture will allow them to expand processor and memory configurations without requiring an I/O architecture upgrade for quite a while. Finally, their partnerships with well-known manufacturers allow them to ride the technology wave very closely and gives them the ability to react quickly.

Hitachi

Hitachi may not have been the first company to offer blade and virtualization solutions, but they are the only ones who are incorporating the knowledge they have gained over 20 years of developing mainframes into their blade and virtualization offerings. With annual revenues of $80 billion worldwide, Hitachi is able to focus resources on their BladeSymphony solutions, leveraging their close partnership with Intel.

Mainframe-Class Virtualization

Hitachi has taken a different approach to virtualization with their BladeSymphony line (see Figure 16.8). Instead of loading a hypervisor onto a blade each time a blade is powered on, they have included their hypervisor, in firmware, on the blade itself. Their embedded virtualization technology improves the all-around performance of the hypervisor during startup (no booting from across the network) and throughout execution — both of which are performed at hardware speeds.

Figure 16.8: Hitachi BladeSymphony product
Source: Hitachi

Scalability

Scalability has been a primary motivator during the design of the BladeSymphony products. Hitachi supports Intel's Xeon (two-way and four-way) and Itanium (two-socket) processors with up to 128GB of memory on each blade, and has the capability of having both in one chassis. Each chassis can hold up to eight front-loading blades, and up to five power supplies for N+1 redundancy. To scale up the system even further, two eight-socket (16-core) Itanium blades can be combined to create symmetric multiprocessing, giving customers a broad range of options when scaling for their applications.

Hitachi's I/O design also focused on scalability and flexibility. Rather than having proprietary switch modules for all I/O interfaces, they support a GbE switch that comes with the chassis, and 16 slots for standard PCI-X or PCI

Express (two slots per blade), which support standard NICs, HBAs, and HCAs. When two blades are combined in an SMP configuration, the SMP "system" has access to all four I/O slots.

Centralized Management

Hitachi's BladeSymphony Management Suite provides centralized management at every level of the system: hypervisor, chassis, rack, VLAN, and storage, allowing the customer to visualize and manage all aspects of the servers, the storage, the network, and the rack.

Final Analysis

Hitachi has a long-standing reputation of reliability and scalability of their enterprise products, and they continue this trend with the BladeSymphony line. Using their history in the mainframe space, they are bringing a higher-performing, virtualized, "mainframe-in-a-box" to the market. At press time, Hitachi was finalizing plans to announce additional significant innovations, especially around their embedded virtualization capabilities. For information on these new announcements, check Hitachi's web site, http://hitachi.com/.

Sun

Sun was one of the earliest companies to offer blade solutions, then they exited the market when their customers told them they did not want extreme density at the cost of slower performance and throughput. Sun waited until the technology evolved to the point of being able to match or better the processing power and I/O throughput offered in standard rack servers. In 2006, they launched their Sun Blade 8000 line of blade solutions (see Figure 16.9).

Racks Plus

Sun provides all the benefits of blades — better space and power utilization, serviceability, maintainability — with their Sun Fire 8000 line. In creating their blade solution, they strove to reach parity or improve on what was available in rack servers. In doing so, they went a step further to build in a life span for the chassis of at least five years to allow their customers to take advantage of upgrades in blade performance and capabilities without having to incur the cost of a new chassis to support the improvements. To accomplish this, each Sun Blade 8000 chassis holds up to 10 hot-pluggable blades. Sun is using both AMD Opteron and SPARC processors on their blades for processing power, and six PCI Express interfaces per blade to support 1.92 Tbps throughput of Fibre Channel, InfiniBand, or GbE.

Figure 16.9: Sun Blade 8000 Modular System

Source: Sun Microsystems

Rather than using specialized, shared I/O modules, Sun uses standard PCI Express interfaces to allow each blade to connect to up to two dedicated PCI Express slots each, (for example, to connect to an HBA or HCA). In addition, the chassis includes a shared module, which also uses PCI Express, called a Network Express module, to allow sharing of GbE ports. Because all of these options use PCI Express, Sun's intention is for third-party vendors to be able to develop cards and network modules for Sun blades, using an industry-standard interface.

Transparent Management

Continuing the theme of parity or improvement over the rack-'n'-stack model, Sun strove to make integrating their blade solutions into their customers' management infrastructure transparent. The Sun Fire 8000 blades integrate into the Sun N1 Systems Manager as if they were servers being added onto the network with no additional management interfaces.

Virtualization

Sun has been providing virtualization capabilities for over 10 years within Solaris or as add-on capabilities. Sun sees virtualization as being simply about resource management — sharing a small number of resources with many applications. On the blade systems, Sun offers two types of virtualization: Solaris Containers, which comes standard with the Solaris 10 operating system, and VMware's ESX solution. Solaris Containers use OS partitioning to provide separate virtual Solaris and Linux environments in which to run applications with complete fault and security isolation for each container. Their partnership with VMware allows Sun to provide a hypervisor solution for their customers with support for Solaris, Linux, and Windows guest operating systems. Along similar lines, Sun is working to support the Xen 3.0 hypervisor and to make sure they are a good Xen host and guest.

Final Analysis

Sun's exit and reentry into the blade space is a positive step, since they were losing server share to competitor's blade offerings, but it means they have some catching up to do in the market. Their insistence that blades need to have more value to their customers than simply dense packaging, as well as their forward thinking in designing their solution for the long run, will pay off both for their customers and for Sun.

Virtualization Software

Although virtual machines have been around for a long time (on IBM mainframes in the 1960s and '70s), virtual machines running on x86 servers really came about in the late 1990s. Since then, server virtualization has grown tremendously. Initial growth came through proprietary software; in particular, VMware and SWsoft, followed slowly by Microsoft. More recently, growth has started to come through open source efforts with Xen, and with vendors working on hypervisors and management products based on Xen (XenSource and Virtual Iron).

VMware

VMware, which is now an independent subsidiary of EMC with separate sales, marketing, and R&D, began as a startup company in 1998, when a group of Stanford University students began working on operating systems which could bring virtualization to desktops and servers. Through some clever technology tricks, they skirted the difficulties of virtualizing the x86 environment, and VMware was born. VMware Workstation was the first product delivered, in 1999, targeting the desktops of technical users by running on Windows or Linux (it still exists today as a desktop product).

In 2000/2001, a similar product was released, based on the same concept but on a server. This product became VMware GSX Server, and eventually VMware Server, which VMware made available for free (in response to Microsoft, as described later). VMware Server (formerly GSX Server) offered a hosted approach to server virtualization and included additional features such as remote operation and clustering features.

VMware's next server virtualization solution, called ESX Server, was developed based on a bare-metal hypervisor approach. ESX was designed for enterprise data center class redundancy, with sophisticated features including virtual switches, virtual SMP, network virtualization, SAN multipathing with failover, and a distributed file system with locking capability, called VMFS. VMware continues to dominate the server virtualization market, with over 20,000 customers as of 2006, and ESX as the mainstay in enterprise environments. A Yankee Group survey in 2006 showed 45% of the 1,700 users polled deploying or planning to deploy ESX, with an additional 10% going with VMware Server.

Management as Differentiator

As other virtualization options begin to take hold, VM management will become the key differentiator. At the outset, VMware comes in way ahead, with a full suite of management offerings ranging from base-level management of virtual machines through highly sophisticated functionality, including automated VM failover and automated resource scheduling across VMs.

VMware offered its first virtual machine management product in 2003, with the release of its VirtualCenter management product, allowing management of a group of ESX or GSX servers from a single console (single pane of glass). VirtualCenter provides the ability to start and stop VMs, look at performance and utilization, set thresholds, and easily provision new VMs with templates. VMotion provides the ability to move a running VM from one physical server to another — for example, for maintenance or load balancing. VMware's Distributed Resource Scheduler (DRS) is yet another way to manage loads. DRS allows for the creation of resource pools that can span servers and define CPU and memory policies so that VMs are automatically migrated from one server to another based on utilization targets. Complementing DRS is VMware's HA feature that will restart a VM on another host if the original host fails. Rounding out the list of VMware's enterprise features is its Consolidated Backup tool that provides backup hooks for the major backup software packages. VMware bundles together ESX, VMFS, Virtual SMP, VirtualCenter, HA, DRS, VMotion, and Consolidated Backup as VMware Virtual Infrastructure (VI). VI is purchased by 80% of VMware's customers, according to VMware.

In 2006, VMware also opened up their virtual machine disk-format specification (which describes and documents the virtual machine environment and how it is stored). This allows partner vendors (such as Altiris, BMC, PlateSpin, Surgient, and Symantec) to add value to the VMware environment through development of complementary products, including automation and management tools.

Final Analysis

VMware essentially created the x86 virtualization market and has continued to dominate it, with an estimated 55% share of the market (45% using or planning to use ESX, and an additional 10% using or planning to use VMware Server). As other hypervisor options become available, VMware will no longer be the only game in town, but it still has a substantial lead, particularly in management. Competition will serve only to make things better for the users, as feature wars get serious and low-cost and/or free options drive prices down.

SWsoft

SWsoft's Virtuozzo takes a different approach from most other server virtualization vendors, and has had a great deal of success doing it, with over 1,000 customers using Virtuozzo on more than 10,000 servers and 400,000 virtual environments (the Virtuozzo equivalent of VMs). Virtuozzo is based on operating-system-level virtualization, sometimes called partitioning, and SWsoft currently has over 30 patents pending on its technology. Although SWsoft has no official numbers to quote, as of 2006 they believe they are number two in market share after VMware (though according to Yankee Group the number-two position has gone to Microsoft with 29% share since Virtual Server was made available for free). Strategic relationships with Intel and Microsoft, including investment from Intel Capital (among others), have helped move SWsoft and its version of virtualization toward success.

Performance and Manageability

Virtuozzo's approach melds aspects of both hypervisors and hosted approaches, to offer many of the benefits of both. Based on a thin customized version of Linux 2.6.8 as the core, it introduces very low overhead and is extremely efficient, similar to a hypervisor approach. Unlike hypervisors, however, rather than each virtual environment (VE) containing an entire virtual machine, each VE is a partitioned version of either Linux or Windows, appearing like a separate OS. This lack of duplication in operating systems adds to Virtuozzo's efficiency. According to SWsoft, it is possible to deploy up to hundreds of VEs on a regular two-way server. A server can run VEs with either Linux or Windows, but not both simultaneously. If necessary, any individual VE can use the full resources of the physical server during a spike in activity.

There are numerous manageability benefits as well. Since there is only a single operating system to maintain, management is simplified. For example, one update can patch multiple VEs on multiple servers. VEs can also be moved from one physical server to another, even if the servers do not share storage. This live migration process is also very efficient since it does not involve moving the whole OS. In addition, Virtuozzo offers highly granular resource management, with the ability to modify CPU, memory, disks, I/O allocation, and so on, with a total of over 30 parameters. These capabilities will be the foundation for policy-based management going forward. For example, policies could be set to give preference to a particular VE, or cap a VE at a certain level to prevent a single VE from taking over too many resources. Management controls are established using role-based administration, allowing distributed roles with varying levels of control over specific VEs. Virtuozzo also includes both P2V and V2V tools. In late 2006, SWsoft declared its intention to provide tools to manage other virtualized environments from other vendors, including VMware- and Xen-based virtualization.

Final Analysis

SWsoft has taken a unique and highly efficient approach to server virtualization and it has served their customers well. The performance and manageability benefits of OS virtualization have created a strong customer base and strategic relationships for an emerging company. With the changes in the virtualization space brought on by Microsoft and Xen, SWsoft has expanded their scope to include management of other environments, leveraging their expertise and experience. This direction can only be good for users — giving choices that include the performance benefits of their OS virtualization approach and bringing much of their management capability to other environments.

Microsoft

Although VMware has clearly dominated the server virtualization space from the beginning, Microsoft's entry into any market changes the landscape. Microsoft's initial offering, Virtual Server R1, was in 2004, with general availability in 2005. In 2006 they changed the rules of the game by making Virtual Server R2 available for free. As a result, as of late 2006 Microsoft has grown to around 29% market share. According to Microsoft, they see server virtualization as part of the management of the operating systems, not as an "end-all" solution. The evidence of this is in its productization, with Virtual Server 2004–2006 and the announced Windows Server Virtualization (tied to the Windows Longhorn Server release) in 2007–2008.

Both Hosted and Hypervisor Approaches

Microsoft Virtual Server (MSVS) is based on a hosted approach, using Microsoft Windows Server 2003 as its base platform. The original R1 version was fairly limited and supported only Windows guest operating systems. This changed in R2, with the additional support for both Red Hat and SUSE Linux. Because MSVS sits on top of Windows, it has the advantage of the broad hardware and device support that Windows brings. However, as a hosted approach it brings additional overhead as compared to a hypervisor approach.

Virtual Server R2 added other significant features, such as support for the hardware-assist virtualization chipsets Intel VT and AMD-V, performance improvements to MSVS, particularly running an unmodified guest OS such as Linux. Support for Volume Shadow Copy Support (VSS) was also added, allowing snapshots of running VMs and offline Virtual Hard Disk (VHD) mounting, and thus facilitating offline configuration control.

As part of its longer-term vision with the Longhorn server operating system, Microsoft announced a hypervisor-based offering called Windows Server Virtualization. Plans for availability are within 180 days of Longhorn general availability, which is slated for late 2007, putting Windows Server Virtualization in the early 2008 timeframe. The hypervisor will support both emulation for unmodified guest OSs, as well as support for paravirtualization (or what Microsoft calls "enlightened" OSs), where the guest OS has been modified to be aware that it's running virtual, for improved performance in that environment. Also supported are features such as hot-add of virtual and physical resources, including CPU, memory, networking, and storage.

Managing MS Virtualization

As part of Microsoft's vision for virtualization in the OS, they have created an open licensing option for their Virtual Hard Disk (VHD) format. As of 2006, over 50 partners have participated, most notably XenSource (see the later discussion) as well as other server-management vendors.

In addition to the virtualization software itself (MSVS and Windows Server Virtualization), Microsoft has released software to manage these environments. System Center Virtual Machine Manager (VMM) is a standalone server application used to manage either Virtual Server or Windows Server Virtualization, and is scheduled to be released in 2007. There are some differences in management between the two environments, based on the underlying technologies. For example, with MSVS, moving VMs requires a stop, move, and start, while with the hypervisor that will be a live migration.

VMM offers a variety of features, including monitoring and management, some automated configuration features, P2V utilities, grouping functions, and more. VMM is integrated in the Microsoft System Center family of products, offering the advantage of managing both physical and virtual environments.

In mid 2006, Microsoft announced its acquisition of Softricity Inc., a provider of application virtualization and dynamic streaming technologies. This technology will allow virtualization within the OS environment, creating the equivalent of virtualized or "guest" applications as opposed to guest OSs, virtualizing at the registry level, with some level of isolation. Microsoft announced availability of the Softricity SoftGrid application virtualization platform as two planned offerings: SoftGrid for Desktops and SoftGrid for Terminal Services.

Final Analysis

As a newer entrant into the server virtualization space, Microsoft will still, no doubt, make a huge impact. The initial Virtual Server offering may lack the performance benefits of a hypervisor approach, but has still made strong inroads. This is likely due to the fact that it is available for free, and that it allows Windows users to move into virtualization and start to reap the benefits while staying in the comfort zone of the Windows environment. With the addition of Virtual Machine Manager and Windows Server Virtualization in Longhorn, Microsoft will begin to catch up with the other hypervisor approaches and management tools. The licensing of VHD will create a mini ecosystem around Microsoft virtualization, enabling third parties to succeed in delivering other products, such as advanced management tools for Microsoft and Xen products. It will be interesting to see where the application virtualization goes as well; it may be an area of differentiation, right up the Microsoft alley.

XenSource

XenSource, founded in early 2005, has a dual role as a leader in the Xen open source community — as the distributor of the Xen (free) hypervisor, and as a software vendor — developing and selling value-add virtualization management solutions around the Xen technology. Through both efforts, XenSource evangelizes the benefits of virtualization across all markets. Xen also pioneered the paravirtualization approach to server virtualization, offering significant performance improvements for guest OS environments where the source could be modified to use the paravirtualization API.

The World According to Xen

The Xen community was originally created by the founders of XenSource to develop a virtualization hypervisor that would become ubiquitous across all markets. The Xen project includes such vendors as AMD, Intel, Cisco, Dell, Egenera, HP, IBM, Mellanox, NetApp, Novell, Red Hat, Sun, Symantec/Veritas, Voltaire, and XenSource, with new vendors becoming involved daily. One of the primary goals of Xen is to provide a common feature set for the next-generation virtualization architecture, with near bare-metal performance.

Xen continues to lead the paravirtualization hypervisor effort, and is achieving great success via partnerships with Microsoft, Novell, and Red Hat. SUSE Linux Enterprise 10, Red Hat Enterprise Linux, OpenSolaris, and Solaris 10 are shipping or will soon ship with Xen integrated. XenSource's strategic partnership with Microsoft will allow Xen-enabled Linux guests to run paravirtualized under the Windows Hypervisor (Viridian) just as it does under Xen. (Viridian and Xen are both paravirtualizing hypervisors.) A Xen-enabled Linux guest will use native Xen hypercalls to access virtualization functions, and a small adapter will translate the Xen hypercalls into Viridian hypercalls. With both AMD-V and Intel VT chips offering hardware virtualization assist, guest operating systems now can run unmodified on Xen, as well. The Xen 3.0 hypervisor is quickly becoming the basis for nearly all hypervisor implementations.

Virtualization Management

A hypervisor is only part of the virtualization story. The higher-level management capabilities are the more interesting part. XenSource has developed XenEnterprise to be the complementary management interface for Xen. XenEnterprise helps customers install and configure the Xen hypervisor, what XenSource calls "10 minutes to Xen." It also helps customers move their applications from a purely physical server environment to a virtual environment (P2V), as well as perform other management tasks such as VM provisioning/reprovisioning and guest OS configuration/reconfiguration and scheduling. LiveMigrate provides the ability to move a running virtual machine from one system to another. All management is done in compliance with the DMTF CIM standards for visibility to other management platforms, such as HP OpenView or Microsoft Operations Manager (MOM).

Final Analysis

XenSource is doing a great job of making Xen a de facto industry standard for hypervisor virtualization. Their deep understanding of the technology and its capabilities puts them in an excellent position to partner and create solutions for managing both the hypervisor and the virtual environment.

Virtual Iron

Founded in March 2003, Virtual Iron (VI) is releasing its second generation of virtualization management solutions with Virtual Iron 3.0. With this release, and going forward, VI will be leveraging the Xen 3.0 hypervisor as the base component then adding value within the top levels of the virtualization management stack, all targeted at the enterprise data center.

Stack It Up

Virtual Iron 3.0 contains two levels of virtualization management software: the Virtualization Services Layer and the Virtualization Manager. The Virtualization Services Layer is responsible for managing the multiple guest OSs and providing fault, security, and resource isolation for the guest OSs. VI virtualizes the I/O resources for the multiple virtual machines, providing multipathing and load balancing across the I/O resources. This layer also supports the ability to migrate virtual instances to a new physical server without application downtime — a function called LiveMigrate. This is often used when additional resources are required for the application.

The Virtualization Manager is the high-level interface that allows customers to monitor, automate, and control all virtual resources and the applications that run within the virtual machines. It aids with capacity planning (through a function called LiveCapacity) with performance and availability reports, and allows reconfiguration of guest OS (and VM) resources — processor configuration, memory, network, and storage — without changing the physical hardware. The Virtualization Manager also supports moving virtual machines (servers, as they call them) to other virtual environments when a hardware failure occurs to allow for timely application recovery.

Strong Partnerships

Virtual Iron has some very strong partnerships that have helped them get to this point and will continue to help move them forward. Intel is one of their investors, and they gained early access to Intel's Virtual Technology chip, helping them take advantage of the hardware assist within their solutions. They also have partnered with AMD to support their hardware-assist capabilities. The flip side of this is that Virtual Iron will not run on earlier blades that did not have virtualization hardware assist.

Final Analysis

Virtual Iron came early to the server virtualization market and, like many, got caught up in the race to work around the x86's inability to be virtualized. Once

Intel remedied that situation, Virtual Iron decided to shift over to the Xen 3.0 hypervisor as the basis of their virtualization stack, believing that Xen 3.0 would become a de facto industry standard. VI was then able to leverage 70–80% of the management software from their initial products to deliver solutions quickly to market. This ability to move quickly to get a piece of this growing market and continue to build more capabilities into their management layers will serve them and their customers well.

Complementary Software

In addition to the virtualization vendors, other vendors (both existing and emerging) are delivering interesting complementary technology — particularly in management for virtualized and utility computing. Although it is outside the scope of this book to cover systems management offerings, a few sample products are included here to give a taste of things to come.

PlateSpin

PlateSpin was founded in 2003 to be a VMware-like solution provider. In the process, they built a tool to help their customers move their application environments from a physical server to a virtual server (Power P2V). This tool took off and PlateSpin has been growing at a rate of about 300% every year since. With this success, they redirected their company focus to improve on and expand the capabilities of converting from one environment to another. With this change of focus, PlateSpin changed the name of their first solution to PowerConvert and have introduced a second tool called PowerRecon.

The Power of Conversion Tools

PlateSpin's PowerConvert discovers all servers, both physical and virtual, within the environment. The user then simply drags and drops the physical server onto the virtual server. The software discovers the exact application environment of the physical server (or image) and, with their patented migration technology, creates the same environment on the virtual server with no further involvement necessary from the admin. PlateSpin, in the same way, supports moving from a virtual environment to a physical environment. The underlying technology is able to collect the entire image of the application environment, enabling customers to capture these images to create libraries, if desired, then recall an image from the library to either a physical or virtual server. Many users view the capabilities provided by PowerConvert as essential to moving to a virtualized environment. (VMware appears to agree, and in late 2006, introduced a beta version of a new tool called VMware Converter that offers a number of P2V and V2V conversion aids.)

Workload-Utilization Tools

The power of blades and virtualization can never truly be realized until there are tools to help them automate workload and utilization management. Plate-Spin is well on their way along this path with their PowerRecon solution. PowerRecon discovers and analyzes resources for workload utilization and performance over time. The administrator enters target utilization levels and PowerRecon, given these inputs and collected data, models a best-case scenario then advises where to move environments to reach the targeted workload-utilization levels.

Final Analysis

PlateSpin's solutions of PowerConvert and PowerRecon allow users to, as they say, "Beam servers around like in *Star Trek*" to both migrate from one environment to another and/or create the targeted and balanced workload utilization across the environment. PlateSpin's solutions bring customers one giant step closer to utility computing.

Symantec (Veritas)

Before being acquired by Symantec, Veritas had a strong business in systems and storage management, including their Veritas Cluster Server (VCS), which has been shipping since 1998. Not to be caught resting while the world marches toward utility computing, Symantec is joining other vendors to provide management tools to support workload monitoring and management across both physical and virtual environments.

Clustering for High Availability

Clustering solutions and blades, due to their close proximity and shared resources, are complementary to one another. VCS is an excellent example of this, with their N+1 high-availability clustering solution. VCS is a traditional failover product that will work with blades out of the box, just like any other server. Symantec has also partnered with VMware to provide virtual failover capabilities with the ESX virtualization solution. If there is a hardware failure, VCS will fail over the ESX hypervisor, along with the entire virtual environment, to another server (blade).

Directing Applications

Symantec has created the Veritas Application Director (VAD) to define and manage what resources an application has, then match system resources with the application as well as provide workload balancing across the resources. Over the next few years, expect Symantec to be a big player in this market.

Final Analysis

Symantec/Veritas has a wide range of solutions that are applicable to the blade environment, spanning server, security, and storage management. VCS and VAD are excellent examples of solutions that are particularly complementary. As the blade and virtualization spaces grow, expect to see more solutions from Symantec driving a utility computing model.

PolyServe

PolyServe, founded in 1999, develops software solutions that create a shared data capability to support and help manage utility computing environments. Their three solutions — Database Utility, Virtual Server Utility, and File Serving Utility provide every blade within a defined pool high-speed access to the same data, simplifying failover or movement of either physical or virtual servers.

Share-Everything Data Model

The basis for PolyServe's solutions is a share-everything data model. If every blade already has access to all the data, failover or movement of applications or guest OSs from one server to another becomes much simpler. With their Matrix Server software, PolyServe creates shared data clusters, much like what was available with VAXclusters, but for Windows and Linux. PolyServe uses block-mode access to the data via a SAN, enabling high-performance I/O as well as direct I/O capabilities for databases.

The bulk of PolyServe's business comes from their Database Utility. The Database Utility supports dynamic rehosting of database instances from one server to another, including high availability for database instances. This capability allows users to easily match workloads with appropriate systems. It also supports multiple database instances on a single system to improve system utilization.

PolyServe's Virtual Server Utility is an add-on to Microsoft's Virtual Server. Much like the Database Utility, the Virtual Server Utility supports multiple virtual machine instances and provides support for movement of virtual machines between servers (blades) for workload balancing or for high-availability failover.

PolyServe's third solution is the File Serving Utility, which can be used to scale out file services on the fly. Need more storage? Simply drag and drop resources into the file server pool to add them to the shared file system nondisruptively.

Final Analysis

PolyServe's solutions are highly complementary to both blades and server-virtualization solutions. The ability to create a high-performance, share-everything data environment between blades and/or VMs working with the same data set simplifies many of the complexities associated with high-availability failover scenarios, as well as with moving workloads from one blade or VM to another.

Conclusion

Even though blades and server virtualization are both fairly young — there were no blade server systems before 2001 and no x86 virtualization products before 1999 — there are quite a few vendors involved in making these markets succeed. This chapter is a snapshot in time that outlines many of the vendors developing blade, virtualization, and management solutions as the building blocks for next-generation data centers. New, innovative companies will continue to emerge and bring added value. Some smaller companies will be acquired by bigger companies and, unfortunately, some will disappear. Other larger companies will enter these markets as well, and the landscape will continue to change.

This chapter presented a variety of environments, needs, and product offerings and discussed drivers, evaluation processes and results, and lessons learned throughout the implementation. Chapter 17, "Case Studies," offers another view of blade and virtualization products, from the perspective of users who have implemented them.

Case Studies

Perhaps the best way to understand the drivers, benefits, and challenges of blades and virtualization is to examine some real-world user environments. This chapter presents case studies, which include a variety of blade and virtualization vendors and products, across different industries and of different size implementations. Although an attempt was made to include as many blade and virtualization vendors as possible, some vendors were not able to provide reference customers (in some cases, because their products were too new).

Case Study — Service Provider: Software as a Service

At a Glance

Industry: Service provider — Software as a Service

OpSource, Inc.: www.opsource.com

Blades: 1150 HP BladeSystem p-Class blades

Virtualization: VMware ESX, VirtualCenter, VMotion

Environment: Red Hat Enterprise Linux, Windows 2003, SQL Server clusters

Organization

OpSource, founded in 2002 as a web hosting company, began the shift to Software as a Service (SaaS) in 2004. OpSource differentiates themselves from other application management and hosting providers by offering complete service delivery priced on demand, including managed services, call-center support provided under the software company's brand, and application management. Their business is based on their patent-pending OptiTech Services Engine, which supports rapid integration and deployment of SaaS offerings.

Drivers

As a key part of their transition to SaaS, OpSource felt it was critical to have a uniform platform from which they could deliver their services, with the least amount of time possible to provision new customers and new services. Using their previous platforms of rack-mounted servers, it was taking them 30 days to provision a new customer, with most of that time taken up by racking and stacking the necessary hardware and software. Their key driver was to reduce the time to provision (which has now been reduced to 10 days).

Additional drivers were to increase manageability and flexibility in managing their server farms, including managing their Service Level Agreements (SLAs). With their entire business reliant on their server hardware, they needed ways to improve physical server maintenance, with minimal disruption to their customers. They were also looking to improve the efficiency of their hardware, including increasing their server utilization and growing their ability to serve customers while managing their power consumption requirements.

Implementation

They began looking at blades as a solution in early 2004 and went into production in late 2004. They evaluated virtualization during 2005 and went into production in late 2005.

Evaluation Process

Their evaluation process began with investigating blades versus rack-mounted servers — specifically, how the strengths of blades matched up with their requirements. They evaluated IBM, Dell, and HP blades in 2004. Their in-house testing was focused on time to provision. At the time, they were using Altiris management software as their primary provisioning tool. Their power comparisons were based on specs rather than actual testing.

For virtualization, they evaluated VMware, Xen 2.0, and Virtuozzo.

Results

Their conclusion overall was that blades were easier to install, easier to stock unified spares for increased availability, and easier to swap, with more predictability in the amount of time needed to swap (reducing their quality-assurance time).

According to OpSource, they selected HP blades for two main reasons: power and management software. Their decision on power was based on a comparison of HP p-Class blades versus IBM BladeCenter, which were both the high-end chassis at the time of the evaluation. (Note that both HP and IBM have made considerable strides in power efficiency with their next-generation blade chassis.) Their evaluation of management software put HP Systems Insight Manager "head and shoulders above everyone else." They viewed acquisition costs as a distant third criterion. Initially, they viewed all vendors as roughly equal on price, although as the incumbent now, HP offers them better pricing.

Their choice of VMware was based on their evaluation showing a higher level of both performance and sophistication with the VMware suite. They ruled out Microsoft Virtual Server due to the overhead of its hosted approach versus hypervisor solutions, and its lack of management capabilities. They felt that Xen (release 2.0 at the time) was "not yet bullet-proof enough." Virtuozzo was more attractively priced than VMware, but they felt that it lacked the sophistication of VMware, especially in its management features, such as VMotion.

Environment

Their production environment now includes 1,150 blades out of a total of 1,200 servers. The blade configuration consists of HP BladeCenter p-Class blades, 12 per enclosure, 24 per cabinet. They are not fully populating with p-Class due to power consumption. OpSource is currently testing c-Class, which they hope will allow a denser population due to increased power efficiency and the use of AMD processors.

The blades currently being used are BL25 blades, with 300GB SCSI drives, and BL35 blades, with 60GB ATA drives. All blades have redundant drives. OpSource's small users may run completely on one blade, including storage; however, their larger customers (some with more than 100 blades) are connected to a SAN, which uses EMC and 3PAR storage, and/or BlueArc NAS. For those customers with high-transaction applications, OpSource uses ONStor Bobcats to front-end the SAN.

SAN connections use a pass-through from the blades to external McData switches, and Ethernet connections come through Nortel Ethernet switch modules in the chassis. They also use an external F5 switch for load balancing.

The OS environment includes Red Hat Enterprise Linux, Windows 2003, some SQL Server clusters, and some Red Hat clusters. Their rack-server environment supports Oracle RAC, which they run on HP DL servers. So far, they have not moved these to blades due to sensitivity to I/O latency. This will be re-evaluated with the c-Class evaluation.

Most of OpSource's environment is running on VMware Infrastructure, with ESX, VirtualCenter, and VMotion. Their average ratios exceed five virtual servers to one physical server.

Benefits

When asked how well blades are addressing their needs, the response was, "Fantastic! We don't even want to think about anything but blades. Nothing else makes sense for us." Their overriding issue is flexibility — the blade architecture and virtualization allow them to move physical and virtual servers around the data center easily and quickly, facilitating maintenance and reducing time to provision. This flexibility has resulted in "definitely less hours, less planning, less heartache, and maybe less people." They rated efficiency as their number-two benefit, citing power, space, and server utilization.

In terms of reliability and availability, they have had "zero problems with blades" beyond the normal kinds of problems with any server. Their experience included some failures in power supplies and disk drives, but they were within normal limits and were handled by redundancy.

If they had not gone to blades and virtualization, they believe they would be using 50% more space and 50% more power.

Lessons Learned

The only limitations they have experienced are in the size and number of hard drives, and in the number of NICs and HBAs. They believe these are addressed (for now) with the c-Class. They see the cost of VMware as high, making it hard to argue for ROI without including analysis for all the OpEx savings. They calculate their breakeven at four or five servers consolidating down to one.

Their experience is that the move to virtualization has been "slower than they had thought, with lots of things to consider." They see it now in terms of learning a new operating system environment (which it is), and highly recommend VMware training and other vendor services, such as a study of your environment and best practices recommendations.

Their final words: blades and virtualization have been great for them, but are not right for everybody. Their advice, "Measure twice and cut once. Decide what's right for you first, and then focus on implementation decisions. Once you've deployed virtualization, you can't change easily. And if you need 10 hard drives, or incredible graphics, blades may not be right."

Case Study — U.S. Government Installation

At a Glance

Industry: Large government installation in the United States

Blades: 250 IBM blades in 12 BladeCenter chassis in 3 racks

150 Egenera blades across 7 BladeFrames

Virtualization: VMware ESX, VirtualCenter, VMotion in test

Environment: Red Hat Enterprise Linux, Windows 2003, SUSE Linux

Red Hat Cluster Suite — Global File System (GFS)

Oracle RAC, SAS, Microsoft SQL

Organization

This government installation provides IT services for a large government organization. In 2004, it undertook a major project to develop a utility computing model that would bring their decentralized infrastructure back into one centrally managed IT facility.

Drivers

This project was started to address both organizational and IT technical issues, recentralizing and standardizing the design, implementation, purchasing, and management of IT resources. IT issues included multiple hardware and software platforms from too many different vendors; SAN islands; and various disparate file system layouts, operating systems, and versions. The goal of the new utility architecture was to standardize applications on blade servers with AMD processors, Red Hat Linux and MS Windows operating systems, and a centrally managed SAN.

Implementation

The project was based on a two-step implementation. The first step was to consolidate applications and standardize on two hardware platforms. The second step was to implement server virtualization to further reduce the number of physical servers.

Evaluation Process

The blade evaluation process began with a market-research study in 2004, followed by an extensive RFP sent out to the four major blade vendors at the time (IBM, HP, Sun, and Egenera), and included "a massive bake-off," in the words of the project manager. The Sun solution at the time was the Sun Grid Computing solution, comprised of 1U rack servers with Topspin InfiniBand high-speed interconnect.

The blade evaluation included functionality testing, performance testing, and cost-benefit analysis of both the hardware and its related tool sets. The testing was conducted in an in-house blade lab, which was established specifically for this process. The acquisition strategy was to choose two vendors to implement, to avoid a sole-source installation. The virtualization evaluation has just started, with a test of VMware as the first step.

Results

As a result of the blade evaluation process, IBM and Egenera were selected for implementation. Due to the high-speed interconnect of the Egenera Blade-Frames at 2.5Gb/s node-to-node communication, and the higher-speed processors and large memory options on Egenera blades, Egenera is used for the higher-end applications, such as Oracle RAC and SAS. (The IBM Blade-Center H, IBM's high-performance solution, was not available at the time of the initial evaluation.)

The remaining applications with no particular high-speed requirements are implemented on IBM BladeCenter. These applications include web servers, Windows infrastructure (Active Directory, SQL Server), NetBackup media servers, security applications, and so on.

Overall, IT feels that both products are "handling the load pretty well, with no complaints about performance." They are very pleased with the automated failover capabilities of Egenera, and would like to replicate them on IBM BladeCenter, which they feel does not have the same level of functionality. For example, if an Egenera BladeFrame detects a hardware failure, the Egenera PAN Manager automatically restarts the same functions on a different blade.

Environment

The new configuration includes 130 Egenera blades deployed cross 7 Blade-Frames, with 24 per rack (and 20 more blades on order at press time). The Egenera blades are configured with four-way AMD dual-core 32GB RAM. The IBM BladeCenter implementation includes 150 blades, with 12 chassis in 3 racks, with 100 more on order, including the BladeCenter H chassis. (This provides up to 70 servers per rack.) The BladeCenter chassis also include integrated Cisco Ethernet switch modules and Brocade SAN switch modules. The IBM blades are either two-way dual-core 16GB RAM AMD blades or single-core Intel blades, with GbE and 2Gb fibre channel HBAs. All blades are diskless and boot from the SAN, which includes 900 TB of IBM, 3PAR, and some HP EVA storage.

Operating systems have now been standardized to include Red Hat Enterprise Linux, Windows 2003, and some SUSE Linux. Clustering includes Microsoft Cluster Services and Red Hat Clustering.

Benefits

The biggest benefits have been in space, deployment time, and standardization. The space savings are on the order of 70% (now using only 30% of the space previously required), presenting new options for hosting other applications in that same space. Deployment time for new servers has gone from two to six months (for ordering equipment, installing cabling, dealing with power and floor space, and so on) to a few hours ("now we pop a blade into a chassis"). Standardizing on both hardware and software has simplified their infrastructure, streamlined deployments, and simplified management tremendously. In addition, they save on hardware maintenance and vendor agreements.

Their new utility computing environment provides "failover and redundancy, faster repair, and easier management."

Lessons Learned

One of the biggest issues in their deployment was in power and cooling. Because of the size and importance of this project, they had the luxury of starting fresh and engineering the data center for high-density computing. Upgrades included additional Power Distribution Units (PDU), (providing ~25kW power per rack of blade servers (65KBTU) per rack), additional chillers (they had a supercomputer in there previously, so water cooling was already in place), hot/cool zones to support optimal airflow for heat dissipation (120 tons of additional cooling), and vented floor tiles that funnel cooling in front of each rack from the chillers. In total, their implementation requirements were as follows:

- Lots of power
  - Egenera — 20kW/frame, up to 24 blades per frame, 4-socket, dual-core processors = 192 cores per frame/rack.
  - IBM — 24kW/rack (6-chassis configuration); they use mostly 5-chassis/rack, 14 blades/chassis, 2-socket, dual-core = 280 cores/rack, partially populated
- Generating lots of heat
  - Egenera — 65K BTU/frame
  - IBM — 68K BTU/rack (6-chassis configuration)

The lesson to be learned here is that if the room is properly designed, implemented, and managed, the density of blades is not a problem.

However, this involves planning and proper room-level power and cooling. Most blade vendors offer professional services to evaluate power and cooling issues and make recommendations. But according to the organization, "It's worth it." Tools are also available to help with ongoing monitoring, such as IBM PowerExecutive and PAN Manager's temperature monitoring. "Invest early in resolving potential cooling issues."

Other challenges arose around the complexities of the Egenera virtualization layer, particularly with respect to troubleshooting: "When everything is working, there is no problem, but when something goes wrong, that extra layer makes it difficult to troubleshoot. But it's worth it due to the failover and high performance we get with Egenera."

Another important lesson — test all applications thoroughly before deploying them. Understand their requirements at all levels. If there is a CPU-heavy back-end database, put it on more powerful blades. If the middleware is I/O-intensive, make sure that there is enough bandwidth to handle it and don't stack all those blades in the same chassis and saturate the uplinks. Watch your CPU load and I/O load.

If you use both high-speed and lower-speed blades, spread out the high-speed, higher-heat blades across multiple chassis/racks for better cooling. If the software supports it, use resource pools to facilitate managing like blades as a group.

Finally, according to the technical lead at this organization, who has postponed the virtualization implementation until after the initial blade implementation, "Think twice about implementing blades and virtualization at the same time. It increases the complexity and slows the migration. But doing it in steps may cost more." You'll need more blade hardware if you have not yet virtualized and haven't consolidated to fewer servers. And to virtualize you may need newer servers with virtualization-assist hardware. Clearly, there are pros and cons both ways.

Case Study — Managed Service Provider: Virtualized Utility Services

At a Glance

Industry: Managed service provider — virtualized utility services

SAVVIS: www.savvis.net

Blades: Over 1,000 Egenera blades on over 40 BladeFrames

Virtualization: VMware ESX on rack-mount servers

Environment: Windows, Linux, Sun Solaris, AIX on rack-mount servers

Microsoft SQL clustering, Oracle RAC

Organization

SAVVIS is a service provider focused on delivering managed services on a virtualized utility platform. SAVVIS serves more than 5,000 customers, with 25 data centers, 1,000 virtual servers, 1,400 virtual firewalls and load balancers, with more than 370 TB of virtualized storage and 21,000 managed network end points. Their business is to deliver managed IT services as an infrastructure (databases, middleware, web services), not applications.

Drivers

SAVVIS, with their virtualized utility services, offers infrastructure in virtual forms for less cost than physical forms. By avoiding additional hardware purchases (reducing both CapEx and its associated ongoing OpEx), they can deliver better-priced offerings to their customers.

Implementation

As they considered their move from traditional rack-mount servers in 2004, they were not interested in what they viewed as "traditional" blades, which they saw as a footprint-only improvement. Their interest was in the additional virtualization that Egenera offered, "decoupling compute and memory resources from storage and networking."

Evaluation Process

Their litmus test consisted of three things in both the Linux and Windows environments. First was the ability of the management interface to integrate with their provisioning systems. Second was scalability and ease of management for large numbers of servers. Third was control and reporting capabilities. As a service provider, they needed to simplify and automate the process of translating an order into a physical instance, with full configuration management at every step.

Results

Their results were positive, and they have launched their utility service around blades with virtualization, virtualized switching, and virtualized storage.

Environment

Their blade environment consists of more than 1,000 Egenera blades across 40 BladeFrames, fully populated with 24 blades per frame. Although they buy blades configured as requested by their customers, the profile most requested is the 2-processor, 8GB RAM blade. Operating systems include Windows and Linux, which communicate with 370TB of 3PAR SAN storage across their Cisco MDS fabric. In addition to blades, they run VMware on their traditional HP DL servers. They use a proprietary provisioning system, which interfaces with the provisioning functions in PAN Manager as well as 3PAR. There is some traditional clustering using Microsoft SQL clusters and Oracle RAC, as well as through PAN Manager failover and HA features.

Benefits

The benefit of their virtualized utility services model is flexibility and rapid response. Egenera's design of "decoupling the processor and memory from everything else makes the hardware functions of the blade more fungible."

Lessons Learned

One of the big lessons SAVVIS learned was to be careful with the configuration-management process, including putting procedures in place to handle this new virtualized world, where there is no longer a one-to-one relationship between a box and the environment running on it. They advise new users to pay attention to management systems overall. Their experience is that building virtual machines and virtual environments is the easy part; the management and troubleshooting is harder.

With regard to power and cooling, they run fully populated frames without problems. (They do not run Egenera's CoolFrame.) They are working on operating as a "green" environment.

Their last word of advice to users: "Go to a service provider!"

Case Study — Large University in Australia

At a Glance

Industry: Large university in Australia (Over 50,000 students)

Blades: 88 HP BladeCenter p-Class blades across 11 enclosures in 2 racks

40 Dell PowerEdge blades across 2 enclosures — in test

Virtualization: VMware ESX, VirtualCenter, VMotion

Environment: Windows 2003 Server, Novell NetWare

Organization

This large university provides IT resources for both the academic and administrative areas of the university.

Drivers

In 2003, as part of an effort to reduce costs and better utilize their hardware, they began to look at consolidating on a standard platform. Their goal was also to reduce their data-center footprint.

Implementation

They began their efforts with the move to blades in 2003 and then added virtualization in 2005.

Evaluation Process

Since their preferred hardware supplier for servers was HP, their initial evaluation of blades was HP BladeCenter only. The evaluation process was simple and straightforward, with no formal testing or benchmarking. For virtualization, they went with VMware as the market leader and had not really even heard of other options in Australia.

Results

Based on "gut-feel testing" the HP BladeCenter met their requirements to support all necessary software environments while reducing their physical space required. Since the initial evaluation, Dell was added to the university's preferred-supplier list, and presented an attractive pricing offer. They are currently evaluating Dell to decide between Dell and HP for future growth.

Environment

Their production blade implementation is a pure HP BladeCenter p-Class environment, with 88 blades. These BL20p blades, with 2–4GB of memory, reside within two racks — one with 6 enclosures and another with 5 enclosures (with 8 blades per enclosure). One enclosure is populated with 8GB RAM blades which are dedicated to VMware. Blades are configured with local disk ranging from 36GB to 146GB. Some also connect to the SAN via a Brocade switch module. The blades with larger local disks are used for Novell NetWare Directory Services (NDS) and GroupWise email. They are planning to evaluate both Woodcrest processors for p-Class as well as the c-Class products.

In addition, there are two more enclosures of Dell PowerEdge blades, with a total of 20 blades, running 8GB RAM each, with redundant 70GB SAS drives. They are planning to attach these blades to the SAN, but have not yet. They are also planning to connect the PowerEdge Cisco switch to their Nortel switches, but have been waiting for help from Dell (they have had no exposure to Cisco prior to this).

In addition to VMware ESX, they run Novell NetWare and Windows Server 2003. There is no Linux or Unix, and no clustering in use. Management is done through HP System Insight Manager and Dell OpenManage.

Benefits

On a scale of 1 to 10, the university scored blades and virtualization as an 8 in terms of how well this combined solution is addressing their needs. Benefits include better space utilization due to consolidation, better management (they eliminated their remote sites), and central control.

Lessons Learned

Overall, they view blades as not much different than servers as far as reliability, availability, processor options, and/or limitations. The only lesson they learned with blades is that they will populate only four enclosures out of five per rack due to heat. They still feel this is a winner and is better than racks.

With respect to VMware, they learned that training is important and useful. To get full benefit out of VMware and properly configure for the best utilization when consolidating under VMware, training was important.

Case Study — Academic Clinical Research Organization

At a Glance

Industry: Academic clinical research

Blades: 16 HP BladeSystem p-Class blades

Virtualization: VMware ESX; VirtualCenter, VMotion

130 virtual servers, of which 86 are on 14 blades

Environment: Supporting 600 onsite users and 400 remote users

Red Hat Linux; Windows NT 4.0, 2000, and 2003; Solaris 8 and 10 for x86

Organization

The world's largest academic clinical research organization combines clinical expertise and academic leadership of a teaching hospital with the full-service operational capabilities of a major contract research organization. This requires an IT organization that is driven by their clients' needs. If a client wants a certain application for a study, IT must be prepared to implement the application or face the possibility of losing the contract.

To support the work of this organization yet balance the cost and size of the computing infrastructure, the IT department has been working on server consolidation, workload balancing, and disaster-recovery projects.

Drivers

The CIO hated having a room full of servers, all of which were running at less than 5% CPU utilization. A 15% utilization level was the sign of a runaway process that needed attention, rather than a server being well-utilized. In early 2004, they had 80–90 physical servers (which cost them roughly $7,000–10,000 each) and the rat's-nest cabling that comes with so many servers. On top of that, it was becoming more difficult to get money for new servers. They were reaching their uninterruptible power supply (UPS) capacity on power, breakers, and outlets, with cooling quickly becoming an issue as well. In an attempt to remedy this situation, IT set goals of reducing the number of physical servers by a factor of four, increasing CPU utilization of the remaining servers to at least 50%, and improving overall availability in case of hardware or power failures.

Implementation

A two-phased approach was used to address their goals. The first phase was to try running applications in a virtual environment rather than in a purely physical environment. If this worked, they would be able to run multiple virtual environments on fewer systems and retire some of their servers. The second phase was to test blade systems as a possible upgrade path for their servers. They liked the idea of virtualization but did not think highly of blade technology before the evaluation process — primarily because of the higher start-up costs associated with the blade chassis.

Evaluation

They started their proof of concept in March 2004 with the installation of VMware ESX to test virtual capabilities. They also considered Microsoft Virtual Server but needed a smaller footprint with less overhead.

Initially, there were some problems with a couple of the clinical applications not running in a virtual environment. According to the user, "The software didn't play nice if it wasn't on its own box."

Evaluating performance was difficult, as they didn't have good benchmarks. To test performance, they made changes then looked for anecdotal feedback from users. For example, they would migrate a physical server to a virtual machine running with other virtual machines, and wait to see if users noticed. Mostly, they didn't.

Results

In January 2005, they brought in the HP BladeSystem p-Class for evaluation to help overcome their cabling problems. They soon found that the cable issue was resolved, plus they had a more reliable, redundant, and flexible platform on which to run their virtual environments.

Environment

In January 2005, VMware ESX on blades went into production. The blade chassis is configured with 16 blades. Fourteen blades are dedicated to running ESX. Two blades are running Windows, acting as NAS heads for the SAN, clustered for high availability running Microsoft Cluster Services in an active-active configuration. Each blade has single-core processors with either 5GB or 8GB RAM and two 36GB onboard SCSI drives mirrored for reliability (purchased before ESX supported boot from SAN). A Nortel GigE switch module is used for the LAN and an external Brocade switch is used for the SAN.

Their virtual environment extends beyond their BladeSystem to support a total of 130 virtual servers running on 50 physical servers. Of those physical servers, the 14 blades running ESX are currently supporting 86 virtual machines running Red Hat Linux or Windows supporting SQL Server 2000, among other applications.

Benefits

The migration to blades and virtualization allowed them not only to address their initial problems, but also to realize additional benefits. While they have not yet reduced the number of physical servers by a factor of four, they were able to remove four racks (~40 servers) from their floor, and nearly double the number of virtual servers managed (over the initial 80–90 physical servers). Today, their physical servers run between 24% and 70% utilization, depending on the application mix.

With virtual machines, IT no longer has to go through the long cycle of justifying new servers every time a new application is introduced; they simply add another virtual machine. Unfortunately, they still have the same justification issues if a new blade is needed, and especially if a new chassis is also required.

With the blade system, they are in a better position in terms of availability — if something fails, the VMs can be moved to another blade. For example, during the implementation a loop failed on the SAN. The VMs all lost connectivity for a second, but the servers stayed online. When the loop failed over, all went fine with no staff intervention, and the VMs and their applications continued.

Additionally, the combination of the blade system and virtualization has eased management across the board. The remote console allows the network services group, located in a different building than the data center, to have remote access to the networking functions. With the speed and ease of deployment and overall management, they have increased the number of servers; with no added staff (they manage their servers with three Windows administrators, one Linux administrator, and one IT strategist).

Finally, they recognized $200,000 over 18 months in cost avoidance by paying $100,000 initial investment for the BladeSystem and VMware ESX, rather than $300,000 in physical servers.

Lessons Learned

Many lessons were learned, mostly around moving from a physical environment to a virtual environment. Overall, they now feel that "Blades and virtualization go well together."

They did hit a couple of rough spots along the way. For example, at press time VMware's VMotion requires matching processors in order to move VMs from one blade to another. If the blade chassis contains blades with different processors, there may be limits to which processors VMs can be moved.

Due to the fairly recent advances in virtual server capabilities, not all software vendors support their applications in a virtual environment. IT often heard, "Run it in on a physical server then call."

For one of their primary (large) applications, they discovered that there cannot be two virtual instances of that application running on the same physical system, even in separate VMs, but it can run with other applications. This problem was caused by memory over allocation. They found that "you can over-allocate memory somewhat, but too much will cause problems!" They realized that some of their applications were pickier about memory than others. They don't use VMotion on those applications.

Initially, the organization used VMotion to keep applications running while they would apply patches to the systems in real time. Now that their server farm is larger, VMotion is used mostly at night to perform rolling upgrades of the OS while keeping applications running.

When asked what advice they would give to someone just beginning to look at blades and virtualization, the response was, "I'm a big fan of VMware and I have changed my mind on blades. I would like to switch everything to blades and virtualize it all."

Case Study — Concrete Accessories Manufacturer

At a Glance

Industry: Concrete accessories manufacturing

Blades: HP BladeSystem

Virtualization: VMware ESX, VirtualCenter, PlateSpin PowerConvert, and PowerRecon

Environment: 2 data centers in 2 cities

150 servers

800 users

50 remote sites

HPUX (HP Systems), Linux (x86)

Organization

This company is a large manufacturer and distributor of metal accessories and forms used in concrete construction, and a leading manufacturer of metal accessories used in masonry construction. The company's products are used in two segments of the construction industry: infrastructure construction, such as highways, bridges, utilities, water and waste treatment facilities, and airport runways; and non-residential buildings, such as schools, stadiums, prisons, retail sites, commercial offices, hotels, and manufacturing facilities. They have been using virtualization in their data centers for over a year.

Drivers

Like many companies, they found that the cost of maintaining "a bunch of old systems that needed to be around for history, but not much more" was putting a strain on their data-center space as well as their personnel. "Our data center is very small. In the old days, it was big enough to hold just one mainframe." Power was always a problem and heat was becoming a problem. Plus, management was pushing to gain better utilization from the systems they have rather than purchasing new systems. This drove the IT group at this company to investigate and implement virtualization and blades, though not yet together.

Implementation

In early 2004, this company set out to find smarter support for their legacy systems, as well as better space, power, and cooling management while improving computer utilization. They looked to virtualization and blades to help achieve these goals.

Evaluation

This company didn't have much time to test many different configurations. They started their evaluation of what was available in the market in 2004 when there were not many choices. For their virtualization solution, it came down to a choice between VMware's GSX or ESX solutions. They liked GSX but wanted the broader support afforded by the ESX solution in combination with the PlateSpin PowerConvert and PowerRecon tools.

Results

The company decided on VMware's ESX solution and uses it in combination with the PlateSpin tools. They have converted 15 physical servers to virtual, "which is a big deal for us." These included moving a couple of old tape backup machines and an old domain server to virtual, as well as upgrading and moving their Active Directory system and their Exchange Server. "We simply drag and drop a standard image with PlateSpin. We use VirtualCenter to deploy base images and instead of deploying hardware machines, we deploy a virtual machine."

Environment

Virtualization has been in production for about a year; however, it's not used to support their mission-critical applications yet. They say, "Virtualization has been working well for us; it's very stable."

This company also has an HP BladeSystem that is used to support their Citrix desktop environment. They have plans in 2007 to purchase more HP BladeSystems and implement virtualization on them as part of their consolidation efforts.

Benefits

They were able to remove 15 physical servers from their data-center floor using VMware's ESX and PlateSpin solutions. This combination "takes the worry and much of the cost (OpEx) out of maintaining legacy services within the environment." They say, "The combination of virtualization and migration technologies has simplified these operations."

Before using PlateSpin, transitioning an application to another server would take weeks; now "it only takes (depending on the size of the storage) two to three hours to migrate a system."

Lessons Learned

This IT group says they are "less interested in hardware and more interested in the services." They "don't want to deal with provisioning a physical server."

Case Study — Pharmaceutical Company

At a Glance

> **Industry:** Pharmaceutical
>
> **Blades:** None currently
>
> **Virtualization:** VMware GSX (Server)
>
> PlateSpin PowerConvert migration software
>
> **Environment:** Four-processor HP servers
>
> Stratus for high availability
>
> Microsoft Windows

Organization

This pharmaceutical company, founded by physicians, is dedicated to finding, developing, and bringing to market new medicines and related products that promote health and healing. The company has long been focused on pioneering research to address persistent pain. They have used virtualization in their data center for more than six years.

Drivers

This company, like all pharmaceutical companies, is highly regulated. Due to the regulations, the company is required to maintain legacy environments with the ability to re-create results. In an environment where every application has its own server, they were running out of floor space. In addition, filling their floor with computers running at sub-5% utilization wasn't good for business.

Implementation

In 2000, in an attempt to better manage all their legacy systems, the Production Services group of this company evaluated virtualization software, as there were no blade solutions at that time.

Evaluation

When they started their evaluation, there were not many options. They tested VMware's GSX and looked at Connectrix before Microsoft purchased them, but as a pharmaceutical company their support requirements were stringent. They tested HP and Stratus systems at the same time. Their list of test criteria included the following:

- Hardware/system reliability; they cannot put 5 or 10 of their production applications on a system that is prone to crashes
- Price points
- Decent I/O performance for the virtual servers
- Support for at least 15 virtual machines per physical server
- The ability to quickly move their applications from a physical server to a virtual server
- Ease of management within a Windows environment (they use MOM extensively)

Results

The company went with HP servers for their non–mission-critical applications and Stratus for their mission-critical servers. For their virtual environment, they found that the combination of VMware's GSX (now called Virtual Server) and PlateSpin's Power P2V (now called PowerConvert) met their needs very well. VMware's GSX provided the ability to run, during their tests, 15–18 virtual servers per system with reasonable I/O performance. PlateSpin's Power-Convert, with the ability to move a physical environment over to a virtual environment with a simple point and click (actual elapsed time was several hours) made the migration to virtual a trivial task. For their legacy applications, with PowerConvert they have been able to create a library of system images to recall into either a physical or virtual environment — again, within one or two hours (depending on the size of the image).

Environment

When they first put GSX into production, VirtualCenter was not yet available for managing the environment. "Three or four months later we bought it and it's been great!" Today this company runs nearly all their applications (except for the I/O-intensive applications) in a virtual environment using VMware's GSX with 9 or 10 virtual servers per physical server. Some of the applications running virtual include Citrix, their Blackberry Enterprise Server, and many of their in-house applications. They also have a few applications, such as SQL Server 2000, running partly on virtual and partly on physical servers.

They have started a second evaluation as they look to upgrade to VMware's ESX Server. They are also looking at Microsoft's Virtual Server. They like it but say "it looks like VMware's management is about four years ahead of Microsoft right now." As a large Microsoft shop, they would like to have their virtualization management interface tie into MOM. They are also looking at the granularity of system control available with both. They would like to run 12–15 virtual servers per physical servers in production. Finally, when virtual servers need to be moved due to spikes in activity, this is done manually or with specialized scripts today. They are hoping to automate this movement with VMotion, which is not supported with VMware's GSX release or with Virtual Server.

As to their opinions on PowerConnect, they say, "PlateSpin is awesome; we couldn't have done it without them. They talk to their customers and actually incorporate needed features. They are our standard now." In some instances, the company has moved an application to a virtual server and found out the virtual environment is not a good fit. "What other tool would enable you to easily move the application back to the physical environment?"

Benefits

The company currently supports over 150 virtual servers on 12 physical servers. Utilization across the GSX virtual environment is over 60% and moving to 70–75% but no more than 80%. They say, "Applications have spike times — this is where the extra headroom comes in."

The organization has seen financial benefits through cost avoidance; instead of paying roughly $9,000 for a physical server, they have an equivalent virtual server for about $5,000, for a savings of $4,000/server. That, multiplied by the 150 virtual servers currently supported, comes to a $600,000 savings. They are working on getting the virtual server cost down to $3,000 per server, for a savings of $900,000.

Several years ago pharmaceutical companies hit some hard times, and this company was forced to lay off 70% of the workforce, reducing the Production Services group from 250 people to 70. Since that time, the group has not hired any additional help but they have continued to manage many more virtual servers and a few more physical servers.

An added benefit they received with the PlateSpin solution was the ability to create a snapshot of the entire server environment, which is now part of their disaster-recovery plan.

Lessons Learned

One of the biggest lessons/battles the group had to overcome was when they recentralized their systems back into the data center: "This was, culturally, a very difficult move, but now the departments can focus on their work rather than administering their distributed systems."

They also recommend that you really know your systems — what hardware configurations do and don't work with your applications, how much memory each application requires, and so on. They advise that you "monitor the application and systems requirements and interdependencies" before moving to virtual. When it's time to migrate to virtual environments, use P2V, V2V, and V2P tools to streamline the migration process: "You can't possibly move as many applications/server as we have from physical to virtual without P2V tools, like PlateSpin PowerConvert." Finally, they add, "Once you get your applications into a virtual environment, understand that the applications may behave differently than in a physical environment. That's where the V2P tool is priceless — have a good back-out plan!"

When asked if there was any advice they could offer to those just starting down the virtualization path, the response was, "If you are not doing it already, you are behind — get on the ball!"

Conclusion

This chapter has described a variety of user environments in which blades and server virtualization products have been evaluated and road-tested. It has offered real-world configurations, opinions, and lessons learned from IT professionals who are working in the trenches. Chapter 18 takes the next step, offering some insights into what's on the horizon with blade and virtualization technologies.

A Look into the Future

It is impossible for anyone to look into a crystal ball and know without a doubt what the future will bring. However, after carefully researching this book, talking with both vendors and customers, and taking a lesson from history, we see trends emerging around blades, virtualization, and the management software that ties it all together.

There is no doubt that, even with its rocky start, the blade server market is here to stay. IDC predicts the blade market will be at $9.6 billion in 2008 and go from roughly 500,000 blades shipped in 2005 to between 2.5 and 3 million blades shipped in 2009. IDC expects this will make up 30% of the total server market.

Virtualization technology of all flavors, especially server virtualization, is also taking off. Several surveys completed in mid 2006 showed that 40–50% of those surveyed had already implemented server virtualization, and the number is expected to increase significantly in the next two years.

Bigger, Better, Faster, Cheaper

It shouldn't be surprising that the trends we described at the beginning of the book will continue to be seen in future blade server and virtualization solutions. Bigger — greater capacity, more processors, more memory, more bandwidth on a single blade; better — virtualization and management tools to support the "always on" requirements of utility computing, improvements in architecture, and efficiencies in power and cooling; faster — processors, memory architectures, and I/O architectures to keep data flowing to the processors; cheaper — with economies of scale, the cost of blade solutions will fall and, in fact, some virtualization software now can be obtained for free. Interestingly, the flip side of bigger is a trend toward smaller. While capacities continue to grow, physical size is getting smaller — smaller components to fit more on a blade, smaller number of physical racks, and a smaller (thinner) virtualization footprint in memory. These trends are affecting and will continue to affect chip architectures and production, which will, in turn, create the ripple effect in memory and disk I/O, as well as virtualization and management software.

Hardware

The birth and the future of blades comes largely from improvements at the lowest level — modularization, miniaturization, and chip improvements — creating the opportunity for ultrahigh-density computing.

Chips

Processors used in the data center are pushing and will continue to push the envelope on power and cooling issues. Over the past few years, the performance of processors has been growing linearly, while the power required to create the performance has been growing exponentially. When you consider the cost to power the hardware and then double it to account for cooling that hardware, high-performance computing expenses become prohibitive. Chip vendors are highly focused on creating solutions that provide increasing levels of performance, with more-efficient power and cooling. Performance per watt will continue to be a fierce competition between chip vendors.

Increasing the number of cores per socket has brought significant improvements in this area. Generally speaking, with dual-core you can expect to achieve roughly an 80% performance gain (not quite 100% due to overhead) over a single processor in the same real estate, using less than two times the power and cooling. The chip vendors are continuing this *doubling* of processors to increase performance without doubling the power and cooling requirements; quad-core chips are due out in early 2007, 8-core chips in early 2008, 16-core after that, and so on. As long as the chip vendors can leverage this ability to deliver performance efficiently, they will continue along these lines.

The chip vendors are also working hand-in-hand with the virtualization software companies to continue to evolve server virtualization through improvements in hardware-assist capabilities. These improvements will continue to move functions currently performed by software down onto the chip, reducing overhead and making hypervisor virtualization significantly more efficient. This has the added benefit of making the hypervisor software much less complex. An example of this is support for nested-page tables for smooth transitions between the hypervisor and virtual machine guest operating systems. Rather than the software having to manage page tables, the processor can do this more efficiently.

These advancements from the chip vendors will cause a ripple in the rest of the blade and virtualization markets. Processor improvements will force memory, blade, and I/O vendors to focus on providing balanced architectures with faster I/O bandwidth. In addition, all of these vendors will have to keep an eye toward power improvements, which will also reduce cooling requirements.

Memory

Blade vendors will be looking to their memory suppliers for larger amounts of memory to keep these multicore processors fed with data. The memory market, for quite a few years, has been driven only by economics, with ever-decreasing costs for memory. As power and cooling (and the costs for that energy) increase, it will be interesting to see how memory vendors respond to these new demands for balanced performance per watt. Over the next few years, watch for a transition from DDR2 (Double Data Rate 2) memory to the next generation, DDR3. How that transition will take place and exactly what it will look like are not yet clear.

I/O

With CPU bandwidths and memory sizes increasing, attention also must be paid to data paths. For example, AMD plans to double data-path bandwidth over the next few years. In addition, blades and virtualization are creating a shared disk environment that was never designed to be shared. This will force a change in the way both operating systems and the hypervisors handle disk I/O (for example, a change in protocols and drivers to allow disk to be shared nicely), as well as the way storage vendors build their disk subsystems. Enhancements in virtualized I/O will continue to improve the way blade systems share common components. Watch for changes in PCI Express as well.

There is no doubt that the combination of blades and virtualization technologies will stress all the system components as well as the management capabilities. In the past when this has happened, technological breakthroughs have been found. It will be exciting to watch as server virtualization consolidates workloads and increases utilization, while processors, memory, and I/O race to keep up.

Power and Cooling

Power and cooling will continue to drive changes at the chip level as well as at the blade and chassis level, creating more efficiency in both power and cooling. In terms of mass movement, although liquid provides a far better cooling medium than air (think of the differences between an old VW bug and a Porsche) the economics of liquid cooling will continue to be a deterrent to many. Liquid cooling at the chip level may appear in niche products.

Chassis

Like the component vendors, the blade system vendors will be looking to deliver bigger, better, faster, and cheaper solutions. It is unlikely, however, that there will be cross-vendor interoperability between blades or chassis any time soon. The only chassis standard that exists in this space is the AdvancedTCA standard used in the telco market. There just hasn't been the pressure from customers to create an interoperable chassis.

Chassis and blade management will continue to evolve, with vendors leapfrogging each other with new functionality, similar to some of the newer power and cooling monitoring and management capabilities.

Virtualization and Management

With advances in server virtualization including hardware assists, and both open source and Microsoft entries in the hypervisor space, the virtualization landscape is changing. As server virtualization gains significant traction as a result of this change, expect to see rapid changes in both the virtualization technology and the software infrastructure for managing virtual environments.

At press time, the industry leader in server virtualization is VMware, with Virtual Infrastructure 3. There are two primary reasons for this. The first is that they were clever enough to create a hypervisor for the x86 architecture (that could run unmodified guest operating systems) before there were virtualization hardware assists. The second and more compelling reason is that they have also developed sophisticated management tools for managing the virtual environment.

The next few years will see other virtualization vendors, as well as traditional management vendors, scrambling to catch up to and surpass VMware's management functionality. There will continue to be enhancements in virtualization software products, but the real battleground will be in the management. In addition, management software that spans individual virtualization approaches (and manages virtualization software from multiple vendors) will become a key part of the competitive landscape.

Ubiquitous Hypervisors?

Although VMware was the first hypervisor, the release of the Xen 3.0 hypervisor (the first to take advantage of hardware assist, developed by a team of engineers from top computer companies, and available free on open source) has changed the playing field. XenSource, the marketing arm for the Xen hypervisor, is highly motivated to make Xen a ubiquitous hypervisor. They are working very closely with the industry's leading hardware and software vendors to create a joint hypervisor solution in which part of the solution is implemented in the silicon, making the hypervisor extremely efficient when running with these chipsets.

Regardless of whether it is a single hypervisor that becomes ubiquitous, or whether hypervisors in general become ubiquitous, having server virtualization as a baseline will have far-reaching effects and will change the way IT operates in many ways.

Managing Virtual Environments

The goal of a virtual management infrastructure is to provide utility or autonomic computing that will result in stabilizing or lowering operational expenses associated with provisioning and managing computer systems while providing on-demand response to fluctuating user needs. These management systems will, given defined initial operational policies, adjust themselves automatically according to the needs of the business — adding or removing resources if the resources are available on the local system, or automatically moving to a system within the pool that has the resources required — and will continue to learn from successes and mistakes/failures. This will require the virtual environment to be self-aware; that is, the VM will have a sense of the CPU, memory, disk and network speeds, sizes, and attachments required to perform optimally. This will, of course, be an evolutionary process that will begin with human intervention but could move to requiring little to no intervention.

VMware has held the lead in the management arena, with other vendors working to close the gap. The bar has been set already, and advanced functionality in management should include such features as the ability to aggregate or disaggregate processors across VMs, monitor VM performance as well as system performance, set policy for dynamic and intelligent management of resources, move running VMs in response to resource-allocation requirements or system maintenance requirements, and provide high availability for virtual machines with failover to another system, as well as the ability to back up VMs.

In addition, the move toward full utility computing will demand more. Within virtualization software, there should be increased support for all operating systems, including further 64-bit support, Mac support (OS X), and legacy support (older Microsoft Windows Server releases, for example), with management consoles accessible from anywhere (that is, not tied to any OS, but operating from a browser). Don't be surprised when you can order a system with a hypervisor preinstalled on the system or even on a chip, along with software and licenses for the operating environments you plan to run virtualized.

Management software will provide even better monitoring and alerting capabilities, so a quick check will show a runaway process versus everything running smoothly. Policy-based management will continue to advance in terms of automation, eventually eliminating scripting from the process. Preinstalled systems will tie into the management infrastructure automatically; adjust to the operating environment, patch level, security software, and quality of service parameters currently being used in the business; and register themselves as resources to be added to the pool. Like plugging in your toaster and turning it on, you may have to adjust a few things (so you don't burn the toast), but it should just work. This is the goal of utility computing.

Enlightened Operating Systems

Over the next few years, you can expect that many of the operating systems prevalent today will be modified or paravirtualized to be aware they are running in a virtual environment (just as an operating system would be modified to support any new hardware or firmware). These enlightened operating systems (to use Microsoft's term), will be able to take advantage of hooks within the hypervisor and hardware to improve performance of both the operating system and their applications running in a virtual environment.

Conclusion

Nobody knows exactly what the future will bring, but we know that some things will stay the same. The "bigger, better, faster, cheaper" miniaturization and centralization/decentralization themes in computing will not go away any time soon. Blade systems and virtualization are key building blocks for next-generation data centers to deliver bigger, better, faster, and cheaper computing in a smaller, consolidated footprint and move us closer to the utopia of true utility computing.

We hope that this chapter, and this book overall, have provided a comprehensive look at blade and virtualization technologies, architectures, considerations, solutions, and prospects. As you continue to explore the changing landscape, this information can provide a foundation on which to build as you begin to assess your own needs and select the best solutions for your environment. We wish you the best in building your next-generation data center.

Vendor and Product Information

This appendix includes vendor and product information on blade server systems, virtualization software, and other related hardware and software products, including blade switches, management software, power and cooling products, and processor chipsets. The information included in this appendix has been provided directly by the vendors and does not include any analysis from the authors. More-detailed discussions and analysis of selected products are included in Chapter 16, "Key Vendor and Product Analysis." For updated information on any of these vendors and their products, refer to the individual vendor websites.

Dell

At a Glance

Company name: Dell Inc.
  HQ address: 1 Dell Way
  Round Rock, TX 78682
  Contact info: 1-800-WWW-DELL
  Website: www.dell.com
  Date founded: 1984
  Dates of blade system and/or virtualization SW FCS:

- PowerEdge 1655MC: 2003

- PowerEdge 1855: November 2004

- PowerEdge 1955: June 2006

Number of employees: ~75,000
Revenue and customer base: 57.4 billion for previous four quarters ending in Q2FY07; #25 on the Fortune 500
Industry awards/recognition: Numerous; please see dell.com for the latest.
Targeted markets: Dell products are factory-customized for almost any solution.
Types of solutions offered:

☑ Blade servers	☐ Virtualization software
☐ PC blades/thin clients	☑ Clustering software
☐ Processor chipsets	☑ Management software
☑ Blade switch modules	☑ Power & cooling solution
☑ High-speed interconnects (InfiniBand, 10 GigE, FC)	

Company Description

Dell Inc. listens to customers and delivers innovative technology and services they trust and value. Uniquely enabled by its direct business model, Dell sells more systems globally than any computer company, placing it at number 25 on the Fortune 500. Dell's climb to market leadership is the result of a persistent focus on delivering the best possible customer experience by directly selling standards-based computing products and services.

Dell was founded in 1984 by Michael Dell, the longest-tenured executive to lead a company in the computer industry. The company is based on a simple concept: by selling computer systems directly to customers, Dell could best understand their needs and efficiently provide the most effective computing solutions to meet those needs. This direct business model eliminates retailers that add unnecessary time and cost or can diminish Dell's understanding of customer expectations. The direct model allows the company to build every system to order and offer customers powerful, richly configured systems at competitive prices. Dell also introduces the latest relevant technology much more quickly than companies with slow-moving, indirect distribution channels, turning over inventory in just under five days on average.

Product Information

PowerEdge

The first blade server without compromise — Dell delivers on the promise of high density computing with a blade server featuring the latest high performance server technologies, plus total cost of ownership and density advantages over traditional Dell 1U servers.

Dell believes customers should get true server functionality without compromise, as compared to other blade server vendors that require customers to make a significant trade-off between density and features.

The PowerEdge 1955 delivers true server functionality, including up to two dual- or quad-core Intel Xeon processors, 1333MHz front side bus, up to 32GB fully buffered dimms (FBD), and SATA or SAS hard drives.

Dell also believes customers shouldn't be forced to choose a systems management strategy based on their hardware vendor of choice or the form factor of a server. Why should managing blade servers be any different from managing other servers? Dell's partnerships with industry leaders allow choice and flexibility with integration into leading third-party enterprise management applications and existing management infrastructures such as Microsoft, Novell, and Altiris.

Physical deployment of servers can be greatly accelerated by utilizing blade servers. Adding an additional server to the existing chassis is as simple as sliding a blade server into the chassis and powering up the blade.

Dell provides customers the blade solution they seek: always better density and equal features to a 1U server plus management and TCO advantages.

Partners (Technology, OEMs, and Resellers)

Dell works with numerous partners, including the following:

- Intel
- Microsoft
- Novell
- Altiris

- VMware
- EMC
- F5
- Broadcom

Blade System(s) and/or Virtualization Software Supported

- Dell PowerEdge 1955
- VMware (ESX, GSX, etc.), Microsoft Virtual Server, Xen

Operating Systems Supported

Factory-installed O/S

- Microsoft Windows Server 2003, Standard Edition
- Microsoft Windows Server 2003, Web Edition
- Red Hat Linux Enterprise v4, Enterprise Server
- Red Hat Linux Enterprise v4, Workstation Server
- SUSE Linux Enterprise Server 10

Validated O/S, NFI

- Red Hat Linux Enterprise v4, Advanced Server

Egenera

At a Glance

Company name: Egenera
   HQ address: 165 Forest Street
   Marlborough, MA 01752
   Contact info: 508-858-2600
   Website: www.egenera.com
   Date founded: 2000
   Date of blade system FCS: October 2001
   Number of employees: 350+
   Revenue and customer base: Private
   Industry awards/recognition:

- AlwaysOn Winner (four consecutive years)

- *Red Herring* 100 Winner (three consecutive years)

- Ernst & Young Entrepreneur of the Year

- YankeeTek Ventures Innovator of the Year

- Waters Editorial Best Server Solution

- *InfoWorld* Innovator to Watch 2005

Targeted markets: Large enterprise, service providers, government
Types of solutions offered:

☑ Blade servers	☑ Virtualization software
☐ PC blades/thin clients	☑ Clustering software
☐ Processor chipsets	☑ Management software
☐ Blade switch modules	☑ Power & cooling solutions
☑ High-speed interconnects (InfiniBand, 10 GigE, FC)	

Company Description

Egenera delivers business agility through data center virtualization and utility computing with an integrated system of diskless blades and virtualization software — the Egenera BladeFrame system.

Product Information

BladeFrame and PAN Manager

The Egenera BladeFrame system delivers a new computing architecture that virtualizes processing, storage, and networking — lowering server count, slashing TCO and complexity, and delivering utility computing. It combines diskless, stateless processing blades with powerful virtualization software, in a fully redundant, highly available system. Egenera simplifies the data center with a unique computing architecture — the processing area network or PAN. Egenera's PAN architecture combines diskless Egenera Processing Blade (pBlade) modules; a high-speed fabric; and software that virtualizes compute, storage, and networking resources. The virtualization of data center resources means that servers are no longer tied to specific operating systems or applications, and can be easily shared and automatically repurposed based on business priorities and SLAs. By turning servers from fixed resources into dynamic assets, enterprises can dramatically reduce the number of servers they need, use a single server as backup for many servers, and reduce data center complexity by up to 80%. Egenera holds four patents focused on virtualized I/O, clustering, and power management.

Partners (Technology, OEMs, and Resellers)

Egenera has an exclusive OEM agreement with Fujitsu Siemens Computer for sales in Europe, the Middle East, and Africa; a partnership with Liebert for CoolFrame cooling system; and strategic enterprise alliances with the following companies:

- 3PAR
- AMD
- BEA
- EMC
- IBM
- Intel
- Microsoft
- NetApp
- Novell
- Oracle
- Red Hat
- SAP
- Veritas

Egenera also has more than 50 partners that offer interoperable or certified solutions and numerous reseller/system integrator relationships in the federal government market and outside of North America.

Blade System(s) and/or Virtualization Software Supported

- VMware (GSX, with ESX available by 2007), SWsoft, Microsoft Virtual Server, Xen (2007)

Operating Systems Supported

- Red Hat Enterprise Linux
- SUSE Enterprise Linux
- Microsoft Windows
- Sun Solaris
- Specific solutions for Oracle Grid, 9i and 10g RAC applications; Microsoft Exchange and SAP

Hewlett-Packard

At a Glance

Company name: Hewlett-Packard
HQ address: 3000 Hanover Street
Palo Alto, CA 94304-1185
Contact: Eric Krueger; Eric.krueger@hp.com; 281-518-6083
Website: www.hp.com
Date founded: 1939
Dates of blade system and/or virtualization SW FCS:

- BladeSystem: 2001

- p-Class: 2002

- c-Class: 2006

Number of employees: 140,000 in 178 countries
Revenue and customer base: $86 billion in revenue, generating $7 billion in organic growth for fiscal year 2005
Industry awards/recognition:

- 2006 *Windows IT Pro* Readers' Choice Award — HP BladeSystem

- #1 globally in x86, Windows, Linux and UNIX servers according to IDC Q3 2005

Targeted markets: HP blade target markets include corporate data centers, distributed/branch sites, large grid and cluster farms, and small server rooms in industries including manufacturing, financial services, telecommunications, public sector, and IT service providers.
Types of solutions offered:

☑ Blade servers

☑ PC blades/thin clients

☑ Processor chipsets

☑ Blade switch modules

☑ High-speed interconnects (InfiniBand, 10 GigE, FC)

☑ Virtualization software

☑ Clustering software

☑ Management software

☑ Power & cooling solutions

Company Description

HP is a technology solutions provider to consumers, businesses, and institutions globally. The company's offerings span IT infrastructure, global services, business and home computing, and imaging and printing. For the four fiscal quarters ending July 31, 2006, HP revenue totaled $90 billion. More information about HP (NYSE, Nasdaq: HPQ) is available at `http://www.hp.com`.

Product Information

HP BladeSystem Enclosure

The next-generation HP BladeSystem is a data center in a 17″ box. The c7000 enclosure consolidates and provides shared access to power, cooling, and interconnectivity managed from a single, secure interface. The new BladeSystem enclosure was designed to support 8 to 16 blades, including one-, two-, and four-processor server blades, storage blades, and client blades. Each enclosure is 10U (17.5″ high, allowing for 4 enclosures in a standard 42U rack.

Different types of HP blades can be mixed and matched in the same enclosure, and support a wide variety of industry standard operating systems and applications. All power, cooling, and interconnect resources are modular and hot-pluggable and can be added or reconfigured to match the requirements of the blades inside. The Onboard Administrator provides fast setup and efficient management via an interactive LCD screen on the front of the enclosure and built-in management modules in the back for effective KVM and remote control of all infrastructure resources within the enclosure.

To address key pain points of infrastructures, three new technologies were also integrated to deliver more efficient and flexible approaches to interconnectivity, power and cooling, and management — HP Virtual Connect architecture, HP Thermal Logic technologies, and HP Insight Control management.

Server and Storage Blades

HP server blades are designed to match the same key features of traditional HP rack and tower servers. Today, HP provides a choice of server blades that support Intel Xeon and Itanium and AMD Opteron processors in a variety of one-, two-, and four-processor designs. Based on industry standards, HP server blades also support the same industry standard operating systems and applications for Windows, Linux, and HP-UX as their equivalent rack and tower servers.

The balanced architecture of the new HP ProLiant c-Class server blades are designed to provide more memory and interconnect capacity to both processors with enough headroom to also support dual- and future multicore processor designs, as well as more demanding applications and virtualized server environments. All HP server blades support enterprise-class features such as

- Hot-plug drives and built-in RAID for high availability
- At least 32GB of memory capacity for high performance

- Multiple I/O expansion options for Ethernet, Fibre Channel, Infini-Band, and more

- iLO 2 management controller built in

To add incremental storage capacity to each server, HP also offers a modular storage blade expansion unit to add up to six more hot-plug drives to each server for different application requirements.

PC Blades/Thin Clients

The Consolidated Client Infrastructure (CCI) solution from HP centralizes desktop computer and storage resources into more easily managed, highly secure data centers. IT and business management will appreciate this solution for raising levels of security and privacy, enabling dramatically lower desktop operational supports costs, and improving service quality, accessibility, and ease of management. End users will enjoy the convenience, familiarity, and performance of a traditional desktop environment. HP also supports a variety of virtual client PC solutions on HP BladeSystem based on VMware and Citrix.

Blade Interconnect Modules

HP offers a variety of interconnect options that support standards such as Ethernet, Fibre Channel, and InfiniBand to connect the BladeSystem to external networking and storage. The built-in Virtual Connect architecture includes a 5 terabit fault-tolerant backplane and supports four redundant fabrics across eight high performance interconnect bays. All interconnect options are hot-pluggable and can be installed in pairs for full redundancy.

- Standards-based: Ease of installation, configuration, and interoperability with existing network infrastructures and management.

- Familiar brands: A variety of interconnect choices are available from Cisco, Brocade, Blade Network Technologies, HP, QLogic, Emulex, and Voltaire.

- Connectivity options: Choices to support 1Gb to 10Gb Ethernet, 4Gb Fibre Channel, 4X DDR InfiniBand, RDMA, TCP Offload, iSCSI, PCI, and future I/O technologies.

- Built-in redundancy: Hot-plug interconnects that can be removed and replaced without need to cable/recable network connections.

- Cable reduction: Cut cables up to 94%, providing up to 32-to-1 network cable reduction per enclosure.

Management Software

Insight Control software builds upon HP Systems Insight Manager, HP Control Tower, and select ProLiant Essential software designed for blade infrastructure provisioning, monitoring, and control across multiple enclosures, even multiple data centers. To simplify purchase and deployment, the software is delivered in convenient packages such as the Insight Control Data Center Edition.

The ProLiant Essentials Virtual Machine Management Software installs into the Insight Control environment and unifies the management of physical and virtual resources. Use the ProLiant Essentials Virtual Machine Management Software (PEVMS) to boost virtual machine availability and monitor virtual machine host and guest health and performance, as well as to schedule regular virtual machine guest backups. In order to balance application workloads across multiple physical platforms, PEVMS enables movement of virtual machine guests between physical hosts in both SAN and direct-attached storage environments without service interruption through VMware VMotion integration.

The software also delivers virtual-to-virtual (V2V) migrations to simplify conversions between different virtualization platforms and virtual-to-physical (V2P) migrations to transition virtual machines back to physical systems as necessary — even physical-to-physical (P2P) for rapid server migrations and consolidations.

HP Thermal Logic Power and Cooling Technology

Thermal Logic pools and shares power and cooling as a resource, adapting both to maximize efficiency, reliability, and scalability to meet demand. Single- and three-phase configurations are supported in N+1 and N+N redundancy modes. Each enclosure also includes built-in sensors to actively monitor and automatically adapt power load and cooling capacity based on changes in demand and environment to maintain the highest energy efficiency, redundancy, and scalability based on demand. Versus rack-mount servers, HP blades can save up to 40% on overall power utilization.

Thermal Logic technology provides instant thermal monitoring for real-time heat, power, and cooling data at a system and rack level. Built-in HP Active Cool fans optimize airflow, acoustics, and performance while delivering more airflow with less power versus traditional technology. The fans pull air across the system via the PARSEC architecture for parallel, redundant, scalable airflow design to deliver cooling where it's needed most.

For greater power savings, the HP Dynamic Power Saver shifts power loads and tunes power supplies on or off for maximum efficiency and reliability. To save more energy and match to application workloads, customers can adjust processor performance on each blade.

Partners (Technology, OEMs, and Resellers)

As of August 2006, HP lists more than 120 software, hardware, and reseller partners worldwide as members of the HP BladeSystem Solution Builder program. Key partners include the following:

- AMD
- Blade Network Technologies
- Brocade
- Cisco Systems
- Citrix
- Emulex
- Intel
- Mellanox
- Microsoft

- Novell
- Oracle
- PolyServe
- QLogic
- Red Hat
- SAP
- VMware
- Voltaire

Blade System(s) and/or Virtualization Software Supported

- HP BladeSystem Series
- VMware, Xen, Microsoft Virtual Server

Operating Systems Supported

- Windows
- Linux
- NetWare 6.5 (BL460c and BL20p blades only)
- Solaris 10 (Opteron-based server blades)
- VMware

Plans/Direction

The HP blade strategy is to deliver the same choice of servers, storage, and networking options common in today's rack- and tower-based IT infrastructure in a blade design. The goal is to consolidate the core elements of the data center, including power and cooling, into standard modules within a shared management enclosure. The blade enclosure becomes the modular building block of the next-generation data center. All elements would be virtualized and all management processes automated. The BladeSystem would support blades with multicore processors, plus storage, network, PC, and workstation blades. HP describes this modular agenda as "blade everything."

Hitachi, Ltd.

At a Glance

Company name: Hitachi, Ltd.
   HQ address: 6-6, Marunouchi 1-Chome, Chiyoda-ku, Tokyo, 100-8280 Japan
   Contact info: Ken Kawada; ken.kawada@hal.hitachi.com
   Website: http://www.hitachi.com or http://www.bladesymphony.com
   Date founded: Founded 1910; incorporated February 1, 1920
   Date of FCS for blade solution(s): December 10, 2004
   Date of GA for virtualization solution(s): August 31, 2006
   Number of employees: 355,879 (as of March 31, 2006)
   Revenue and customer base: $80.896M (for the fiscal year ending March 31, 2006); Hitachi has more than 200 customers in Japan and around the world who have selected BladeSymphony to support its IT computing requirements.
   Industry awards/recognition:

- SAP Award of Excellence
- Oracle Award 2006 Excellent Partner

Targeted markets:
Hitachi offers a wide range of systems, products, and services in market sectors including information systems, electronic devices, power and industrial systems, consumer products, materials, and financial services.
   Types of solutions offered:

☑ Blade Servers	☑ Virtualization software
☑ PC blades/thin clients *	☑ Clustering software *
☑ Processor chipsets	☑ Management software
☑ Blade switch modules	☑ Power & cooling solutions*
☑ High-speed interconnects (InfiniBand, 10 GigE, FC)	

* Japan only

Company Description

Hitachi, Ltd., (NYSE: HIT / TSE: 6501), headquartered in Tokyo, Japan, is a leading global electronics company. Fiscal year 2005 (ended March 31, 2006) consolidated sales totaled 9.464 billion yen ($80.9 billion). The company offers a wide range of systems, products, and services in market sectors including information systems, electronic devices, power and industrial systems, consumer products, materials, and financial services.

Product Information

BladeSymphony

Hitachi's BladeSymphony Server is an enterprise-class server system designed to deliver unmatched performance, reliability, and scalability. With its symmetric multiprocessing (SMP) blade interconnect technology, server modules can be coupled together to increase system performance while maintaining a single operating-system environment. In addition, server modules can be combined to run different operating systems within the same chassis. Together with Hitachi's embedded virtualization technology, BladeSymphony enables customers to consolidate and maximize their server needs onto a single and robust system platform.

With Hitachi's two-socket (four-core) Intel Itanium 2 Processor Server Modules, BladeSymphony's blade chassis can support up to two eight-socket (16-core) SMP environments, with each environment supporting up to 128GB of memory. Hitachi is the first to offer a system platform capable of supporting both Intel Xeon Processor and Intel Itanium 2 Processor server modules within the same chassis. Intel Xeon Processor blade server modules are also available in two-way and four-way offerings.

Whether the customer's business model involves Internet-based commerce, high-bandwidth streaming, electronic mail, capacity planning, transactional data processing, or database management, BladeSymphony solutions not only simplify and streamline the enterprise while reducing its total cost of ownership, but also place a whole new world of processing power in its hands for future profitable growth.

Partners (Technology, OEMs, and Resellers)

- Intel
- Brocade
- Microsoft
- Red Hat
- Oracle
- SAP
- Kabira

Blade System(s) and/or Virtualization Software Supported

- VMware ESX Server
- Hitachi Server Virtualization Feature

Operating Systems Supported

- Microsoft Windows Server 2003
- Red Hat Enterprise Linux
- Novell SUSE Linux

Plans/Direction

Hitachi's plan and direction are focused on continuously improving and expanding its blade offerings to satisfy requirements of customers today, as well as introducing innovative features and functions for needs of customers tomorrow. At or around the time of this book's publication, Hitachi plans to release a new range of products revolving around dual-core technology, which will also support an innovative system-embedded virtualization technology delivering mainframe-class virtualization (high performance and high availability) to open-platform systems.

IBM

At a Glance

Company name: IBM
 HQ address: New Orchard Road
 Armonk, NY 10504
 Contact info: 914-499-1900
 Website: www.ibm.com
 Date founded: Founded 1888; incorporated 1911; added to NYSE 1916
 Date of blade system FCS/GA: BladeCenter introduced in 2002
 Number of employees: 329,373
 Revenue and customer base: $91.1 billion (2005 year end)
 Targeted markets: IBM's clients include many different kinds of enterprises, from sole proprietorships to the world's largest organizations, governments, and companies representing every major industry and endeavor. The majority of the company's enterprise business, which excludes the company's original equipment manufacturer (OEM) technology business, occurs in industries that are broadly grouped into six sectors:

- Financial Services: Banking, financial markets, insurance

- Public: Education, government, healthcare, life sciences

- Industrial: Aerospace, automotive, defense, chemical and petroleum, electronics

- Distribution: Consumer products, retail, travel, transportation

- Communications: Telecommunications, media and entertainment, energy and utilities

- Small and medium business: Mainly companies with fewer than 1,000 employees

Types of solutions offered:

- ☑ Blade servers
- ☑ PC blades/thin clients
- ☑ Processor chipsets
- ☑ Blade switch modules
- ☑ High-speed interconnects (InfiniBand, 10 GigE, FC)

- ☑ Virtualization software
- ☑ Clustering software
- ☑ Management software
- ☑ Power & cooling solutions

Company Description

IBM strives to lead in the invention, development, and manufacture of the industry's most advanced information technologies, including computer systems, software, storage systems, and microelectronics. They translate these advanced technologies into value for their customers through their professional solutions, services, and consulting businesses worldwide.

IBM systems facilitate the sharing of servers, storage, and networking resources to create true on-demand operations that enable businesses to collaborate more efficiently and securely. IBM Systems and Technology Group delivers innovative solutions for the increased collaboration between companies and institutions that has begun to blur the traditional lines of information technology. New technologies like virtualization, open standards, and encryption help organizations and their partners share information in real time and collaborate seamlessly on innovative applications ranging from designing automobiles and aircraft to discovering new medicines.

Product Information

IBM BladeCenter

The industry's top-selling blade server — IBM BladeCenter — integrates servers, networks, storage, and applications in highly efficient one-inch systems that sit in a rack like books in a shelf. BladeCenter uses integrated switches to decrease cabling by 80%, and vastly simplifies management and power usage through IBM Director and PowerExecutive. With BladeCenter, IBM and co-designer Intel have provided a standard design that allows other companies to build specialized blades, switches, and solutions to do specific tasks.

The IBM BladeCenter is currently based on three different types of blade chassis: the original BladeCenter, BladeCenter T for telco environments (NEBS Level 3–compliant), and BladeCenter H for high performance environments. There are currently three major lines of blade servers: HS for Intel CPU x86–based blades (HS20 for dual socket, HS40 for quad socket), LS for AMD Opteron–based blades, and JS for IBM's PowerPC 970 RISC–based blades.

The **JS20** was the first blade server to run one of the three major UNIX operating systems, IBM's own AIX. The follow-on product **JS21**, which employs single- or dual-core PowerPC 970 processors, was the first blade server to offer built in virtualization, offering Dynamic Logical Partitioning (DLPAR) capabilities.

The IBM BladeCenter was one of the first blade architectures to integrate not just computing (server) blades, but also I/O modules (InfiniBand, iSCSI, Ethernet, and Fibre Channel) from leading switching vendors such as Cisco, Brocade, QLogic, McData, and Nortel.

Partners (Technology, OEMs, and Resellers)

The BladeCenter ecosystem includes more than 700 partners. Relevant partners include the following:

- Brocade
- Cisco Systems
- Citrix Systems
- Intel

- NetApp
- Nortel
- Novell
- VMware

New members joining Blade.org (Sept. 2006) include

- Altiris
- AMD
- Avnet
- BladeFusion
- Broadcom
- CGAtlantic
- Clovis Solutions
- Devon IT
- Emulex
- Force10 Networks
- Fulcrum Microsystems
- HCL Technologies
- iVivity
- Myricom
- NetEffect
- Neoware

- OpenService
- PathScale
- QLogic
- Qumranet
- Red Hat
- Sensory Networks
- Server Engines
- Stargen
- Teak Technologies
- Tehuti Networks
- Universal Network Machines
- Universal Scientific Industrial
- Virtual Iron
- Voltaire
- Wyse Technology
- Zeus Technology

Blade System(s) and/or Virtualization Software Supported

- IBM BladeCenter Series
- VMware, Microsoft Virtual Server, Xen

Operating Systems Supported

- Windows
- Linux
- AIX 5L

Plans/Direction

Since its launch in 2002, IBM BladeCenter has grown to be the world's number-one blade — now with nine consecutive quarters as industry leader according to Gartner in August 2006. IBM's leadership in the blade segment will continue as as they grow their ecosystem of collaborators developing solutions for a blade platform with Blade.org.

Microsoft

At a Glance

Company name: Microsoft Corporation
HQ address: One Microsoft Way
Redmond, WA 98052
Contact info: 425-882-8080
Website: www.microsoft.com/virtualization
Date founded: Founded 1975; went public March 13, 1986
Dates of blade system and/or virtualization SW FCS:

- September 13, 2004: General availability of Virtual Server 2005

- October 2004: Availability of Virtual Server Migration Toolkit

- April 2005: MOM 2005 Management pack for Virtual Server 2005

- December 2005: General availability of Virtual Server 2005 R2

- April 2006: Beta 1 of Virtual Server 2005 R2 Service Pack 1

- May 2006: MOM 2005 Management Pack V2 for Virtual Server 2005 R2

- August 2006: Beta 1 of System Center Virtual Machine Manager

Number of employees 71,553
Revenue and customer base: $44.28B
Targeted markets: Multinational
Types of solutions offered:

☐ Blade servers	☑ Virtualization software
☐ PC blades/thin clients	☑ Clustering software
☐ Processor chipsets	☑ Management software
☐ Blade switch modules	☐ Power & cooling solutions
☐ High-speed interconnects (InfiniBand, 10 GigE, FC)	

Company Description

Founded in 1975, Microsoft (Nasdaq: MSFT) is the worldwide leader in software, services, and solutions that help people and businesses realize their full potential.

Product Information

Virtual Server 2005 R2

In conjunction with Windows Server 2003, Virtual Server 2005 R2 provides a virtualization platform that runs most major x86 operating systems in a guest environment, and is supported by Microsoft as a host for Windows Server operating systems and Windows Server System applications. Virtual Server 2005 R2's comprehensive COM API, in combination with the Virtual Hard Drive (VHD) format and support for virtual networking, provide administrators complete scripted control of portable, connected virtual machines and enable easy automation of deployment and ongoing change and configuration.

Additionally, its integration with a wide variety of existing Microsoft and third-party management tools allows administrators to seamlessly manage a Virtual Server 2005 R2 environment with their existing physical-server management tools. A wide array of complementary product and service offerings are available from Microsoft and its partners to help businesses plan for, deploy, and manage Virtual Server 2005 R2 in their environment.

Microsoft System Center Virtual Machine Manager

Microsoft System Center Virtual Machine Manager is the latest addition to the System Center family of management products and provides centralized management of Windows Virtual Machine infrastructure. Virtual Machine Manager enables increased physical server utilization, centralized management of virtual infrastructure, and rapid provisioning of new virtual machines by the administrator and users.

Partners (Technology, OEMs, and Resellers)

More than 25 partners; please check www.microsoft.com/windowsserversystem/virtualserver/partners/default.mspx for more information.

More than 50 vendors license Microsoft's virtual hard disk (VHD) format.

Blade System(s) and/or Virtualization Software Supported

- Hardware: All x86- and x64-based (AMD, Intel) systems
- Intel Celeron, Pentium III, Pentium 4, Xeon; AMD Opteron, Athlon, Athlon 64, Athlon X2, Sempron, or Duron processor

Operating Systems Supported

Supported host operating systems:

- Microsoft Windows Server 2003 Standard Edition, Enterprise Edition, or Datacenter Edition or later
- Windows Server 2003 Standard x64 Edition, Enterprise x64 Edition, Datacenter x64 Edition or later versions
- Windows Small Business Server 2003 Standard Edition or Premium Edition
- Windows XP Professional Service Pack 2 or later (for nonproduction use only).

The following operating systems are supported guests of Virtual Server:

- Windows Server 2003 Standard Edition (Windows Server 2003 SP1 support for Virtual Server 2005 R2 only)
- Windows Server 2003 Enterprise Edition or later
- Windows Server 2003 Web Edition or later
- Windows Small Business Server 2003 Standard Edition or later
- Windows Small Business Server 2003 Premium Edition or later
- Windows 2000 Server
- Windows 2000 Advanced Server
- Windows NT Server 4.0 with Service Pack 6a
- Windows XP SP2 (for Virtual Server 2005 R2 only)

Virtual Server 2005 R2 Enterprise distributions:

- Red Hat Enterprise Linux 2.1 (update 6)
- Red Hat Enterprise Linux 3 (update 6)
- Red Hat Enterprise Linux 4
- Novell's SUSE Linux Enterprise Server 9

Standard distributions:

- Red Hat Linux 7.3
- Red Hat Linux 9.0
- Novell's SUSE Linux 9.2, 9.3, 10.0

Plans/Direction

System Center Virtual Machine Manager, which is a standalone server application used to manage a virtualized data center running either Virtual Server 2005 or Windows Server Virtualization, is scheduled to be released in the second half of 2007. Virtual Machine Manager is integrated in the System Center family of products so customers can manage both physical and virtual environments.

Microsoft will release a beta of Windows Server Virtualization to select partners and customers at the end of 2006. Windows Server virtualization will provide integrated virtualization capabilities in Windows Server "Longhorn." Windows Server virtualization is scheduled to be generally available within 180 days after the release of Windows Server "Longhorn."

On July 17, 2006, Microsoft announced it has completed the acquisition of Softricity Inc., a leading provider of application virtualization and dynamic streaming technologies. Microsoft will make available the SoftGrid application virtualization platform at a reduced price in the streamlined form of two core offerings: SoftGrid for Desktops and SoftGrid for Terminal Services.

PANTA Systems, Inc.

At a Glance

Company name: PANTA Systems, Inc.
   HQ address: 10400 Ridgeview Court, Suite 200
   Cupertino, CA 95014
   Contact info: info@pantasys.com
   Website: www.pantasys.com
   Date founded: 2002
   FCS date of first blade solution: 2005
   Number of employees: 80
   Revenue and customer base: Private
   Customer base: Customers in enterprise and high performance computing
   Targeted markets: Enterprise and high performance computing
   Types of solutions offered:

☑ Blade servers

☐ PC blades/thin clients

☐ Processor chipsets

☐ Blade switch modules

☐ High-speed interconnects
   (InfiniBand, 10 GigE, FC)

☐ Virtualization software

☐ Clustering software

☐ Management software

☐ Power & cooling solutions

Company Description

PANTA has developed leading-edge technology that enables the next-generation "dynamic" data center, providing IT organizations with improved quality of service, rapid response to changing requirements, and lower total cost of ownership. Traditional servers can't provide the quantum improvements demanded in this next generation.

   PANTA has multiple enterprise and high-performance computing customers using its first-generation product. PANTA has also established over two dozen partnerships, and has multiple patents pending, covering software, hardware, and systems-level innovations.

Product Information

PANTAmatrix

PANTAmatrix is the first server platform to combine industry-leading off-the-shelf technology to provide a highly scalable, dynamically configurable, and power-efficient computer system. The system has a balanced architecture that allows compute and I/O performance to be scaled independently, with no bottlenecks occurring. The scalability and dynamic configuration capabilities make it a perfect fit for the new "dynamic" data center, in which application services are no longer bound to dedicated servers, and industry-standard systems take over the role of expensive proprietary solutions even for the most demanding applications. PANTAmatrix is particularly suited for applications that benefit from multiprocessing, are data- and I/O-intensive, or are latency-sensitive; examples include database, data warehousing, and streams processing.

Partners (Technology, OEMs, and Resellers)

- Akibia
- AMD
- American Council for Technology
- Cisco Systems, Inc.
- Coral8
- DataDirect Networks
- The EMS Group
- EverGrid
- IBRIX
- JB Cubed
- Mellanox
- mental images
- Microsoft
- Novell
- NVIDIA
- Open Fabrics Alliance
- Oracle
- Pathscale
- Rand Federal
- Scalable Informatics
- SilverStorm
- System Fabric Works
- Tatung
- Voltaire

Blade System(s) and/or Virtualization Software Supported

- Microsoft Virtual Server, Xen 3.0
- PANTA System Manager

Operating Systems Supported

- Windows
- Linux

Plans/Direction

Contact PANTA directly for details.

PlateSpin Ltd.

At a Glance

Company name: PlateSpin Ltd.
  HQ address: 144 Front St. W, Suite 385
  Toronto, Ontario, Canada, M5J 2L7
  Contact info: info@platespin.com; 416-203-6565
  Website: www.platespin.com
  Date founded: April 2003
  First GA date(s) of software solutions: April 2003
  Number of employees: 100+
  Revenue and customer base: Customer base: 1,500+
  Industry awards/recognition:

- 2006 International Business Award for Best Company Overall
- Named the fourth-fastest-growing IT company in Canada by Branham Group
- Named one of the Top Five Movers and Shakers in the Canadian IT Sector for 2006 by Branham Group

Targeted markets: Fortune 500, Global 2000 data centers
Types of solutions offered:

- ☐ Blade servers
- ☐ PC blades/thin clients
- ☐ Processor chipsets
- ☐ Blade switch modules
- ☐ High-speed interconnects (InfiniBand, 10 GigE, FC)

- ☑ Virtualization software
- ☐ Clustering software
- ☑ Management software
- ☐ Power & cooling solutions

Company Description

PlateSpin provides the most-advanced data center automation software designed to optimize the use of server resources across the enterprise to improve business service levels and lower costs. PlateSpin's agentless software remotely collects and analyzes servers to create the optimum match between application workload and hardware resources and liberates software from hardware platforms, allowing servers to be streamed over the enterprise network from any source to any destination.

Global 2000 companies use PlateSpin solutions to lower costs and solve today's most pressing data-center initiatives, such as server consolidation, disaster recovery, hardware migration, and test-lab automation. For more information please visit www.platespin.com.

Product Information

PlateSpin PowerConvert

PlateSpin PowerConvert is a software solution that allows servers to be streamed between physical servers, blade infrastructures, virtual machines, and image archives over the network. PlateSpin's powerful OS Portability (patent pending) is the first and only technology that decouples data, applications, and operating systems from servers, reconfigures and optimizes resources, and automatically streams them to any physical or virtual platform. Administrators can remotely, drag-and-drop servers across dissimilar infrastructures around the world to optimize server resource capacity, saving time and money.

PlateSpin PowerRecon

PlateSpin PowerRecon is agentless software that measures, analyzes, and determines the optimal fit between server-resource supply and workload demand. By remotely capturing server-resource capacity and workload demand statistics, PlateSpin PowerRecon ensures that the right server infrastructure has been matched to the right application workload to maximize performance while minimizing hardware cost. It takes the guesswork out of capacity planning, server consolidation, and continuous server optimization projects.

Partners (Technology, OEMs, and Resellers)

Technology partners include

- DoubleTake
- VMware
- Microsoft
- IBM
- Akimbi
- Novell
- Red Hat

Resellers include

- Dell
- Unisys
- Fujitsu Siemens

Please see http://plateSpin.com/partners for more extensive list.

Blade System(s) and/or Virtualization Software Supported

- IBM BladeCenter and any blade system that supports the configuration
- VMware, Microsoft Virtual Server, Virtual Iron

Operating Systems Supported

- Windows 2000, 2003, XP Pro
- Red Hat Linux
- SUSE Linux

Plans/Direction

PlateSpin is a leader in providing analysis, planning, and migration software for server consolidation using blades and virtual machines. PlateSpin's technology can be easily applied to solve other problems in the data center, such as disaster recovery, hardware migration, test-lab automation, and continuous server optimization.

PolyServe, Inc.

At a Glance

Company name: PolyServe, Inc.
  HQ address: 20400 NW Amberwood Drive, Suite 150
  Beaverton, OR 97006
  Contact info: 877-POL-SERV; 877-765-7378
  Website: www.polyserve.com
  Date founded: 1999
  GA date(s) of software:

- PolyServe Matrix Server: April 2002

- PolyServe Database Utility (Oracle): April 2002

- PolyServe File Serving Utility (Linux): April 2002

- PolyServe Database Utility (SQL Server): November 2003

- PolyServe File Serving Utility (Windows): November 2003

Number of employees: 105
Revenue and customer base: More than 500 customers worldwide
Industry awards/recognition:

- *InfoWorld* 2006 Technology of the Year Award: Best NAS Killer

- Microsoft 2006 Best of TechEd: Most Innovative Award

Targeted market: Fortune 1000
Types of solutions offered:

☐ Blade servers	☑ Virtualization software
☐ PC blades/thin clients	☑ Clustering software
☐ Processor Chipsets	☑ Management software
☐ Blade switch modules	☐ Power & cooling solutions
☐ High-speed interconnects (InfiniBand, 10 GigE, FC)	

Company Description

PolyServe software consolidates servers and storage into manageable, scalable, and available database and file-serving utilities. This approach overcomes the limits of server virtualization to extend consolidation benefits to mission-critical applications, and addresses all three major data-center cost footprints: hardware, software, and storage. Customers typically see their server and software installs cut in half, configuration and management time slashed by as much as 75%, and total cost of ownership lowered by more than 50%.

Founded in 1999, PolyServe has strategically placed itself at the confluence of three fundamental technology trends:

- The rise to dominance of low-cost Intel architecture–based servers

- The emergence of Microsoft Windows and Linux in the data center

- The maturation of sophisticated and affordable storage area network (SAN) solutions

PolyServe provides the software that unifies many servers and storage devices to form a modular utility that acts as, and can be managed as, as single entity.

More than 500 organizations worldwide are deploying PolyServe's products to build computing utilities for mission-critical database services and file services. PolyServe maintains strategic partnerships with HP, Microsoft, IBM, Dell, and Novell.

Product Information

PolyServe Database Utility for SQL Server

In many organizations tens to hundreds of instances of SQL Server are deployed on dedicated servers. Server utilization rates hover in the low teens. More than twice as many servers are being managed than are truly required to meet application needs. The ease of use and affordability of SQL Server have created an expensive situation: SQL Server sprawl.

The PolyServe Database Utility for SQL Server is the first server-consolidation solution to effectively address SQL Server sprawl and meet the high performance and availability needs of mission-critical SQL Server. While server virtualization approaches address only hardware costs, PolyServe reduces server and storage requirements while streamlining management — delivering up to a 70% reduction in total cost of ownership.

PolyServe's unique approach to server consolidation avoids the pitfalls of server virtualization alternatives, like performance overhead and unreliable server failover. The Database Utility provides "bare metal" performance of Microsoft SQL Server and protects against both planned and unplanned downtime. And it provides a framework for managing SQL Server infrastructure that reduces management time by up to 75%.

By addressing all the cost elements associated with managing SQL Server, PolyServe can reduce your TCO by up to 70 percent. Eliminating passive servers and consolidating the associated storage yields immediate hardware savings.

PolyServe File Serving Utility for Windows

Consolidation of Windows file servers provides IT departments a way to both drastically reduce the cost of operations and provide more efficient management of the incredible storage growth everyone is facing.

Digital data has been growing at a triple-digit rate for many years and is showing no signs of slowing. At first, businesses reacted by deploying inexpensive and easy-to-manage Windows file servers with direct-attached storage (DAS) wherever a workgroup server was needed. Eventually, IT departments started deploying SANs and some NAS appliances to rein in storage growth. This has created a headache of multiple (possibly thousands of) pools of storage throughout the data center with inconsistent deployment and management practices. This is called server sprawl, a very expensive and complex IT architecture that makes it nearly impossible to meet availability and performance SLAs.

The PolyServe File Serving Utility for Windows enables IT to consolidate many disparate storage "puddles" and associated file servers into one cost-effective, scalable, and easy-to-manage file-serving cluster. The File Serving Utility runs on Windows Server System, enabling administrators to maintain their current IT practices rather than forcing them to switch to a proprietary architecture. Based on industry-standard building blocks — servers, storage, FC SAN, or iSCSI — it provides the best price-performance in scalable file serving.

PolyServe File Serving Utility for Linux

IT organizations are looking for ways to meet their growing performance needs, but don't have a lot to spend. Large Unix servers and enterprise NAS appliances are expensive and costly to maintain. Many technologists have already discovered that a cluster of inexpensive Intel servers with PolyServe's File Serving Utility can more than adequately meet their performance needs at a dramatically lower price than other alternatives. In addition, they can achieve greater application and data availability and simplify backup and restore operations, further lowering operating expenses.

By enabling file-serving protocols, such as CIFS and NFS, to be scaled across a cluster of servers, PolyServe's File Serving Utility software delivers unprecedented, absolute I/O throughput and performance, with no single points of failure and integrated fault tolerance. By building on industry-standard servers and storage, solutions can be tuned for very high-performance applications or optimized for price-performance — nearly one-eighth the cost of traditional NAS appliances at a given throughput. And unlike UNIX servers or NAS appliances that suffer from a single point of failure and a single performance bottleneck, the PolyServe software supports multiple servers serving the same or different files concurrently with no single point of failure, and aggregate performance far in excess of traditional NAS appliances.

PolyServe Database Utility for Oracle

IT organizations are being driven to meet ever more stringent Service Level Agreements (SLAs) while managing within budget constraints for new equipment, software, and staff.

The PolyServe Database Utility for Oracle allows IT to consolidate Oracle databases from many active-passive cluster pairs into fewer larger shared data clusters. It provides a more reliable and cost-effective failover architecture, on-demand server and storage scalability, improved database management, and a path forward to Oracle RAC.

PolyServe Database Utility for Oracle RAC helps customers install Oracle RAC faster, manage larger clusters more easily, and realize more benefits from Oracle than if OCFS is used. PolyServe Database Utility for Oracle RAC is used in conjunction with two of the largest RAC implementations in the world. It is also part of a 10,000-user, 10-terabyte, 10-server cluster proof of concept showing Oracle9i RAC scalability and manageability for the largest commercial workloads.

The PolyServe Database Utility for Oracle RAC is a critical component of any Oracle RAC deployment. According to most analysts, mainstream customers will not deploy Oracle RAC without the presence of a robust cluster file system such as that at the core of the PolyServe solution. Oracle itself recommends the use of a cluster file system in conjunction with Automatic Storage Management — a new feature in Oracle Database 10g.

Partners (Technology, OEMs, and Resellers)

- Microsoft
- Dell
- HP
- Novell
- IBM
- Red Hat

For a complete list of all partners, please visit `http://www.polyserve.com/partners.php`.

Blade System(s) and/or Virtualization Software Supported

- IBM, HP, Dell, any Intel-architecture blade
- Microsoft Virtual Server

Operating Systems Supported

- 32-bit: Windows Server 2003 or later; 64-bit: Windows Server 2003 R2
- Red Hat Enterprise Linux (RHEL) 4.0 Support: 32- and 64-bit
- SUSE Linux Enterprise Server (SLES) 9 Support: 32- and 64-bit

Rackable Systems

At a Glance

Company name: Rackable Systems
  HQ address: 1933 Milmont Drive
  Milpitas, California 95035
  Contact info: sales@rackable.com
  Website: www.rackable.com
  Date founded: 1999
  Date of blade system FCS: December 2004
  Number of employees: 194 full-time (as of April 2006)
  Revenue and customer base: 2005 revenues: $215 million; more than 200
customers
  Industry awards/recognition:

- 2004 *LinuxWorld* Conference & Expo Product Excellence Award for
  Most Innovative Hardware Solution (for Scale Out Server Series)

- 2004 *LinuxWorld* Conference & Expo Product Excellence Award for Best
  Cluster Solution (for DC Power Technology)

- 2005 *LinuxWorld* Conference & Expo Product Excellence Award for Best
  Server (for C2002 High Efficiency Server)

- 2005 *LinuxWorld* Conference & Expo Product Excellence Award for Best
  Utility/Grid Computing Solution (for Parallel File System Solution)

Targeted markets: Internet, semiconductor design, enterprise software, federal government, financial services, entertainment, oil and gas exploration,
biotechnology, and pharmaceutical
  Types of solutions offered:

- ☑ Blade servers
- ☐ PC blades/thin clients
- ☐ Processor chipsets
- ☐ Blade switch modules
- ☐ High-speed interconnects
  (InfiniBand, 10 GigE, FC)

- ☐ Virtualization software
- ☑ Clustering software
- ☑ Management software
- ☑ Power & cooling solutions

Company Description

Rackable Systems is a leading provider of server and storage products for
large-scale data-center deployments.

Their rack-mount servers, storage, and hybrid blade server designs are configured in industry-first, half-depth, "back-to-back" rack mounting. In addition to superior density, their platforms feature improved thermal efficiency, optimized power distribution, simplified serviceability and superior remote management — with a tremendous breadth of configuration options to support specific application requirements for a broad range of customers.

Founded in 1999, they serve leading Internet, enterprise software, federal government, financial services, and HPC customers worldwide, including Amazon.com, Electronic Arts, Microsoft, NVIDIA, Sony, Tellme Networks, Webex, and Yahoo! Innovative designs, patented technology, and commitment to customer service have enabled them to successfully address the needs of many of the world's most complex data centers.

Product Information

Scale Out Blade Server Series

Rackable Systems' Scale Out Series servers incorporate the key benefits of back-to-back rack-mount server designs with the best features of blade solutions — improved serviceability, ease of management, and density — to provide a vastly superior "open blade" alternative for large-scale data-center deployments.

The Scale Out Series achieves maximum server density with up to 352 processing cores per cabinet of today's fastest CPUs. DC Power technology enables power savings of up to 30%, in addition to dramatically increasing system reliability. Leveraging patented, breakthrough cooling technologies, Rackable Systems' Scale Out servers maximize key benefits of industry-standard, open-architecture components and designs.

Partners (Technology, OEMs, and Resellers)

- 3Ware
- Adaptec
- AMD
- Asus
- Cisco
- Cyclades
- Digi
- Intel
- TDI
- LSI Logic
- Maxtor/Seagate
- Mellanox
- Microsoft
- Oracle
- QLogic
- Red Hat
- SUSE
- SilverStorm
- Tyan
- Western Digital

Blade System(s) and/or Virtualization Software Supported

- Rackable Systems — Scale Out Series
- VMware ESX, Microsoft Virtual Server, Xen, SWsoft Virtuoso

Operating Systems Supported

- Microsoft Windows
- Red Hat Enterprise Linux
- Sun Solaris
- SUSE Linux (SLES)

Plans/Direction

Rackable Systems continues to provide innovations and product leadership to meet the growing challenges of today's and tomorrow's data-center environments. With an ongoing focus on thermal management, reduced power consumption, and highest system reliability, Rackable Systems remains committed to deploying servers and storage designed to achieve the best possible total cost of ownership for even the most complex data centers.

Sun Microsystems

At a Glance

Company name: Sun Microsystems, Inc.
   HQ address: 4150 Network Circle
   Santa Clara, CA 95054
   Contact info: Paul Read; Paul.Read@sun.com
   Website: http://www.sun.com
   Date founded: 1982
   FCS Date of Blade Hardware: August 2006
   GA date of virtualization software: September 2006
   Number of employees: 35,000
   Revenue and customer base: $13.1 billion (FY ending June 2006)
   Targeted markets: Most markets, including telco, finance, government, recreation, high performance computing, oil and gas, and travel
   Types of solutions offered:

- ☑ Blade servers
- ☑ PC blades/thin clients
- ☑ Processor chipsets
- ☑ Blade switch modules
- ☐ High-speed interconnects (InfiniBand, 10 GigE, FC)

- ☑ Virtualization software
- ☑ Clustering software
- ☑ Management software
- ☐ Power & cooling solutions

Company Description

A singular vision — "The Network Is the Computer" — guides Sun in the development of technologies that power the world's most important markets. Sun's philosophy of sharing innovation and building communities is at the forefront of the next wave of computing: the Participation Age. Sun can be found in more than 100 countries and on the Web at http://sun.com.

Product Information

Sun Blade 8000 Modular System

Sun's no-compromise approach to blade design means that its blades can compete with rack-optimized servers on level terms. The blade chassis is designed to last several years, with the power, cooling, and infrastructure to accommodate new technologies as these become available. At announcement, the Sun

Blade 8000 Modular System set several world records for performance, and given its processor performance, large memory, and exceptional I/O it is the leading platform for virtualization and consolidation.

The Sun Blade 8000 offers uniquely high levels of availability. All key components are hot-swap, including blades, disks, power supplies, fans, monitoring modules, network modules, and PCIe ExpressModules. No other blade vendor offers hot-plug of PCI cards, for example.

Sun's initial offering is a four-processor, eight-core server powered by AMD Opteron processors. Planned offerings include SPARC technology, two processor blades, and multicore systems. This will mean the customer has a range of blades tailored for most applications.

Sun's unique combination of high performance, high throughput, long product life, and outstanding availability makes it a leading choice for core applications, database, consolidation, and virtualization.

Solaris Containers

As an integral part of the Solaris 10 Operating System, Solaris Containers isolate software applications and services using flexible, software-defined boundaries. A breakthrough approach to virtualization and software partitioning, Solaris Containers allow many private execution environments to be created within a single instance of the Solaris OS. Sun is leading the industry with this partitioning technology now being referred to as OS virtualization. Each environment has its own identity, separate from the underlying hardware. This causes it to behave as if it is running on its own system, making consolidation simple, safe, and secure.

Because Solaris Containers are independent from the underlying hardware environment, application services can be re-created on other systems as needed. Each application runs in its own private environment — without dedicating new systems — and many application resources can be tested and deployed on a single server without fear that they will impact one another.

System and network resources can be allocated and controlled on a fine-grained basis, helping simplify computing infrastructures and improving resource utilization. As a result, companies can better consolidate applications onto fewer servers without concern for resource constraints, fault propagation, or security breaches, simplifying service provisioning. In addition to the consolidation benefits of Solaris Containers, customers find value in the technology's seamless and rapid time in deployment. Data center managers can use Solaris Containers to quickly roll out new versions, or copies of the old version, to fit new demand. Solaris Containers enable users to securely run multiple software-isolated applications on a single system, allowing easy consolidation of servers.

Software Management

The Sun Blade 8000 provides comprehensive manageability. Every Server Module has its own built-in Integrated Lights-Out Manager (ILOM) Service Processor, enabling direct access, management, and monitoring — just like a rack-mount server. In addition, a Chassis Monitoring Module is supplied for chassis-level monitoring of all components.

As the numbers of systems in an organization grow, the complexity of managing such large and often diverse environments becomes increasingly apparent. Sun is helping customers to speed up system deployment and reduce operating costs using Sun N1 System Manager. N1 System Manager provides complete hardware lifecycle management by enabling customers to discover, provision, monitor, update, and manage hundreds of Sun Fire x64 and SPARC servers and blade systems from a single management console.

Sun N1 System Manager is bundled with every Sun Blade 8000 Modular System. This software offers a hybrid user interface with both GUI and CLI capabilities. Administrators can automatically discover bare-metal systems based on subnet or IP addresses; logically group systems together; and perform actions across the group simultaneously; provision operating systems, firmware, software packages, and patches to selected nodes; and monitor hardware and operating system attributes; while providing lights-out management for remote systems.

Partners (Technology, OEMs, and Resellers)

Sun's many partners include

- AMD
- QLogic
- Intel
- Mellanox
- Red Hat
- Novell
- Microsoft
- Oracle
- SAP

Blade System(s) and/or Virtualization Software Supported

- Sun Blade
- Solaris Containers
- VMware (ESX, GSX), Xen 3.0.1

Operating Systems Supported

- Solaris 06/06 (x86)
- Red Hat Enterprise Linux Advanced Server 4, U3 (64-bit)
- SUSE Linux Enterprise Server 9, SP 3 (64-bit)
- Windows Server 2003, SP1 (32-bit) — Enterprise and Standard editions
- Windows Server 2003 (64-bit) — Enterprise and Standard editions

Plans/Direction

Sun plans to support a broad range of servers, from entry models up to multi-core SMP models. These will support x64 processors as well as SPARC. The consistent design emphasis will be on combining high performance with efficiency, long product life, and extremely high availability.

SWsoft

At a Glance

Company name: SWsoft
   HQ address: 13755 Sunrise Valley Drive, Suite 600
   Herndon, VA 20171
   Contact: info@swsoft.com
   Website: www.swsoft.com
   Date founded: 1999
   GA date of virtualization software: 2001
   Number of employees: 600
   Revenue and customer base: Privately held (revenues not disclosed); 10,000
customers total; 1,000 Vituozzo customers
   Industry awards/recognition:

- *LinuxWorld* Product Excellence Award 2006 winner

- *eWeek* Analyst's Choice, April 2006

- Top 100 IT Vendor of 2006 (by *IT Week* magazine in June 5 issue)

- *InfoWorld* "Excellent" rating (April 21, 2006 issue)

- *TechWorld* "Recommended" (July 24, 2006)

Targeted markets: Enterprises, hosting companies
Types of solutions offered:

☐ Blade servers   ☑ Virtualization software

☐ PC blades/thin clients   ☑ Clustering software

☐ Processor chipsets   ☑ Management software

☐ Blade switch modules   ☐ Power & cooling solutions

☐ High-speed interconnects
   (InfiniBand, 10 GigE, FC)

Company Description

SWsoft is a recognized leader in server automation and virtualization software. With more than 10,000 customers in over 100 countries, SWsoft's suite of award-winning products delivers proven performance, manageability, and value. SWsoft is a high-growth company funded by Bessemer Venture Partners, Insight Venture Partners, and Intel Capital.

The company offers comprehensive solutions to meet virtually every need of the world's largest service providers and enterprises. SWsoft's proven solutions range from server virtualization to data-center automation, server management, and website creation tools.

Product Information

Virtuozzo

Virtualization technology has the ability to increase data-center density many times. By consolidating tens or hundreds of virtual environments on one physical server, IT managers can reduce hardware costs while increasing utilization. The ability to effectively manage and automate a growing catalog of virtual assets ensures that complexity is reduced and that virtualization delivers cost savings.

With Virtuozzo OS-level server virtualization technology, a single Linux or Windows OS instance can be dynamically partitioned into multiple, highly efficient virtual environments. The low overhead of Virtuozzo allows for demanding workloads such as database and application servers to run inside virtual environments with near-native performance and scalability.

Also, Virtuozzo is the first and only virtualization technology that addresses the challenge faced by today's data centers of operating system sprawl, where a number of different operating systems require support, maintenance, and updating. Overall, Virtuozzo provides efficiency and manageability that result in the lowest total cost of ownership and fastest ROI for customers.

Partners (Technology, OEMs, and Resellers)

- Intel
- AMD
- HP
- IBM
- NEC
- Bull

- Microsoft
- Red Hat
- Novell SUS
- iSysTek
- Thinclient
- Interquad (UK distributor)

For more information on their partners visit the following websites:

- http://www.virtuozzo.com/en/partners/enterprise/na/
- http://www.virtuozzo.com/en/partners/enterprise/uk/
- http://www.virtuozzo.com/en/partners/enterprise/eu/
- http://www.virtuozzo.com/en/partners/enterprise/af/

Blade System(s) Supported

Anything that supports the architecture for SWsoft Virtuozzo. Please consult `http://www.swsoft.com/en/products/virtuozzo/specs/`.

Operating Systems Supported

- Windows
- CentOS 3.4, CentOS 4.0
- Fedora Core 1, Fedora Core 2, Fedora Core 4
- Red Hat 9, Red Hat Enterprise 3, Red Hat Enterprise 4
- SUSE SLES 9

Plans/Direction

In August 2006, SWsoft announced its strategic vision to provide IT organizations with the tools to manage other virtualized computer resources from additional vendors.

All future releases of SWsoft's Virtuozzo management tools will include support for other vendors' virtualization solutions, including VMware virtual servers — giving data-center managers unprecedented control of virtualized resources and enabling them to use various virtualization technologies without being tied to a single vendor's management tools.

SWsoft will introduce its first wave of support of another technology in late 2006 with VMware virtual machine management. Xen and other technologies will soon follow.

Verari Systems

At a Glance

Company name: Verari Systems
 HQ address: 9449 Carroll Park Drive
San Diego, CA 92121
 Contact info: David Driggers, 858-874-3800 or dave.driggers@verari.com
 Website: www.verari.com
 Date founded: 1991
 FCS date of blade solution: June 2002
 GA date of virtualization solution: September 30, 2006
 Number of employees: 250
 Revenue and customer base: Undisclosed
 Industry awards/recognition: AeA 2006 High Tech Award
 Targeted markets: Financial services and banking, internet and media, oil and gas, electronic design automation, entertainment
 Types of solutions offered:

☑ Blade servers

☑ PC blades/thin clients

☑ Processor chipsets

☑ Blade switch modules

☑ High-speed interconnects (InfiniBand, 10 GigE, FC)

☐ Virtualization software

☑ Clustering software

☑ Management software

☑ Power & cooling solutions

Company Description

Verari Systems is an open-architecture blade company. They offer complete solutions for Fortune 500 companies. Their blade products cover all of their product lines, including servers, workstation, storage, and desktop replacements. Their platform is an open architecture that utilizes best-of-breed commercial off-the-shelf (COTS) components. This architecture forms the building blocks for their blades, reaping the cost benefits of economies of scale and performance benefits of cutting-edge technology.

Product Information

Verari Systems BladeRack 2 Platform

The BladeRack 2 platform is the most power-efficient blade server solution available in the HPC market today. This platform provides reliable and scalable density, performance, and capacity in an integrated solution.

BladeRack 2 is capable of supporting the fastest, most powerful volume CPUs on the market today, as well as offering investment protection through upgrades of newer and faster processors. BladeRack 2 comes standard with integrated cluster management and monitoring through Verari Command Center.

The simplicity and elegance of the BladeRack 2 design will easily withstand the constantly increasing computing requirements of the future.

Verari Systems BladeRack 2 Blade Servers

Verari Systems offers a wide variety of blade servers for the BladeRack 2 platform. For an up-to-date listing, please visit `http://www.verari.com`. Some of their most popular offerings are listed here:

VB1150 and VB1055 Series (StorageBrick)

The VB1150 and VB1055 series tie together to become the most advanced StorageBrick assembly available on the market today. The advanced blade architecture provides the utmost control and flexibility, allowing for up to 12 drives in one blade and placing up to 450TB of storage in a single rack.

VB1200 and VB1500 Series

Verari Systems takes performance to a new level with the VB1200 and VB1500 server for the BladeRack 2. These blade servers incorporate all of the functionality and processing power that Intel and AMD are known for and give consumers the multiple configuration options that they have come to expect from Verari Systems. The VB1505 supports the fastest state-of-the-art processors available today and allows for extreme investment protection. No other blade computing platform available today has the ability to provide such capable and powerful options.

Partners (Technology, OEMs, and Resellers)

Verari Systems takes pride in its leading partner relationships with companies such as

- Intel
- AMD
- Engenio
- Western Digital
- Arima
- Tyan

- NVIDIA
- Microsoft
- SUSE
- PathScale
- Red Hat

Blade System(s) and/or Virtualization Software Supported

Verari Systems' BladeRack Series blades are supported within their platforms. Various blade solutions supported are for servers, workstations, storage, and desktop replacements. Their latest offerings can be found on their website: `http://www.verari.com/bladeRack.asp`

Verari Systems is certified and authorized to install a wide variety of software packages. Currently, Verari Systems' blade servers can run popular packages such as VMware and Landmark's GeoProbe.

Operating Systems Supported

Operating systems supported include the following:

- CentOS
- Fedora Core
- Microsoft Windows 2003 Server
- Red Hat
- Enterprise Linux
- SUSE Linux

Plans/Direction

Verari Systems is leading the way into enabling the data center of the future with core technologies that matter to today's Fortune 500 companies. These technologies include virtualization, integrated storage, remote desktop over IP, remote management, and portability. Over the course of the next several years, Verari Systems will continue to refine its patented Vertical Cooling Technology, industry-leading energy efficiency, and increased density solutions.

Virtual Iron

At a Glance

Company name: Virtual Iron
  HQ address: 900 Chelmsford Street
  Lowell, MA 01851
  Contact: Antonio Faillace, info@virtualiron.com
  Website: www.virtualiron.com
  Date founded: March 2003
  GA date of virtualization solution:

- Virtual Iron 1.0 – August 2005;

- Virtual Iron 3.0 – November 2006

  Number of employees: 50
  Revenue and customer base: Confidential
  Industry awards/recognition: Please go to http://www.virtualiron.com/
news_events/industry-recognition.cfm.
  Targeted markets: Enterprise Global 2000 customers
  Types of solutions offered:

- ☐ Blade servers
- ☐ PC blades/thin clients
- ☐ Processor chipsets
- ☐ Blade switch modules
- ☐ High-speed interconnects (InfiniBand, 10 GigE, FC)

- ☑ Virtualization software
- ☐ Clustering software
- ☐ Management software
- ☐ Power & cooling solutions

Company Description

Virtual Iron provides enterprise-class software solutions for creating and managing virtual infrastructure in the data center. The company's software enables companies to dramatically reduce the complexity and cost of managing and operating their industry-standard data-center infrastructure.

Product Information

Virtual Iron is focused on delivering advanced virtualization capabilities that leverage industry standards, open source, and processors with built-in hardware-assisted virtualization, unlike other proprietary expensive solutions in the market.

Global 2000 companies use Virtual Iron's software for consolidation, rapid provisioning, business continuity, workload management, and policy-based automation to deliver dramatic improvements in utilization, manageability, and agility.

With Virtual Iron solutions customers can

- Improve the utilization of current systems and get more out of today's fast industry-standard hardware via partitioning and consolidation

- Quickly and economically set up development, test, and production environments via rapid provisioning capabilities

- Recover from failures quickly, reliably, and cost-efficiently via high availability and disaster-recovery capabilities

- Optimally match the capacity of your resources to workload demands (optimize your equipment for efficiency) via workload- and capacity-management capabilities

- Reduce the human labor needed (thereby reducing human error) via policy-based automation

Partners (Technology, OEMs, and Resellers)

Please go to: http://www.virtualiron.com/partners/index.cfm.

Blade System(s) Supported

Virtual Iron supports industry-standard servers from IBM, HP, Dell, and Sun based on Intel VT and AMD-V processors.

Operating Systems Supported

- 32- and 64-bit Red Hat 4
- Red Hat 3
- Novell SLES 9
- 32-bit Windows 2000
- Windows 2003

VMware, Inc.

At a Glance

Company name: VMware, Inc.
  HQ address: 3145 Porter Drive
  Palo Alto, CA 94304
  Contact info: Sales: 1-877-486-9273 or sales@vmware.com
  Website: www.vmware.com
  Date founded: Founded in 1998 and is run as an independent subsidiary of
EMC (acquired January 2004)
  GA date of virtualization software (first commercial shipment): 1999
  Number of employees: 2000
  Revenue and customer base:

- 2005 revenue: $387 million; current run rate: $630 million

- 20,000 enterprise customers

Industry awards/recognition:

- *eWeek* Influential Products of the last 25 Years, July 2006 (VMware x86
  Virtualization)

- 2006 Horizon Awards Winner, August 2006 (VMware's VMware DRS)

- JOLT Product Excellence Award, March 2006 (VMware Technology Network Subscription)

- *InfoWorld* Technology of the Year — Best Desktop and Server Virtualization Products, January 2006 (VMware Workstation, VMware ESX
  Server, VMware VirtualCenter)

- *Redmond Magazine* Readers' Choice Award, May 2006 (VMware Workstation)

- *Network Computing* 12th Annual Well-Connected Awards, April 2006
  (VMware GSX Server 3.2)

- SD Times 100, 2006 (VMware, Tools and Environments)

- *ServerWatch* Product Awards, June 2006 (VMware ESX Server, the Most
  Innovation Virtualization and Clustering Tool)

- *Lotus Advisor* Editors' Choice Awards, 2006 (VMware Workstation)

Types of solutions offered:

- ☐ Blade servers
- ☐ PC blades/thin clients
- ☐ Processor chipsets
- ☐ Blade switch modules
- ☐ High-speed interconnects (InfiniBand, 10 GigE, FC)

- ☑ Virtualization software
- ☑ Clustering software
- ☑ Management software
- ☐ Power & cooling solutions

Company Description

VMware was founded in 1998 to bring virtual machine technology to industry-standard offerings. VMware shipped its first product, VMware Workstation, in 1999 and entered the server market in 2001 with VMware GSX Server and VMware ESX Server. VMware went on to launch VMware VirtualCenter with VMotion, moving beyond platform virtualization and leveraging that platform to handle system-infrastructure services in an automated, distributed, and ultimately more powerful way.

In 2004 VMware extended the enterprise desktop platform to solve security and remote management problems with the introduction of VMware ACE. In June 2006, the company shipped VMware Infrastructure 3, which is a fully distributed and automated comprehensive virtualization software suite allowing large-scale enterprises and small businesses alike to optimize and manage their IT environments with unprecedented ease and power.

More than 4 million users and 20,000 enterprises, including 99 of the Fortune 100, use VMware software for projects ranging from creating small- and medium-sized business solutions to forming the strategic backbone of enterprise infrastructure for Global 1000 companies. VMware desktop and server customers have become evangelistic about the flexibility, ROI, and new capabilities they have benefited from in deploying VMware's high-quality products for test and development, desktop manageability, security, and interoperability. In addition, customers have realized across-the-board strategic gains with savings in power, space, hardware, and time coupled with new and leapfrog-better system infrastructure services such as load balancing, high availability, and backup.

Product Information

VMware Infrastructure 3

VMware Infrastructure 3 is the most widely deployed software suite for optimizing and managing industry-standard IT environments through virtualization.

- **VMware ESX Server:** ESX Server abstracts processor, memory, storage, and networking resources into multiple virtual machines, giving you greater hardware utilization and flexibility.

- **VMware VMFS:** A high performance cluster file system optimized for virtual machines.

- **VMware Virtual SMP:** VMware Virtual SMP allows a single virtual machine to use up to four physical processors simultaneously.

- **VMware VirtualCenter:** VirtualCenter intelligently optimizes resources, ensures high availability to all applications in virtual machines, and makes your IT environment more responsive with virtualization-based distributed services such as VMware DRS, VMware HA, and VMware VMotion.

- **VMware VMotion:** VMware VMotion keeps your IT environment up and running, giving you unprecedented flexibility and availability to meet the increasing demands of your business and end users.

- **VMware HA:** VMware HA provides cost-effective high availability for any application running in a virtual machine, regardless of its operating system or underlying hardware configuration.

- **VMware DRS:** VMware DRS continuously monitors utilization across resource pools and intelligently allocates available resources among the virtual machines based on predefined rules that reflect business needs and changing priorities.

- **VMware Consolidated Backup:** VMware Consolidated Backup provides an easy-to-use, centralized backup facility that leverages a centralized proxy server and reduces the load on production ESX Server hosts.

Developer Products

- **VMware Workstation:** VMware Workstation is powerful desktop virtualization software for software developers/testers and enterprise IT professionals that runs multiple operating systems simultaneously on a single PC.

- **VMTN Subscription:** VMware Technology Network (VMTN) Subscription provides access to a powerful suite of VMware products, support, and upgrades in a convenient, low-cost annual subscription. VMTN Subscription is ideal for anyone involved in software development and testing.

Additionally, VMware acquired Akimbi in June 2006 and will be launching software lifecycle management products soon.

Enterprise Desktop Products

- VMware ACE: VMware ACE gives security administrators the ability to lock down PC endpoints and protect critical company resources against the risks presented by unmanaged PCs.

- VMware Virtual Desktop Infrastructure (VDI): With VDI, companies can host individual desktops inside virtual machines that are running in their data centers. Users access these desktops remotely from a PC or a thin client using a remote display protocol. Since applications are managed centrally at the corporate data center, organizations gain better control over their desktops.

Free Virtualization Products

- VMware Player: VMware Player lets you evaluate new or prerelease software contained in virtual machines, without any installation or configuration hassles. You can also share existing virtual machines with colleagues or friends — just use VMware Player to run any virtual machine.

- VMware Server: VMware Server installs on any existing server hardware and partitions a physical server into multiple virtual machines by abstracting processor, memory, storage, and networking resources, giving you greater hardware utilization and flexibility.

- VMTN Virtual Appliances: A virtual appliance is a fully preinstalled and preconfigured application and operating system environment that runs on any standard x86 desktop or server in a self-contained, isolated environment known as a virtual machine.

Partners (Technology, OEMs, and Resellers)

VMware global OEM alliances include

- Dell
- Egenera
- Fujitsu Siemens Computers
- Hitachi
- HP
- IBM
- NEC
- Sun
- Unysis

VMware global technology alliances include

- AMD
- BMC Software
- Computer Associates
- Citrix
- Dell
- EMC
- Hitachi

- HP
- IBM
- Intel
- Novell
- Oracle
- Red Hat
- Symantec

Blade System(s) Supported

Please see `http://www.vmware.com/support/pubs/vi_pubs.html`.

Operating Systems Supported

- Windows
- Linux
- Netware
- Solaris
- Other x86 operating systems

Plans/Direction

VMware is providing a strategically better way to run industry-standard systems; they reduce complexity while also showing significant ROI in three to six months from purchase of the VMware Infrastructure. They have seen customers save millions of dollars in their first year of deployment. VMware has a robust, secure, and highly functional virtualization platform and leveraging that, VMware has add-on solutions that solve system infrastructure management and cost issues in a significantly better way than is possible without their virtualization platform.

As they go forward over the next two years they will continue to invest in their platform and also work with their partners to keep that platform fully supportive of all of their innovations around processors, chipsets, servers, I/O subsystems, etc. They will also continue to develop add-on solutions that leverage the platform; they have a rich roadmap of functionality that they will deliver around ways to take the complexity out of system infrastructure management while increasing the service level quality.

There is a lot of attention on the virtualization space and their challenge is to educate customers about the deep and significant value they will get from deploying their infrastructure software, indisputably in a class of its own. They find that once people deploy a pilot of our products and solutions, they fairly rapidly move to widespread deployment and become quite evangelistic about the benefits.

XenSource, Inc.

At-A-Glance

Company name: XenSource, Inc.
  HQ address: 2300 Geng Road, Ste 250
Palo Alto, CA 94303
Contact info: John Bara, 650-798-5900
Website: www.xensource.com
Date founded: January 2005
GA date of virtualization solution: August 22, 2006
Number of employees: 60
Revenue and customer base: Not disclosed
Industry awards/recognition:

- Gartner Cool Company 2005

- *InfoWorld* Top 15 Tech Startups to Watch 2006

- Fortune 25 Breakout Company 2005

- *CRN* 5 Executives to Watch 2006 — Ian Pratt

Targeted market: x86 Server Virtualization
Types of solutions offered:

☐ Blade servers   ☑ Virtualization software

☐ PC blades/thin clients   ☐ Clustering software

☐ Processor chipsets   ☐ Management software

☐ Blade switch modules   ☐ Power & cooling solutions

☐ High-speed interconnects
(InfiniBand, 10 GigE, FC)

Company Description

XenSource, Inc. develops the leading enterprise-grade platform virtualization solution, XenEnterprise, based on the industry's highest-performance virtualization technology, the open source Xen hypervisor. Founded and run by the Xen development team, XenSource products allow enterprises to realize the TCO savings that result from server consolidation, increased utilization, and reduced complexity in the data center. XenEnterprise will be generally available as a packaged and commercially licensed product in Q3 2006.

Product Information

Open Source Xen

Xen is the industry-standard open source infrastructure virtualization software created and maintained by the founders of XenSource, Inc., and developed collaboratively by 20 of the world's most innovative data-center-solution vendors. Xen allows multiple virtual server instances to run concurrently on the same physical server, with near-native performance and per-virtual-server performance guarantees. Xen is designed to exploit hardware virtualization capabilities in the latest Intel and AMD processors to offer the highest performance for all virtualized guest operating systems. Xen is being embedded in leading operating systems. Novell offers Xen in SUSE Linux Enterprise Server 10 and Red Hat has committed to include Xen in the release of Red Hat Enterprise Linux 5.

XenEnterprise

XenEnterprise is a multi-OS virtualization solution for the enterprise market that offers all of the performance advantages of the Xen 3.0 hypervisor and enables enterprise IT groups to rapidly deploy Xen. Based on Xen 3.0, XenEnterprise delivers a full virtualization solution for single or multiple OS environments. The benefits from increased server utilization result in efficiency and savings on data center management and operational costs.

XenEnterprise includes the following key features:

- Easy to use: XenEnterprise offers Xen and guest operating system installers P2V tools and a comprehensive management toolkit in a single package to enable customers to quickly build and manage a running virtualization infrastructure.

- Superior performance: XenEnterprise offers near-native performance and fine-grained resource control for guest virtual servers, and virtualizes all x86 operating systems, leveraging the hardware virtualization capabilities of Intel VT– and AMD-V SVM–enabled processors.

- Lowest total cost of ownership: XenEnterprise delivers dramatic improvements in server utilization, reducing capital expenditures and infrastructure-management costs.

Partners (Technology, OEMs, and Resellers)

Their technology partners include

- Microsoft
- Red Hat
- Novell
- Sun
- Intel
- AMD
- IBM

- HP
- NEC
- Fujitsu Siemens
- Egenera
- Stratus
- Cassatt

Their master distributors include

- COMPUTERLINKS
- DataSolutions
- InterQuad

- ITway
- Tech Data

Blade System(s) and/or Virtualization Software Supported

- Egenera, Sun, HP, IBM

Operating Systems Supported

- Linux, all of the BSDs, Solaris, and Microsoft current and future
- Windows (with the Viridian "Longhorn" architecture and XenSource additions, will be supported)
- Every OS for x86, except a few smaller ones

Plans/Direction

XenSource's long-term strategy revolves around the concept of volume virtualization for x86 servers. Their intent is to build the world's best high performing hypervisor, deliver it broadly and affordably, and provide value-added components on top of their virtualization platform.

Standards and Specifications

This appendix provides information on various standards and specifications related to blade systems and virtualization.

Distributed Management Task Force (DMTF) Specifications

More information about any of the following DMTF standards and activities can be found at `http://www.dmtf.org`.

CIM Infrastructure Specification

The DMTF Common Information Model (CIM) infrastructure is an approach to the management of systems and networks that applies the basic structuring and conceptualization techniques of the object-oriented paradigm. The approach uses a uniform modeling formalism that, together with the basic repertoire of object-oriented constructs, supports the cooperative development of an object-oriented schema across multiple organizations. The CIM Infrastructure Specification document describes an object-oriented meta model based on the Unified Modeling Language (UML). This model includes expressions for common elements that must be clearly presented to management applications (for example, object classes, properties, methods, and associations).

CIM Schema

CIM is a conceptual information model for describing computing and business entities in Internet, enterprise, and service-provider environments. It provides a consistent definition and structure of data, using object-oriented techniques. The CIM includes expressions for common elements that must be clearly presented to management applications, like object classes, properties, methods, and associations, to name a few. CIM uses a set of terminology specific to the model and the principles of object-oriented programming. The standard language used to define elements of CIM is Managed Object Format (MOF).

Server Management Command Line Protocol (SM CLP) Specification

The principal goal of this specification is to define a lightweight, human-oriented command-line protocol that is also suitable for scripting environments. This includes a direct mapping to a subset of the CIM schema. The command-line protocol will specify the syntax and semantics used to allow the manipulation of the managed elements and associations within servers, as collections or individually.

Server Management Managed Element (SM ME) Addressing Specification

This document describes the Server Management (SM) Managed Element (ME) Addressing standard. SM ME Addressing provides an easy user-friendly way to address CIM objects (classes and instances). This specification may be used to define valid targets for SM CLP commands. It is intended that this specification be usable by other protocols.

Web Services for Management (WS Management)

This specification describes a general SOAP-based protocol for managing systems such as PCs, servers, devices, Web services and other applications, and other manageable entities.

Open Grid Forum (OGF) Specifications

More information about any of the following OGF standards and activities can be found at http://www.ogf.org.

Open Grid Services Architecture (OGSA)

The document focuses on requirements and the scope of important capabilities required to support grid systems and applications in both e-science and e-business. The capabilities described are execution management, data, resource management, security, self-management, and information. The description of the capabilities is at a high level and includes, to some extent, the inter-relationships between the capabilities.

OGSA WSRF Basic Profile

The OGSA WSRF Basic Profile 1.0 is an OGSA Recommended Profile as Proposed. This profile describes uses of widely accepted specifications that have been found to enable interoperability. The specifications considered in this profile are specifically those associated with the addressing, modeling, and management of state: WS-Addressing, WS-ResourceProperties, WS-ResourceLifetime, WS-BaseNotification, and WS-BaseFaults.

Configuration Description, Deployment, and Lifecycle Management (CDDLM) Foundation Document

This document provides a high-level overview of the CDDLM space by describing requirements, analyzing use cases, and providing an overview of the related work within OGF, other standard bodies, and in industry and academia in general. The document sets the stage for the follow-up documents that will present in more detail the language, component model, and basic CDDLM services.

Application Contents Service (ACS) Specification

To install and operate complex systems such as n-tier systems more efficiently and automatically, it is necessary to specify and manage, as a unit, a diverse set of application-related information. The Application Contents Service (ACS) provides central management of such application information. The ACS specification will focus on two main topics: Application Repository Interface (ARI), specifying repository service and its interface to Application Contents; and Application Archive Format (AAF), specifying archive format to register a set of Application Contents to the ACS as a unit. The Application Contents include application binaries and related information, such as program binaries, configuration data, procedure descriptions for lifecycle management, requirements descriptions for the hardware and underlying middleware, policy rules, and anything needed to create a task on grid systems.

Job Submission Information Model (JSIM)

This document describes the Job Submission Interface Model. It is based on the "job" schema in DMTF's CIM, version 2.8. It includes a UML diagram of the classes associated with job submission, the MOF for those classes, and an XML representation of the UML.

Web Services Agreement (WS-Agreement) Specification

This document describes the WS-Agreement Specification, an XML language for specifying an agreement between a resource/service provider and a consumer, and a protocol for creation of an agreement using agreement templates. The specification consists of three parts to be used in a composable manner: a schema for specifying an agreement, a schema for specifying an agreement template, and a set of port types and operations for managing agreement life cycle, including creation, termination, and monitoring of agreement states.

Internet Engineering Task Force (IETF) Specifications

More information about any of the following IETF standards and activities can be found at http://www.ietf.org.

Structure of Management Information (SMI)

Management information is viewed as a collection of managed objects residing in a virtual information store, termed the Management Information Base (MIB). Collections of related objects are defined in MIB modules. These modules are written using an adapted subset of OSI's Abstract Syntax Notation One, ASN.1 (1988). The SMI's purpose is to define that adapted subset and to assign a set of associated administrative values.

Simple Network Management Protocol (SNMP)

The SNMP Version 3 specifies the SNMPv3 framework and consists of several RFCs, which together comprise Internet Standard 62 (STD 62). These can be found online at http://www.ietf.org/rfc.html. Simply plug one of the RFC numbers listed here into the RFC Number field on the web page:

- *RFC 3411* — An Architecture for Describing Simple Network Management Protocol (SNMP) Management Frameworks.

- *RFC 3412* — Message Processing and Dispatching for the Simple Network Management Protocol (SNMP)

- *RFC 3413* — Simple Network Management Protocol (SNMP) Applications

- *RFC 3414* — User-based Security Model (USM) for version 3 of the Simple Network Management Protocol (SNMPv3)

- *RFC 3415* — View-based Access Control Model (VACM) for the Simple Network Management Protocol (SNMP)

- *RFC 3416* — Version 2 of the Protocol Operations for the Simple Network Management Protocol (SNMP)

- *RFC 3417* — Transport Mappings for the Simple Network Management Protocol (SNMP)

- *RFC 3418* — Management Information Base (MIB) for the Simple Network Management Protocol (SNMP)

NETCONF Configuration Protocol

The NETCONF configuration protocol defines mechanisms to install, manipulate, and delete the configuration of network devices. It uses an Extensible Markup Language (XML)–based data encoding for the configuration data as well as the protocol messages. The NETCONF protocol operations are realized on top of a simple Remote Procedure Call (RPC) layer.

International Telecommunications Union (ITU) Specifications

More information about the following ITU standards and activities can be found at http://www.itu.int.

Security for the Management Plane

This set of recommendations provides a framework for the security of the management plane for telecom networks, including next-generation networks (NGN). In particular, it describes security threats and solutions related to the communication of management information between telecom network resources and associated management systems in telecom management networks, and also between management systems.

Principles for the Management of Next-Generation Networks

This recommendation presents the management principles, requirements, and architecture for managing NGNs to support business processes to plan, provision, install, maintain, operate, and administer NGN resources and services. It defines concepts of the NGN management architecture, such as its business-process view, functional view, information view, and physical views, and their fundamental elements. It also describes the relationships among the architectural views and provides a framework to derive the requirements for the specification of management physical views from the management functional and information views. A logical reference model for partitioning of management functionality, the Logical Layered Architecture (LLA), is also provided.

Organization for the Advancement of Structured Information Standards (OASIS) Specifications

More information about the following OASIS standards and activities can be found at `http://www.oasis-open.org`.

Web Services Distributed Management (WSDM): Management Using Web Service (MUWS)

MUWS defines a web-service interface for management providers. This can be used to manage any manageable resource and any manager. WSDM MUWS defines how to represent and access the manageability interfaces of resources as web services. It is the foundation of enabling management applications to be built using web services and allows resources to be managed by many managers with one set of instrumentation. This specification provides interoperable, base manageability for monitoring and control managers using web services.

Web Services Distributed Management (WSDM): Management of Web Service (MOWS)

MOWS defines a specialization for the case in which the manageable resource is a web service. Specifically, WSDM MOWS defines the manageability model for managing web services as a resource, and how to describe and access that manageability using MUWS

Solution Deployment Descriptor (SDD)

This is a standardizing XML schema that describes the characteristics of an installable unit (IU) of software that are relevant for core aspects of its deployment, configuration, and maintenance.

Storage Network Industry Association (SNIA) Specifications

More information about the following SNIA standards and activities can be found at http://www.snia.org.

Storage Management Initiative Specification (SMI-S)

SMI-S supplies profiles of Resource Information Models specific for storage and is a discipline-specific management standard for the storage industry. This technical specification defines the method for the interoperable management of a heterogeneous SAN and describes the information available to a WBEM (Web-Based Enterprise Management) client from an SMI-S–compliant CIM server. This technical specification describes an object-oriented, XML-based, messaging-based interface designed to support the specific requirements of managing devices in and through SANs.

PCI Industrial Computer Manufacturers Group (PICMG) Specifications

More information about the PICMG AdvancedTCA standards and activities can be found at http://www.advancedtca.org.

AdvancedTCA Specifications for Next-Generation Telecommunications Equipment

AdvancedTCA addresses the requirements for the next generation of carrier-grade communications equipment incorporating new technologies in high-speed interconnect technologies; next-generation processors; and improved reliability, manageability, and serviceability, including blade systems.

Glossary

1U   **U** is a standard unit of measure used to designate the vertical usable space in racks. **1U** is equivalent to 1.75 inches.

aggregate   To collect together. In computing, it means to combine (usually similar) components to increase performance/bandwidth.

AIX   **Advanced IBM UNIX** (AIX) is IBM's version of UNIX based on UNIX System V.

ANSI   **American National Standards Institute** oversees development of voluntary standards such as the Fibre Channel standard.

API   **Application Programming Interface** is a source code interface that allows other programs to communicate with a piece of software, generally to request services or status. Often part of a software development kit (SDK).

APPC   **Advanced Program-to-Program Communication** is an IBM-defined protocol developed as part of SNA, and allows computer programs to communicate with each other as peers over an SNA network using a logical unit (LU) device type defined as LU 6.2.

ARCnet   **Attached Resource Computer Network** became popular in the 1980s and was the first widely available networking environment (LAN) for microcomputers.

ARPANET Advanced Research Projects Agency Network, developed by the U.S. government, was the first operational packet-switching network and the father of the global Internet.

ATA Advanced Technology Attachment is a standard interface used for connecting disk drives and CD-ROMs in personal computers (aka IDE, ATAPI, UDMA).

ATCA Advanced Telecom Computing Architecture is the industry-standard set of specifications for telecommunications equipment. It includes specification for a telco blade architecture that has similarities to enterprise blade-server systems, but with ruggedization, DC power, NEBS compliance, and other differences.

ATM Asynchronous Transfer Mode is a cell-relay network protocol that encodes data traffic into fixed-sized cells instead of variable-sized packets. It is a connection-oriented protocol, requiring a connection to be established before data exchange begins. Used as a high-speed interconnect in the Egenera backplane.

backbone Top level of a hierarchical network.

backplane A circuit board with connectors or "sockets" that sits at the back of a chassis into which other circuit boards plug. They are referred to as either active or passive. An active backplane performs some level of processing of the signals that go through it. A passive backplane performs no processing of the signals that go through it. Sometimes used generically as the connecting architecture of a chassis, even though the connection may actually be a midplane.

BAN A **Blade Area Network** connects blades on a high-speed network to create dynamic pools of processing resources.

Blade.org Organization created by IBM and Intel to help deliver IBM BladeCenter solutions by providing access to the IBM BladeCenter specification and offering support for third-party developers and hardware vendors.

BladeS The **Blade Systems Alliance** (http://www.bladesystems.org) is an independent, not-for-profit organization of server-blade manufacturers, software suppliers, system integrators, analysts, consultants, end users, and other interested parties whose focus is to serve as a clearinghouse for information about blade systems, to provide a means for extending and improving standards, and to promote their use in enterprise applications.

BMC A **baseboard management controller** is a fairly low-cost controller used on some servers; it can generate various alerts and allow for system restarts when the operating system is hung.

BSD **Berkeley Software Distribution** (aka Berkeley UNIX) was one of the first variants of UNIX developed and distributed by The University of California at Berkeley.

bypass airflow Created when cool air is not getting to the air intakes of the computer equipment but is instead bypassing the intended route through leaks, cable cutouts, holes under cabinets, or improperly placed vented tiles.

CAN A **Cluster Area Network** connects computing clusters together to increase performance and availability (aka cLAN).

CapEx **Capital expenditures** are expenses associated with the purchase or upgrade of equipment (physical assets).

CD-ROM **Compact disk Read-Only Memory** is a data-storage medium that once written to can only be read, unlike tape or hard disk drives, which can be written to many times (as can CD-RW, compact disk read-write).

CFM **Cubic feet per minute** (cfm) is a unit for measuring air flow, which is critically important in cooling data centers, particularly with high-density such as blade systems.

CFS A **Cluster File System** is a peer-to-peer shared file system used with clusters.

chassis A blade chassis is the frame into which blade components are slid. Includes the midplane or backplane. Components can include CPU blades, network components, storage blades, I/O interfaces, and so on.

CIFS **Common Internet File System** is a protocol developed by Microsoft for file-sharing across systems.

CIM The **Common Information Model** is an object-oriented information model defined by the DMTF that defines not only a common set of objects, but also their properties, methods, and associations. This allows management systems to have a common set of objects to manage using a well-understood set of semantics.

CLI A **command-line interface is** a way to interact with a computer to initiate a program or application by typing in the program/command/ application name and any arguments.

cold aisle Cold aisles are used in a data center layout where, instead of all equipment facing the same direction, equipment is installed in rows facing each other. Cold aisles are the aisles where the equipment racks are facing each other and are created with vented floor tiles that allow cool air to come up from under the raised floor, so the cool air goes into the front of the racks and out the back into the hot aisles.

CPU The **central processing unit** (aka processor) interprets program instructions and acts on data.

CRAC A **computer room air conditioner** is a large-scale air-conditioning unit designed for cooling data centers.

DAS **Direct-attached storage** is storage, such as disk or tape, that is directly attached to the computer rather than being accessed through a network (SAN/NAS).

DASD A **Direct Access Storage Device** is a disk storage device, which can be accessed directly rather than sequentially, like tape.

daughter card Also know as a mezzanine card, a daughter card is a special-purpose card that attaches to (and sits on top of) a processor board, blade, or motherboard. Examples of daughter cards include network cards, high-end graphics cards, HBAs, and HCAs.

DFS **Distributed File System** is a file system whose metadata is replicated across several systems so the data can be seen and shared by all the systems. Distributed file systems are often used in cluster environments.

DFT **Distributed Function Terminals** are terminals that include some level of intelligence or distributed capability, off-loading some of the processing functions from the computer to which they are attached.

disaggregation Breaking up into pieces. Server disaggregation is slicing up the server resources to be shared by multiple virtual environments.

DMA **Direct memory access** allows certain hardware subsystems (disk, network, graphics, and so on) to read and write to memory bypassing the CPU.

DMTF The **Distributed Management Task Force** is the industry organization leading the development of management standards and integration technology for enterprise and Internet environments.

dual-core A chip in which two processing units (cores) are combined to fit into a single chip socket to deliver close to twice the computing power (typically 1.8 times) in the same footprint. This may involve slowing down the clock speed of the chip (in GHz), which results in cooler operation.

dual-ported A computer component with two ports for communicating. Two ports are used for redundancy; in case one port fails, the other port can continue to work (referenced with HBAs, HCAs, and NICs).

E-port An **expansion port** is the type of port used between two Fibre Channel switches. The link between two E-ports is also known as an InterSwitch Link or ISL.

enlightened   An enlightened operating system is one that has been modified to know when it's being run as a virtual machine and operates differently to utilize a specific interface to the virtualization software it is running under. This is also known as paravirtualization.

ESCON   **Enterprise System Connection** is an optical serial communications interface from IBM that connects mainframes and peripheral devices, including disk and tape. ESCON replaced bus and tag channel technology and was replaced by FICON, which runs over Fibre Channel.

external storage   Any storage or storage subsystem not housed within the system enclosure.

fabric   A network topology where devices (computers, storage, and so on) are connected via switches (aka switched fabric).

FC   **Fibre Channel** is a high-speed networking technology usually associated with storage area networks (SANs).

FCAPS   An acronym used for five management functions — fault, configuration, accounting, performance, and security management.

FCP   **Fibre Channel Protocol** is the interface protocol used for SCSI over Fibre Channel in FC SANs.

FICON   **Fiber Connection** is the Fibre Channel communications interface from IBM that replaced ESCON.

GA   **General Availability** is the date when a product is released by a vendor after testing is complete, and it is made commercially available.

GB   A **gigabyte** is roughly 1 billion bytes (8 bits per byte) and is usually used to describe storage capacities.

Gb   A **gigabit** is roughly 1 billion bits (a bit is a 1 or a 0) and is usually used when describing throughput rates, as in gigabits per second (Gbps).

Gbps   **Gigabits per second** is used to describe the billions of bits that can be moved across a communication link (such as Fibre Channel, Ethernet, and so on) in one second.

GFS   **Global File System** is a peer-to-peer shared file system used with Linux clusters.

GigE (or GbE)   **Gigabit Ethernet** is the Ethernet networking technology that has the capability of transmitting roughly 1 billion bits per second.

HA   **High availability** is the ability of redundant components to fail over to the other if one should stop working.

HBA **Host Bus Adapter** is the adapter/interface (usually a card placed on a computer's PCI bus) between a computer and a Fibre Channel network.

HCA A **host channel adapter** is the adapter/interface (usually a card placed on a host computer's PCI bus) between a computer and an InfiniBand network.

HDD **Hard disk drive** is a nonvolatile magnetic storage medium consisting of one or more platters (aka disks or hard drives).

hosted Refers to the hosted approach for server virtualization. Generally, there is a resident operating system that "hosts" the guest operating systems to create independent operating environments, commonly called virtual machines.

hot aisles Hot aisles are used in a data center layout where, instead of all equipment facing the same direction, equipment is installed in rows facing each other. Hot aisles are located in the back of the racks, with the floor tiles not vented, in order to separate the cool air source in front from the hot air that is sent out into the room.

HPC **High-performance computing** applications require very high-performing cores and floating-point processors, scalable memory, and fast I/O.

HPCC **High-performance computing clusters** are used for HPC applications that are cluster-aware — that is, they can distribute the application workload across a number of systems or processors to get the work done more quickly and efficiently than on a single system/ processor. In addition to the attributes of HPC, HPCC requires inter-processor communications (IPC) capability across high-speed interconnect such as 10GbE, InfiniBand, or Myrinet.

HyperTransport A bidirectional, high-bandwidth, low-latency, packet-based bus used by AMD, as opposed to the shared bus architecture used by Intel.

hypervisor A thin, guest-OS-independent virtualization layer that is loaded onto bare metal, which interacts with the hardware directly and creates virtual machines in which operating systems, either enlightened or not, can run. The hypervisor virtualizes hardware resources, such as memory and CPUs, for the different virtual machines (VMs) and their guest operating systems.

I/O **Input/output** is how data gets into and out of memory.

IEEE The **Institute of Electrical and Electronic Engineers** is a non-profit international professional organization for the advancement of electrical and electronic fields. Among other things, it has a standards body to define global standards.

IEEE 802.3   A collection of standards defining the OSI physical layer, media access control (MAC), and the data link layer of Ethernet.

IETF   The **Internet Engineering Task Force** is a large open international community of network designers, operators, vendors, and researchers concerned with the evolution of the Internet architecture and the smooth operation of the Internet. The IETF is responsible for maintaining the standard for SNMP, one of the major contributions to network management.

in-band management   The traditional method of management in which management access and processing is done by the host system. This means that management requests, functions, and responses are carried out by the operating system and over the data network on which the target system is located.

IBA   **InfiniBand Architecture** is the architectural specification of the InfiniBand networking protocol. It was developed by a group of engineers from Compaq, IBM, HP, Intel, Microsoft, and Sun.

iLO   **Integrated Lights-Out** remote management from HP.

InfiniBand   A scalable, high-speed, switched fabric network, often used in HPCC due to its speed and IPC functionality. InfiniBand (IB) switch modules are available for a number of blade systems. Servers connect to an IB network through a host channel adapter (HCA).

IP   **Internet Protocol** is a data-oriented networking protocol used as part of the Internet Suite for moving data across a packet-switched network. It sits in the network layer (layer 3) of the OSI model.

IPC   **Inter-Process Communications** is the method used to send information between two threads in one or more processes, whether they are running on the same or different processors.

IPoIB   **Internet Protocol over InfiniBand** is IP packets encapsulated in the InfiniBand data link layer, allowing computers on an IB network to communicate to IP devices

IPMI   The **Intelligent Platform Management Interface** is a set of specifications created by a consortium of platform vendors, including Intel and Sun, which provides a set of low-level protocols and data records used to provide out-of-band manageability and access to hardware-management information via a set of in-band application programming interfaces.

IPv6 Internet Protocol version 6 is the latest version of the IP standard used by network devices.

iSER iSCSI Extensions for RDMA is an IETF extension to iSCSI that adds support for a direct-access remote DMA-based transport (such as InfiniBand) under iSCSI, offering better performance than iSCSI over TCP or using a TCP Offload Engine (TOE).

iSCSI iSCSI is a protocol for encapsulating (and encrypting, if necessary) SCSI (Small Computer Systems Interface) commands into IP packets to transfer blocks of data from storage devices connected to an IP network to servers connected to the IP network. The iSCSI protocol is used to create an IP storage area network (SAN) versus a Fibre Channel SAN.

ISL Interswitch Link is the link between two Fibre Channel switches using E-ports on each switch.

ISL trunking Interswitch Link trunking is the grouping of multiple ISLs into a single logical path or trunk. ISL trunking provides frame-level load balancing over the individual ISLs and improves performance by reducing congestion.

IT Information Technology is the group within a company that is responsible for managing and processing information. They support the computers and their associated peripherals, as well as computer processes (used to be called Management Information Systems, or MIS).

KVM Keyboard, video, and mouse generally refers to the interface over which the keyboard, video, and mouse communicate to a server. A KVM switch, which is typically included in a blade chassis, allows a remote user to connect to any blade server within the chassis. KVM over IP allows a remote user to connect over an IP network.

kW Kilowatt is a unit that measures power. It is equal to 1000 watts. Blade systems require roughly an average of 30kW per rack, and growing.

LAN A local area network is a group of computers in close proximity connected together to share data/information.

LCMP Loosely Coupled Multiprocessing was first used to describe a mainframe multiprocessing complex in which processors share disk and communicate through a channel-to-channel adapter (CTCA) but operate independently.

LED A light-emitting diode is the light display on computer, storage, and network devices that shows status.

Longhorn   Code name used by Microsoft for the major release of Windows Server scheduled for 2007. Includes the base code for the Windows virtualization hypervisor, code-named Viridian (aka Windows Server Virtualization), which is scheduled for within 180 days of Longhorn's general availability (GA) release.

LUN   A **Logical Unit Number** is the address of a device, or a virtual partition of a RAID group.

MAC   A **Media Access Control** address is the six-byte unique identifier for each network card or device in an Ethernet network

Mac   **Macintosh computer** made by Apple.

MAN   **Metro area network** is a group of computers located within a metropolitan area and connected together to share data/information.

management module   Redundant hardware components within the blade chassis that communicate with every other component within the chassis to provide management functions, including power on and reboot.

MB   A **megabyte** is roughly 1 million bytes (8 bits per byte) and is usually used to describe storage or memory capacities.

Mb   A **megabit** is roughly 1 million bits (a 1 or a 0) and is usually used when describing throughput rates, as in megabits per second (Mbps).

MBps   **Megabytes per second** is used to describe the millions of bytes that can be moved across a communication link (such as Fibre Channel, Ethernet, and so on) in one second.

Mbps   **Megabits per second** is used to describe the millions of bits that can be moved across a communication link (such as Fibre Channel, Ethernet, and so on) in one second.

mezzanine card   Also know as a daughter card, a mezzanine card is a special-purpose card that attaches to (and sits on top of) a processor board, blade, or motherboard. Examples of mezzanine cards include network cards, high-end graphics cards, HBAs, and HCAs.

MHz   **Megahertz** (Hz) is an SI (International System of Units) unit for frequency — one cycle per second. Megahertz are 1 million hertz.

midplane   A midplane is a circuit board that sits in the middle of a chassis that other circuit boards plug into, both from the front and the back. They are referred to as either active or passive. An active midplane performs some level of processing of the signals that go through it. A passive midplane performs no processing of the signals that go through it.

mirror   To duplicate, usually for redundancy in case of a failure. Mirroring is usually used in conjunction with disk RAID levels.

MPI   Message Passing Interface is the de facto standard communications protocol for transmitting information between nodes running parallel programs.

MTBF   Mean time between failure is the average amount of time between failures on a device. Used as a measure of reliability.

multicore   A chip in which multiple processing units (cores) are combined to fit into a single chip socket to deliver additional computing power in the same footprint. This may involve slowing down the clock speed of the chip (in GHz), which results in cooler operation.

Myrinet   Proprietary high-speed LAN communications technology for clustered computers. Developed and sold by Myricom.

N-port   A **network port** is used to connect a node to a Fibre Channel switch.

NAS   Network attached storage allows systems to access and share files over an IP network using the CIFS protocol for Microsoft Windows and NFS for UNIX and Linux protocols. NAS devices contain disks (usually RAID disks), and a very thin server that specializes in maintaining file systems intelligence and fast access to data at the file level.

NFS   Network File System is a UDP- or TCP/IP-based protocol for accessing files on a remote system (or NAS storage device) as if they were local files. Most often used with UNIX or Linux.

NIC   A **network interface card** is the component that connects a server to a network. Typically, blade servers come standard with redundant 1Gb Ethernet NICs. These can be upgraded to 10GbE and can have a TCP Offload Engine (TOE) option for improving the speed of communicating with high-speed LANs or iSCSI SANs.

onboard storage   One or more disk drives on a blade.

one-way   Single processor on a blade.

OpEx   Operating expenses are expenses incurred for ongoing operations and maintenance, excluding capital expenses (CapEx). This includes salaries, ongoing facilities costs such as power and cooling, and equipment maintenance.

OS   An **operating system** (aka system software) is the underlying software on all computers that manages the system resources on a computer — for example, the processors, memory, graphics, and so on.

OS virtualization   Complete virtualization at the OS layer, which creates multiple virtual environments of the operating system. Each one has its own run-time environment while sharing both the system resources, which have been virtualized, and a base kernel. Since all virtual environments are sharing the virtualized OS rather than each virtual environment loading its own OS copy, overhead is minimal. OS support is limited to a single operating system — for example, Solaris for Solaris Containers and either Linux or Windows (though not both at the same time) for Virtuozzo.

Out-of-band infrastructure (OOBI) management   Allows a remote management system to monitor and control all components of a system without requiring the use of the host operating system and regardless of the current power state of the system.

P2P   Physical-to-physical is the migration of an entire operating environment from one physical computer to another.

P2V   Physical-to-virtual is the migration of an entire operating environment from a physical computer to a virtual system.

PAN   The term **processor area network** was coined by Egenera as a grouping of diskless and stateless blades (each blade consisting of processors and memory only) connected by a high-speed interconnect network to operate as a pool of shared resources, much like storage on a SAN.

paravirtualization   Virtualization approach in which the guest operating systems are modified to know they are running in a virtual environment, and interface with a special API to communicate with the virtualization layer, allowing performance to be significantly improved. The performance benefits, however, must be weighed against the need to modify the guest operating system.

pass-through   Option to allow a server blade to have a pass-through connection from within the chassis through the midplane and out the back, for a direct connection to an external switch, rather than an internal connection to a switch module within the chassis.

PCI   Peripheral Component Interconnect, brought to market initially by Intel as a local bus standard. It was designed as a 64-bit bus, although most vendors implemented it as a 32-bit bus. It can run at either 33 or 66 MHz. Throughput of the 32-bit/33MHz implementation is 133Mbps.

PCI–X   PCI Extended has enhanced the original PCI bus from 133Mbps to 1Gbps and is backward-compatible with PCI cards.

PCI-E, PCIe, PCI Express A two-way serial connection that carries data in packets along two pairs of point-to-point data lanes. Throughput is increased to 200MBps and is compatible with PCI systems.

PICMG **PCI Industrial Computer Manufacturers Group** is a consortium of more than 450 companies that collaboratively develops open specifications for high-performance telecommunications and industrial computing applications. They are the developers of the ATCA specification, which includes a definition of standardization for blade systems in the telecommunications space.

POSIX **Portable Operating System Interface for UNIX** is a set of standards developed by the IEEE to define the API for variants of UNIX. To be POSIX-compliant means programs conforming to this API will run without modification.

PVM A **parallel virtual machine** is an aggregation software tool to enable parallel networking of heterogeneous computers to be used as one big computer.

PXE **Preboot Execution Environment** boot allows a server to boot over a network (as long as you're using DHCP), allowing servers to be diskless and retrieve their boot image from the network. Created as part of a bigger initiative from Intel called Wired for Management (WfM), which was introduced in 1998 to improve the manageability of desktop, mobile, and server systems.

QEMU Free processor emulation software written by Fabrice Bellard. Similar to Microsoft Virtual PC, but on a Mac. Supports Windows, Solaris, Linux, FreeBSD, and Mac OS X.

QOS **Quality of service** is a term that originated in networking to describe a commitment to a certain level of service, regardless of the problems affecting that service, such as dropped packets, out-of-order delivery, and so on. Often associated with a contractual agreement known as a Service Level Agreement (SLA).

RAC Oracle's **Real Application Clusters** allows many computers to run Oracle Database simultaneously, accessing a single database.

RAID A **Redundant Array of Inexpensive (or Independent) Disks** is a grouping of disks in which data is shared across the disks to improve data integrity or data-access speeds.

RAS Stands for **reliability, availability, serviceability**; RAS is an acronym popularized by IBM to describe the benefits of system features — high reliability, high availability (never goes down), and fast (easy) serviceability.

RDMA **Remote direct memory access** allows data to be transmitted from one system's memory to another system's memory without involving the CPU of either system. This is often used in clustered applications and networking protocols.

RDP **Remote Desktop Protocol** is used to connect a user to another computer running Microsoft Terminal Services. This function will be expanded in Microsoft's Vista OS to allow a user to remote an individual application rather than the entire desktop.

RJ-45 connector An 8P8C (8 positions, 8 conductors) modular connector often used in Ethernet.

rings Privileged levels within the x86 architecture used to isolate processing.

RLX The first company to deliver a blade-server system solution. Subsequently acquired by Hewlett-Packard, who continues to sell RLX's Control Tower software.

SAN A **storage area network** is high-speed network connecting computers and storage devices, using block-level data transfers, which allows multiple computers to share a single storage device (can be Fibre Channel- or IP-based).

SAS **Serial Attached SCSI** is an upgrade of the parallel SCSI bus I/O architecture allowing point-to-point data transfer rates of up to 3Gbps (10 Gbps by 2010).

SATA **Serial ATA** is an upgrade of the parallel ATA I/O bus architecture.

scale-out A scale-out architecture is one in which more servers are added to a group of servers sharing a workload, for example in a web-server farm or through a cluster.

scale-up A scale-up architecture is one in which more compute power is added within a server to handle more workload.

SCSI **Small Computer System Interface** is a standard interface and command set used between devices — for example, computers and disks.

server farms Many servers processing millions of similar requests, such as in a web-server environment.

SFF **Small-form-factor** disk drives are 2.5-inch disk drives often used in laptops and on blades themselves.

single-core CPU processor chip using a single chip, as opposed to dual-core or multi-core chips, which use multiple chips in the same socket.

SMASH   Systems Management Architecture for Server Hardware is a suite of management specifications being defined by the DMTF to unify the management of the data center. Its Server Management (SM) Command Line Protocol (CLP) specification enables simple management of heterogeneous servers independent of machine state, operating-system state, server-system topology, or access method, facilitating local and remote management of server hardware.

SMP   Symmetric multiprocessing is a computer architecture in which two or more identical processors have a single connection to a shared main memory. All processors are allowed to work on any task as well as move tasks between processors to balance the workload.

SNA   Systems Network Architecture is IBM's proprietary networking architecture and protocol stack designed for mainframe-based communications, and separating physical from logical communications.

SNMP   Simple Network Management Protocol is the standard protocol used over IP for management of network and other nodes.

SRP   SCSI RDMA Protocol allows the transmission of SCSI commands and traffic over an RDMA-capable communication service such as InfiniBand, Virtual Interface (VI), or other interfaces that support RDMA.

SSL   Secure Sockets Layer is a cryptographic protocol to provide secure communications on the Internet. This is often used in e-commerce.

stripe   To place or send data across multiple media to get parallel transfer and increase transfer speed. Striping across disks in a RAID group is to place data across the disks to increase both read and write performance. Data can also be striped across network paths to achieve faster transfers.

switch module   A network switch (Ethernet, FC, or IB) designed to be placed into a blade chassis.

TCA   A **Target Channel Adapter** is the adapter used by the target I/O device to communicate over an InfiniBand network. It is the I/O device equivalent of a host channel adapter (HCA).

TCMP   Tightly coupled multiprocessing describes a mainframe multiprocessing complex in which processors share real memory and virtual storage disk, and utilize high-speed inter-processor communications.

TCO   Total cost of ownership is a financial measurement which includes hard and soft costs over a period of time (typically three years) and is used to evaluate purchase decisions, including not only purchase costs (CapEx) but also ongoing costs (OpEx).

TCP   Transmission Control Protocol is the session layer (layer 4) of the Internet protocol (IP) suite. It guarantees reliable, in-order delivery of data from sender to receiver. It is more commonly referred to as TCP/IP.

TOE   TCP Offload Engine is a hardware implementation of the TCP/IP stack placed on a network interface card (NIC) to offload the TCP/IP processing from the central CPU to the NIC. This is done to increase both TCP/IP performance and CPU cycles available for business applications.

token ring   LAN technology that was developed by IBM in the early 1980s. It was standardized by the IEEE (802.5) but lost most of the market to Ethernet in the early 1990s.

topologies   Network topologies are configurations of components on a network.

transceiver   A device with both a transmitter (outgoing) and receiver (incoming) in one.

TTY   Teletype was originally a physical typewriter with a communications channel that was used as an early output device for messaging systems such as Western Union. It was subsequently used as an input/output device for early mainframes, and then as a mainframe device-type specification for line-by-line terminals.

two-way   Two processors on a blade: a main processor and a coprocessor. Typically, one processor is used for computing and one is used for I/O.

USB   Universal Serial Bus is a standard serial bus used to communicate between computers and other devices.

V2P   Virtual-to-physical is the migration of an entire operating environment from a virtual environment to a physical computer.

V2V   Virtual-to-virtual is the migration of an entire operating environment (OS, applications, and data) from one virtual system to another virtual system.

VAX/VMS   Virtual Memory System (now called OpenVMS) is the operating system used on the **VAX** and Alpha family of computers, developed by Digital Equipment Corporation (DEC).

VAXcluster   Now called **VMScluster**, is group of systems running the open OpenVMS and acting as a loosely coupled multiprocessing system.

VE   Virtual environment is sometimes used synonymously with the term virtual machine to describe a virtual occurrence of an operating system within a virtualized server. It is also the name used by SWsoft Virtuozzo to describe instances within Virtuozzo, which uses OS virtualization to create multiple virtual environments running within the virtualized OS.

Viridian   Code name used by Microsoft for the Windows virtualization hypervisor, code-named Viridian (aka Windows Server Virtualization), which is scheduled for release within 180 days of Longhorn Server's general availability (GA) release.

virtualization   A logical abstraction of physical assets. Server virtualization allows the creation of multiple independent occurrences of an operating environment (logical or virtual servers) to run on a single physical server (dividing one physical server into multiple virtual servers).

virtualization HW assist   Hardware feature based on the x86 chipset (for example, as implemented in Intel VT and AMD-V) that changes the way the x86 instructions are processed, to simplify server virtualization and make it more efficient by creating a new privileged and protected address space (ring -1) for the hypervisor. This allows the virtual guest operating systems to coexist in their normal address space (ring 0); redirecting communications to the hypervisor without knowledge of the other guest VMs or knowledge that the resources are being shared.

VLAN   Virtual LAN is a method for creating independent, virtual networks within a physical network (disaggregation of the physical network).

VM   A virtual machine is a virtual or logical server running under the control of server virtualization software, such as a hypervisor.

WAN   A Wide Area Network is a network that covers a wide geographic area.

WS-Management   A web services management protocol that can be used to mange CIM-based systems and devices using state-of-the-art technologies such as SOAP (Simple Object Access Protocol), XML (Extensible Markup Language), and WSDL (Web Services Description Language).

WWN   A World Wide Name is a unique 8-byte identifier used in Fibre Channel networks to identify devices on a SAN. The WWN is the SAN equivalent of an Ethernet MAC address.

Bibliography

White Papers

"BladeCenter Storage," paper by W. G. Holland, P. L. Caporale, D. S. Keener, A. B. McNeill, T. B. Vojnovich. Published in IBM J. Res. & Dev. Vol. 49, No. 6, November 2005.

"Cooling Strategies for Ultra-High Density Racks and Blade Servers;" an APC white paper, by Neil Rasmussen. #46, 2005.

"Configuring and Installing HP Blade Servers," a VMware ESX Server technical note, www.vmware.com, 2004.

"Deployment of VMware ESX 2.5.1 Server Software on Dell PowerEdge Blade Servers;" Dell, Inc., May 2005.

"Future Trends of BladeServers;" by Tadashi Okano, *NEC Journal of Advanced Technology*, Spring 2004.

"How Multicore Processing and 64-Bit Operating Systems Enhance a Utility Computing Environment," sponsored by Advanced Micro Devices, Inc. and Egenera, by Kelly Quinn, Jed Scaramella, John Humphreys. October 2005.

"HP Consolidated Client Infrastructure; Enhance Data Security While Lowering Costs," a Hewlett-Packard white paper, November 2005.

"Introducing VMware ESX Server, VirtualCenter, and VMotion on Dell PowerEdge Servers," by Dave Jaffe, Ph.D., Todd Muirhead; and Felipe Payet. Dell Inc. March 2004.

"Magic Quadrant for North American Web Hosting," Gartner Research Note G00123741, T. Chamberlin, L. Leong. October 5, 2004.

"Promises Fulfilled: 'Open Blades' Make Large Scale-Out Solutions a Reality," a Rackable white paper, 2004.

"Server Blades Go Mainstream," an AMD white paper, 2005.

"The Sun Blade 8000 Modular System, Modular Architecture for Business- and Mission-Critical Applications and High-Performance Computing," a Sun Microsystems, Inc. white paper, July 2006.

"Virtualized Architectures on HP BladeSystem Concepts Guide;" HP white paper, 2005.

"Virtualization Overview," a VMware white paper. 2005.

"Virtualization with the HP BladeSystem;" an HP white paper, 2004.

"VMware ESX Server: Scale Up or Scale Out?" an IBM Redbooks paper, by Massimo Re Ferre', 2004.

"Why CIM? CIM in Grid Standards;" Andrea Westerinen, Cisco. March 2004.

Articles

"Chip Changes Propel Virtualization," Steven Hill, a Network Computing Special Report, July 2006.

"Crash Course: Data Center Power; Powerful Designs," by Ron Anderson, *Network Computing*, July 2006.

"Power Surge: The Heat Is Rising — and Costs, Too — As Tightly Packed Servers Consume Gobs of Electricity," by Darrell Dunn, *InformationWeek*. Feb. 27, 2006.

Presentations

"Cut through Data Center Inefficiencies with Blade Server Technology" and "Getting More Out of the Cooling You Already Own," Kenneth Brill, Founder, Executive Director, The Uptime Institute, Ziff Davis Media eSeminars, February 2006.

"Preparing Your Data Center for Blade Servers," Server Blade Summit Tutorial 2B, April 18, 2006; "Future Implications of Blades on Infrastructure," Kelly Quinn, IDC; "Powering and Cooling Blades," Steve Madara, Emerson Network Power; Peter Panfil, Emerson Network Power.

"Responding to the Avalanche of Power Falling on the Data Center: Vendor Trends, and IT Actions;" Jerald Murphy, SVP and Director, Robert Frances Group and Jason Kim, Research Analyst, Robert Frances Group. Server Blade Summit, April 18, 2006.

Websites

http://www.csm.ornl.gov/pvm/

http://www.dmtf.org

http://www.findarticles.com/p/articles/mi_m0BRZ/is_4_24/
  ai_n6070029

http://www.hippster.com/pages/history.html

http://www.ieee.org/web/aboutus/history_center/ramac.html

http://www.netlib.org/pvm3/book/node1.html

http://www.pc-history.org/pc-software.htm

http://www.phy.duke.edu/resources/computing/brahma/Clusters/
  brahma_history.php

http://www.science.uva.nl/museum/papertape.html

http://www.searchservervirtualization.com

http://www.virtualization.info/

http://www.webopedia.com/

http://en.wikipedia.org/wiki/

Index